Parenting by Temperament

Full Revised Edition

by

Nancy Harkey, Ph.D.
and
Teri Jourgensen, MPA

This book is dedicated to Erik and Peter, who taught us how delightfully different two brothers could be.

Acknowledgments

This book had its origin in the development of our Childhood Temperament Sorters, and this could not have happened without help from the faculty and students in the Psychology and Sociology Department at California State Polytechnic University, Pomona. Those efforts went far beyond the call of both duty and collegiality. We will be forever grateful to Marcia Lasswell, Susan Siaw, Laurie Roades, Ruth-Ellen Grimes, James Sturges, Scott Roesch, Larry Goldman, Lou King, Miranda Barone, Ann Englert, Cynthia Teeple, and Bonnie Thorne for heroic efforts in helping with data collection. And to the hundreds of students who found families for us—we can't name you all, but you have our undying gratitude. A small piece of the work of each of you is now embodied in our Childhood Temperament Sorters. We also wish to thank Barbara Way, Dean of the College of Arts, Letters and Social Sciences, as well as Cal Poly University for the financial support that made our data collection possible.

Our most personal thanks must go to all the members of our immediate families, for their continuing support and encouragement and for the wonderful temperament examples that they have given us—each and every one! Thanks to Lorle, Michael, Scott, Candace, Kevin, Sean, Dylan, Travis, Meghan, Erik, and Peter, and all the extended family and friends that brighten their lives and ours.

Table of Contents

OUR THREE GUIDING PRINCIPLES...xi

PART I: THE BASIC DESIGN FOR SUCCESS

CHAPTER 1: WHAT ALL CHILDREN BRING TO THE WORLD 3

CHAPTER 2: THE BEST PARENTING MODEL AROUND........ 17

CHAPTER 3: BEING A LOVING AND RESPONSIVE PARENT 27

CHAPTER 4: DEMANDINGNESS 101.. 41

CHAPTER 5: DEMANDINGNESS 201.. 65

CHAPTER 6: DEMANDINGNESS 301.. 79

PART II: THE IDEA AND MEASUREMENT OF PREFERENCES

CHAPTER 7: EVERY CHILD IS UNIQUE 105

INTERLUDE: TAKING THE TEMPERAMENT MEASURES... 113

PART III: THE FOUR MAJOR PREFERENCE PAIRS

CHAPTER 8: BUZZ AND HUM OR PEACE AND QUIET......... 117

CHAPTER 9: FACTS AND DETAILS OR IDEAS AND
THEORIES.. 127

CHAPTER 10: MERCY OR FAIRNESS...................................... 137

CHAPTER 11: HOW YOU STRUCTURE YOUR DAY, WEEK,
LIFE 147

PART IV: THE CRITICALLY IMPORTANT TEMPERAMENTS

CHAPTER 12: MASTERS OF THE MOMENT (SPS)................. 159

CHAPTER 13: KEEPERS OF THE FLAME (SJS)..................... 167

CHAPTER 14: HUMANITY'S CHAMPIONS (NFS) 175

CHAPTER 15: PASSIONATE ACHIEVERS.................................... 183

PART V: POLISHING THE BASIC DESIGN

CHAPTER 16: PARENT PREFERENCES AND
RESPONSIVENESS.. 197

CHAPTER 17: PARENT PREFERENCES AND
DEMANDINGNESS... 205

CHAPTER 18: THE SP (SENSING AND PERCEIVING PARENT
IN ACTION.. 211

CHAPTER 19: THE SJ (SENSING AND JUDGING) PARENT IN
ACTION 223

CHAPTER 20: THE NF (INUTITIVE AND FEELING) PARENT
IN ACTION.. 233

CHAPTER 21: THE NT (INTUITIVE AND THINKING) PARENT
IN ACTION.. 247

CHAPTER 22: WHAT ABOUT
INTROVERSION/EXTRAVERSION EFFECTS.......................... 259

CHAPTER 23: WHEN MOMS AND DADS DISAGREE............. 265

PART VI: ADDING GRACE TO YOUR PARENTING DESIGN

CHAPTER 24: WORKING WITH YOUR INTROVERTED OR
EXTRAVERTED CHILD... 275

CHAPTER 25: WORKING WITH YOUR SENSING OR
INTUITIVE CHILD 287

CHAPTER 26: WORKING WITH YOUR THINKING OR
FEELING CHILD 295

CHAPTER 27: WORKING WITH YOUR JUDGING OR
PERCEIVING CHILD 303

CONCLUSION: THE HAPPY FAMILY....................................... 317

ABOUT THE BOOK, AUTHORS, WEBSITES............................ 319

INDEX *321*

Our Three Guiding Principles

First of all

No child comes into the world as a blank slate. Nature provides every child with inborn plans for growth and development. Most essential are the needs for closeness, safety and comfort on the one hand, and the needs for exploration and independence on the other hand.

And therefore---

The primary job of a good parent is to help the child to develop both love and community with others, and a strong and independent self. Because this is true for all parents and all children, it is possible to describe an ideal general model for warm, but wise love, and firm but thoughtful discipline that applies to every family.

Secondly:

Every child also differs from every other child in unique and important ways. Like adults, children differ in the things they find most interesting in the world, in the way they resolve problems and structure their time, and in their preferences for high levels of excitement or greater calmness and serenity. Even the balance of closeness seeking and self-assertion will differ innately from child to child.

And therefore---

Although you can—and should-- guide your child's natural desires in positive ways, you do not create them. They have their own developmental plan that unfolds as they grow. One of your most important tasks here is to lovingly parent the child you have been given, and not some other child of your imagination

And Finally:

Just as every child is unique, it follows logically that this is equally true of every parent. Along with a lifetime of experience, you bring to the task of parenting your own innate strengths and weaknesses, delights and aversions.

Some parents love excitement and change; others crave order and predictability. Some parents are gifted at nurture and tenderness; others are more gifted at analyzing problems and finding practical solutions. Some relish the moment; others always take the long view toward the future. Some love to be surrounded by people and action; others love peace and quiet and one-on-one relationships.

For all these reasons, individual parents will naturally approach parenting differently.

And therefore:

A good parenting plan not only has to be adapted to fit the real child being parented, it also needs some adjustment in order to fit the real parent. Sometimes this means some changes in the plan, and sometimes it means some changes in the parent—some stretching or tweaking of your natural style in the direction of the ideal plan. Self-knowledge on the parent's part is essential to this.

Part I

Responsiveness and Demandingness
In a Powerful Blend

What is Responsiveness?

We use this word, with gratitude to Diana Baumrind,[1] to mean tender love and caring, but also something more. That something more is the sum total of several things. One is the effort spent to really get to know your child—what is exciting for him, what is not; what is motivating for her, what is not; what is easy, what is hard. We all learn a part of this over time, but the responsive parent does this more purposefully.

Interacting frequently with your child to share feelings, stories and ideas, and to communicate clearly about values, and family rules is another example. Even maintaining a warm and predictable home environment is a part of this.

What is demandingness?

This includes everything you normally think of as discipline, but again with something more. It implies standards and expectations that have been well thought out in advance, and consequences for misbehavior that are also well-planned. Most of all it includes the concept that discipline is a form of teaching, a gift from a good parent to a growing child.

---

[1] Dr. Diana Baumrind is a research psychologist affiliated with UC Berkeley, and especially known for her work on Authoritative Parenting.

How does the nature of human nature suggest this "powerful blend"?

This is the first question we discuss in this book. To envision an effective blend of love and discipline—responsiveness and demandingness--you need a clear vision of the qualities your child brings into the world.

Chapter 1

What All Children Bring Into the World and What This Means About Parenting

Who is your child, really?

This may strike you as a silly question, but it is not. It is probably the most important thing that you have to know in order to think about this child's development, and your critically important role in that.

First of all—where does human nature come from? Experts differ!

Philosophers, psychologists and parenting experts have given us many versions of the nature of the child over the years. If you had been a young parent in the early 1800s you might have been warned that children often brought "native depravity" into the world with them, and were also in danger of "Satanic influence".[2] In such a case it would be easy to imagine the role of parents—to chase the devil of them! You are not likely to encounter this extreme view of the newborn child today, although there may be a remnant of that in experts who put most of their emphasis on discipline.

In contrast, a very different idea of the nature of the child had began to form in the 1700s, and stood in dramatic opposition to the "native depravity" idea by the 1800s. This was the theory that we all come into the world as a Tabula Rasa, or blank slate for life to write upon.[3] In this view all character is formed through life experience. This was further romanticized into the idea of the "noble savage"—that we

---

[2] Martin, T. (1819) as cited in Kessen, W. (1965) *The Child*. New York: Wiley.
[3] This was particularly advanced by John Locke and Jean-Jacques Rousseau at that time.

particularly come into the world devoid of cruelty, greed, fear, etc. and would remain in this natural state if it were not for the harsh teachings of civilization.

What did Freud Suggest?

In the early part of the 20th century, Sigmund Freud gave us his own blend of these opposing views, in depicting children as having an inborn timetable for sexual stages of development (anal, oral, latent and genital) with all sorts of bad outcomes if parent input wasn't handled extremely well. A little depravity was implied, in that the child would not go through these stages in a healthy manner unless development was handled very carefully. His bleak view also held that aggression of the most destructive kind was innate in all human beings, and held in balance only by forces of civilization. In its raw form this view implied conflict and ceaseless struggle as the model for development. It would seem to be a deeply depressing description of human possibilities.

Never discouraged, however, those favoring innate goodness put their own twist on this, seeing the destructive force in the parent's culturally-learned inhibitions, and the child as born perfectly sound and healthy. This, of course, greatly varied from Freud's own view.

The further development of the "blank slate" and the pretty nice "blank slate"

Right along with Freud's thunderbolt description of human nature, came the Behaviorist movement in the early 1900s. This grew from studies of laboratory animals in which a very large number of behaviors could be conditioned (taught by pairing rewards and negative consequences with natural behaviors). Some psychologists working in this area became convinced that child behavior was similarly conditioned by the rewards and punishments of parents. This, in turn led to the belief that virtually nothing was given by heredity.

Among the most famous of the early behaviorists was John Watson, who claimed "Give me a dozen healthy infants, well-formed, and my own specified world to bring them up in and I'll guarantee to take any one at random and train him to become any type of specialist I might select – doctor, lawyer, artist, merchant-chief and, yes, even beggar-man and thief, regardless of his talents, penchants, tendencies, abilities, vocations, and race of his ancestors."[4]

This is the truest imaginable statement of human nature as a blank slate. There is no suggestion of the "noble savage" who would naturally develop well if not disturbed by civilization, nor is there any suggestion of any native depravity. Rather, the child is open to any potential environmental influence.

Finally, as a rebound from both the darkness of Freud and the neutral blankness of Watson, there has been a more recent movement that suggests once again that human nature is essentially positive from the beginning. This, though more sophisticated, is on the side of the "noble savage" and is seen in the widely accepted "Attachment Parenting" movement of today. As a description of the newborn, we think of this as the "pretty-nice blank slate".

It is a "pretty-nice" model because the child's slate is not simply socially neutral at birth, but includes a natural desire toward cooperation and harmony, and thus a natural tendency toward good and loving behavior in the growing child. In this view, the not-so-blank slate, pretty-nice slate child is seen most of all as innocent and sweet, free of all anger and negativity until adults mishandle things.

The Nature/Nurture divide

As you look at these different views of human nature you can see that they divide along an emphasis on the power of nature (though often a

---

[4] Watson, John B. *Behaviorism* (revised edition). University of Chicago Press, 1930.

dark force in the early models) and the power of nurture. With that, models range from seeing humans as potentially evil, potentially neutral, or potentially good. Many other writers have adopted more moderate views, or have confined themselves to more practical aspects of parenting, and no doubt millions of parents over the centuries have simply approached the parenting task with their best abilities as practical problem solvers. Nevertheless these are deep recurring themes. Humans are bound by their inherent natures or they are free, and they are basically well intended or they are not.

Why does all this matter?

What experts believe about the nature of the child is important. It is directly linked to the parenting strategies they recommend. Similarly, what you believe will determine the strategies you will adopt. Those who strongly subscribe to the pretty-nice blank slate, advocate an enormous amount of loving attention, unconditional acceptance, and a very light, gentle and rare hand in disciplining. This approach is seen as essential in creating a child who will be loving in return, willing to obey sensible rules voluntarily, and correspondingly gentle and understanding with others. As the well-known attachment parenting experts, Sears and Sears, have stated their view clearly, in saying that "A child who feels right acts right" [5] Intense bonding between parent and child is seen as the right road to helping the child "feel right" and therefore "act right". This view permeates everything from discipline (minimal) to co-sleeping with your child to promote bonding. Therefore, the critically important question is about the model. Is it accurate? And, if so, is it accurate for all children?

In contrast, the view offered in such books as "The New Dare to Discipline"[6] tends to put the emphasis on strong discipline as the most crucial factor in good parenting. This seems to assume that

---

[5] Sears, W. & Sears, M. (1995). The Discipline Book, p.12. New York: Little, Brown.
[6] Dobson, J. (1996). The New Dare to Discipline. Carol Stream, Il: Tyndale House.

willfulness and defiance are the most pressing problems for parents, and falls closer to the view of a nature-driven dark side. Is this accurate? And, if so, is it accurate for all children? These are the issues every parent must decide in order to go forward with their own parenting strategies.

And what is our model?

In this book we are going to offer you a very specific view of the nature of your child (and of yourself) and suggest parenting strategies to fit that view. It is a view that is upbeat about the quality of human nature, but very certain that there are large genetic influences. We see parental guidance as very important to a happy childhood and an optimal adult life, but also believe that the child comes into the world with a developmental plan of his own. Children are not blank slates but little bundles of potential development. Your guidance matters, but you are not in this alone. The child brings many resources into the world.

In the best-supported scientific view, each child comes into the world, as her[7] own active agent from the moment of birth, with his own needs, desires and wishes. These wishes include the intense desire to bond to loving parents, and the intense desire to develop all sorts of abilities and the wish to experience and enjoy the world without limits.

Not surprisingly, these two great forces within each child are often on a collision course. This is most dramatically true in the toddler years and again in adolescence, but is an unending theme throughout development. The parent steps in as a loving but *in-charge* mentor, to help the child reconcile these needs and wishes in an effective way.

---

[7] In order not to call your child always by "he" or "her" or "it" or "they" ,we are deliberately shifting back and forth with "she" or "he" pretty much at random. We hope you don't find this too annoying!

In this view, your child needs a world of love, help, and encouragement, but also firm intervention, on many occasions.

However, in this view, there are also unique differences found in each child and adult, differences that we refer to as temperament. Individual temperament influences where the child's greater and lesser passions will be, and the natural strategies she will use to maximize these desires. **The *special* message of this book is that our children are neither blank slates nor carbon copies!**

Your child's early Assets

On the day your child is born, she can discriminate sounds fairly well. One study even found that when a newborn baby's crying is taped and played back, the baby will stop in the midst of crying for a moment and listen. The same infant won't do that for the taped cry of another baby, so there is some recognition there. Your newborn child can recognize the differences between basic colors and show a preference for blue and green. He can show an attention reflex (goes quiet, looks, heart-rate slows) when given something novel to look at or listen to. She suppresses that reflex when shown the same thing over and over—showing both recognition and early ability to be bored. Even more surprising, studies have shown that this infant, in the first 24 hours, will often mimic simple facial expressions (wide open mouth, slight curl of a smile, slight downturn of mouth).

The feeding-rooting reflex is ready to go, and once the food source is found you can see excited anticipatory actions. Baby tenses, kicks arms and legs in excitement and goes for it. Unrequited hunger, on the other hand, brings on screams of desperation.

This is not a blank slate on day one, and that is just the beginning. You don't teach your baby to smile at you in delight around two months; nor to fear strangers and duck, cover, and scream at 6-8 months. You don't teach your baby to reach toward interesting things;

to slap the water in the tub, or squash peas in the high chair. Nor do you teach your baby to crawl, to sit up, or to walk. Your child comes into the world with a profound desire to see, touch, move, experience, and understand. Although your conversation and your response to baby conversation is critical in helping your child acquire language, the desire to talk, and indeed much of the structure of language, is encoded in your child's brain.

What is the parent's role in all this?

We teach our children the rules of our culture, just as we teach them spelling and arithmetic, but the fundamental structures that allow them to learn math, language, and—surprise, surprise—the ability to feel the emotions of others and respond to them, are again built into their growing brains. In order to do all this growing and developing, children have to be profoundly motivated from within. In the early years we help by clearing the obstacles from their path, untying emotional knots, giving comfort in frustration and praise for accomplishment, but we do not provide the drive, or the learning potential in their small brains. We do supply love and encouragement, and discipline--limits and demands. It is our philosophy that over the years, these need to come in nearly equal measures, on average. It is also part of our philosophy, however, that few parents have an "average" child.

Quiet, gentle children may need more love and less discipline. Noisy, assertive children may need, not less love, but more discipline. Understanding and tailoring parenting to your child's unique personality is a major theme of this book, but this can best be understood after looking carefully at the general principles involved in good parenting.

Your baby's inborn motivational tools

Once you abandon the blank or pretty-nice slate model, it is possible to recognize that love and cooperation are not the only motivations your child brings into the world. As we see in everyday observations, young children are both loving and cooperative, and selfish and demanding—depending on the circumstance of the moment. This is not only okay, it is absolutely necessary. ***Because*** they really do have to motivate themselves, children also come equipped with determination, perseverance and a perfectly useful sense that their needs are the most important thing in the world. The screaming newborn is acting from an instinctive reflex that seeks to relieve discomfort, hunger, or distress, but the screaming six month old who has just dropped a spoon from the high chair and wants it back—now--is asserting her absolute intent (and right) to have it so.

Writers may describe this as self-centered, or that even more dreadful sounding word—egocentric. Of course it is. What you may or may not have considered is that this is a *good* thing. Nature sees to it that children have the tools, first to motivate parents to feed and care for them, and then to allow them to try to master everything they come upon, as fast as their little neurons can get it together. The wet or hungry baby who lay there thinking "oh dear, I wonder if anyone would get upset if I cry?" would be in serious risk of malnutrition or at least a lot of soggy diapers.

Why this requires both prevention and discipline

What babies and toddlers do not have, initially, is any recognition of natural limitations. Toddler sees a gorgeous glass vase and speeds toward it. She does not know anything about its breakability, the painful and dangerous effects of broken glass, or the value of the vase to anyone else. You, as you should, say sharply "no", and your toddler is stunned. "What is the matter with mom? Doesn't she see how tantalizing this is? Phooey on that." Toddler child redoubles her speed, you save the day with a swift tackle. Then, depending on her personal reaction (also influenced by her own gene mix), she may sob, scream or lapse into stunned silence. What you may be sure of, if you are foolish enough to leave that vase out there, is that she will try it again, and again.

10

It is very important, especially for your own peace of mind to realize that this behavior is innate, and natural and motivated very strongly by all the drives that will help this child survive and prosper in the adult world. This is how your child learns, and this is how your child's brain grows and matures. However primitive it may be at first, you need to recognize that your child has a built-in will of her own, that is completely independent of anything you have done or will do. When this toddler heads for forbidden objects the first time, she is just following these urges. Around the 20th or fiftieth time you may notice something a little more complicated—she may be keeping one eye on you to see if it is going to work. He now thinks "Does mom really care that much? Does she care as much today as she did yesterday? How about now, while she is on the phone?"

If your two year old could tell you what her true value system is at this point it would go something like "I want you to love me totally, completely, all the time, no matter what I do—*and* let me get my hands on that !#$% vase when I want to." Is this child defying you at that point? Well, yes, by any definition. Does this mean she doesn't adore you? Really the answer there is no. She simply believes that there is no reason why she can't have it all. Disabusing her of this romantic view of life requires plenty of love and plenty of discipline. In order to develop the inner resources to control this behavior your child needs lots of help from you. It also requires lots of time and experience for the young brain to develop the centers that cope with emotional frustration.

Attachment—nature is at work here too.

As is true for crawling, walking, talking, you do not have to coax your child into bonding and falling in love with you. That plan is built in. The fact that newborns can mimic a few of our facial expressions should be a strong clue that nature is at work again. And just as your newborn may stop to listen to the sound of his own crying, he is likely to cry with a kind of primitive empathy at the sound of another baby's cries. In a matter of days after birth, your child has learned to recognize you to some degree, by primitive sight, by the sound of your voice, and even by your familiar smell.

From birth to about six to eight weeks, reflex smiles flash on and off. Here your baby's system is getting practice in making the right moves for a real smile. As yet, it doesn't mean "Hi mom, hi dad", but it soon will. Around that sixth week milestone period, it does become a social "glad to see ya" smile. From there, your relationship is off and running. Your baby will happily do her share from then on with gurgles and sounds, seductive smiles and a repertoire of cute little movements. All these tricks are intended to entice you into playing your half of the attachment dance here. And, believe it, they work very well. Some parents learn quickly, a few need more time, but baby wiles win in the end!

Two kinds of activities are going on in every parent/child encounter. One is endless social learning, especially on the child's part, including strengthening those cute behaviors that seem to delight you and keep you around, learning to have reciprocal conversations even if both of you are just grinning and babbling, and learning to recognize your emotions as they appear and disappear. Right along with this, your child's little brain is growing, developing and storing all this experience. This is the beginning of a system that will be with her for a lifetime.

Unlike the situation for moving, seeing, touching and exploring, where your job is principally to provide a safe place and challenging surroundings for this important work, your role is more central here. Of the many good things that happen with strong parent/child bonding in the first months, there is a positive effect on stress reduction. Newborns show remarkably high levels of stress hormones from birth to about two months, and then this gradually declines. This may be partly the reason that such simple things as diaper changes or stripping for the bath bring on fits of screaming in some children. You may recoil at a comparison of your darling child and a rat pup, but there are some interesting parallels. Maternal licking of the pups has a great calming effect, and it turns out that rat moms that lick more in the early days have pups that are calmer and less easily stressed in later life. Presumably you don't want to lick your little Sam or Sally, but lots of calm, loving touch is a good prescription.

Does this mean that parenting the baby and toddler should be a never ending orgy of emotional communication? Absolutely not. First of all, your child has other business—all that moving and touching and looking and listening to new things. (At six weeks, Ronnie the rat would think his mother was round the bend if she went on licking him. He's into hole digging, play fighting, and scavenging). There is no indication that loving communication is needed constantly, any more than your child needs to constantly eat or constantly sleep. Even more important, if this constant contact begins to drive you up the wall, it will not help you to be a genuinely responsive parent.

What all this means for you

Neither the extreme recommendations for constant tender nurturance, nor the extreme recommendations for tough love for toddlers, really express the balanced back and forth that goes on in good parenting. Children need, in the words of developmental psychologist, Diana Baumrind[8], both responsiveness and demandingness, both love and discipline. What is more, as we see it, they need these ingredients to be tailored to the developing individuals that they really are.

However unfocused in the beginning, your newborn child comes into the world brimming with small abilities and large wants and wishes. These grow and gain greater focus every single day. She is not an empty glass to be filled with your good intentions. He is not clay for your molding. You can help your children to find their own way, doing immeasurable good in the process, or, less happily, you can try

---

[8] Baumrind, D. (1996)/ The discipline controversy revisited. *Family Relations, 45(4)*, 405-415.

to guide them in alternate paths of your choosing, frustrating both you and they in the process.

What is going to matter is that you are sensitive to your child's real needs and responsive to them—that you are there, physically and emotionally, when your child really needs you to be there. It is a quality issue more than a quantity issue, but this is true in a unique way. The quality needs to be there when your child needs it, not at your convenience. And sometimes, the quality that is most needed at a given moment is some discipline and restraint.

Parents will do this in very different ways, depending on their own temperaments and personalities, and that will probably make little difference as long as the following description is true: "Must care deeply for the child's welfare. Must be willing and able to spend time getting to know the child's needs, delights, and natural stresses. Must be able to put aside personal concerns and be responsive to these needs, delights, and stresses on demand." Notice especially that word "delight". We all assume that knowing the child's needs is critical, but if you do not really know what gives your child joy, and what does not, you really don't know that child. Thus, not only loving, but observing, reflecting, really seeing who your child is—is a fundamental part of good parenting.

Finally—Family Harmony: How this book can, and cannot, help

One of the seductions of all parenting books is the reader's hope (and sometimes, the expert's belief) that if you just find the right model, and follow it perfectly, all will go well all the time in this happiest of all worlds. If you want to raise children who grow up with strength, character, and self resilience, that vision of perpetual harmony is simply not realistic. There will be painful parent/child conflicts from time to time, until late adolescence merges into adulthood.

With some children (and some parents) these conflicts will be mild. If so, it will be some tribute to your skillful parenting, but it will also be related to your child's (and your) mellower dispositions. With other pairs it may be very stormy, and the same logic applies; some part of it may be parenting practices that could be improved, but another part will be inborn differences in temperament and personality.

Conflict is the essential result of slowly bringing your child around to the recognition that we live in a social world and have to tailor our actions and our desires to that fact. Conflict will not disappear if you just flood your child with loving attention. It will not go away if you are, instead, stern and ferocious (though it might go underground for a while if you are scary enough).

Conflict is not necessarily a sign that you are doing the wrong thing. It *can* be, if it is constant and disruptive of family life. If so it is time to rethink what is happening. But in its every day garden variety, conflict is an inevitable (and necessary) part of parenting. It can be minimized through an insightful understanding of your own temperament needs as a parent, and the temperament needs of your child--that is what this book is all about--but we cannot, and do not promise to make it simply go away

Parenting by Temperament

Chapter 2

The Very Best Parenting Model Around—
Authoritative Parenting

In Chapter One we indicated that all children come into the world with strong drives for attachment, cooperation and loving connection, but also with strong and pretty self-centered drives for competence, mastery, exploration, and all the pleasures that come from these. What is not there in the beginning is a blueprint for reconciling these drives and desires. That is where parents come in.

Love is what we give our child both because we naturally want to and because the child needs it deeply through all the turbulence of growth and change. It should be unconditional in the sense that trouble does not make it go away or lessen your commitment. It is the bedrock for comfort and joy.

Discipline is what we give our children to aid them in their long journey to maturity. They must learn that no one person can be the center of the universe, that conflicting wants and needs, both within ourselves, and between ourselves and others, require compromise. This is a slow and often grudging lesson that has to be taught over and over until it takes.

Complicating this, the balance of needs for attachment and loving connection, versus the needs for mastery, exploration, and novelty, is truly different from person to person. The parent's greatest ally is the fact that there is a developmental plan for ever-increasing self-control which is built into the genes of every human brain. However, the *brain's* greatest ally is the *wise parent.* Experience as well as growth must point the way for the development of self-control, and supply the motivation for it. That is what discipline is all about.

Authoritative Parenting—A best and Balanced System

In the next four chapters we will present a carefully balanced approach to love and discipline that was developed by the research psychologist, Diana Baumrind. She has conducted over 30 years of research on parenting and child development. In addition, hundreds of other studies have been published, based on her work. We believe that the conclusions from this research are the gold standard in parenting study. There is considerable consensus on this within the psychology community.

The Baumrind Model In this system it is not love or discipline, but both together that fill the child's need for both support and guidance. Responsiveness includes nurturing, loving, listening, responding, and planning for the child's well being. Demandingness includes setting appropriate standards for both conduct and accomplishment, establishing rules and limits, enforcing these as needed, and monitoring behavior in the widest sense (both for avoiding negative behaviors and for getting good things done). Responsiveness and demandingness roughly translate as love and discipline, but have wider meanings. Responsiveness includes not only warm emotion, but effortful understanding of the child's needs and the child's nature. It also includes clear and honest communication, including concerns about rules and limits. Even providing a positive physical environment is a part of this.

Demandingness is more than reacting to unacceptable behavior, and includes serious thought about what is and is not appropriate to demand for a particular child's age and maturity. It also includes planning for effective consequences, and monitoring of ongoing behavior. In our discussions we will use these broader terms, but it helps to realize that the core of responsiveness is loving nurture, and the core of demandingness is thoughtful discipline.

Common parent styles

Over the years Dr. Baumrind concluded that parenting styles could be divided into four major types, based on the emphasis on responsiveness, demandingness, both together, or neither one. The four styles are labeled, authoritative, permissive, authoritarian and unengaged.

Authoritative   This is the ideal. The perfect authoritative parent (if there can be such a thing) is high in responsiveness, thus warm, highly involved in interacting with the child and providing for the child's needs, clear and honest in communication, and strong on the use of reason. The child is encouraged to verbalize his or her own feelings and reactions, but it is clear that the parent is in charge of behavioral outcomes. What seems to be communicated is the idea that the child has a right to hold ideas and beliefs that differ from the parent, but must still conform in behavior. This parent is also high in demandingness. The Authoritative parent therefore confronts behavior rather than ignoring it, gives clear expectations for behavior, monitors this behavior consistently, and disciplines in an equally consistent and immediate way.

Permissive This parent may do all of the good responsive things that the authoritative parent does in being warm and kind to the child, and in using reason in discussing behavioral problems. What he or she does not do is follow through on the demandingness factor. Whether by philosophy or by a simple desire to avoid conflict, this parent trusts that the child will come to understand the reasons for good behavior and gradually move to self-control without argument, punishment, or parent-child stress. Partly as a result, reasoning may be carried much farther than would be the case with the Authoritative parent. When initial discussion doesn't seem to correct the problem, more discussion may be in order. The parent may seek explanations from the child as to why the misbehavior occurred, and may go beyond this to try to set up a democratic child-and-parent approach to what the rules should be. This goes further than the use of reason practiced by the Authoritative parent, but lacks the Authoritative parent's clear willingness to back up reason with force. You might guess that this parent's model of the child is that of the pretty-nice blank slate.

Authoritarian Here the parent is high in demandingness, but low in responsiveness. With this is a strong belief that obedience is next to godliness, and should just happen. There is a very strong emphasis on respect for authority as something the child must learn, and the importance of order and tradition. Reasoning with the child is not part of the Authoritarian approach, and would
actually conflict with the concept. Careful monitoring and structuring of the environment to prevent problems is also often, but not always, missing. The child is supposed to obey, so it should not be the parent's responsibility to be constantly explaining or teaching or watching for problems. Similarly, the warm and friendly parent-child relationship that motivates the child of a responsive parent is lacking. Because absolute obedience is the expectation, punishment tends to be harsh. For whatever reason, it is also more often the case that punishment is variable, based on the mood and amount of anger of the parent. Finally, **_cycles of coercion_** in which the child becomes increasingly hostile and aggressive, and the parent becomes increasingly harsh in discipline are more common with this parenting style.

Unengaged This last style is truly unfortunate. The parent is low in responsiveness, and low in demandingness. At least from the view of any outsider, this is a parent who simply does not care. Providing food, clothing, and physical safety is the limit of responsibility that is accepted. Discipline is probably minimal, except where the behavior directly bothers the parent, and so are the more joyful parent-child interactions. Where this is carried to the extreme, it amounts to child abuse in the form of neglect. We briefly summarize these styles.**here:**

Demandingness, Responsiveness and the Four Parenting Styles

High demandingness, High responsiveness—The Authoritative Parent

This parent not only balances demandingness and responsiveness but also <u>does</u> a lot of both. Shown to be the most effective style

High demandingness. Low responsiveness—the <u>Authoritarian Parent</u>

May have a firm set of rules, limits and punishments, but is low on interacting, low on empathy and understanding and not good at communicating reasons for rules.

Low demandingness, High responsiveness—<u>The Permissive Parent</u>

May be warm and loving, but indulgent and perhaps neglectful about rules and limits and about supervising behavior.

Low demandingness, Low responsiveness—the <u>Unengaged Parent</u>

Whether overwhelmed, emotionally stressed, or truly indifferent, this parent does poorly in both demandingness and responsiveness.

Imagining the Four Styles in Action

An Example: Your two restless sons, age nine and eleven, have been in the house on a rainy day, playing together in a style that is right on the edge of roughhousing. You warn them and they quiet down momentarily, but the activity resumes and finally goes over the top. They crash into each other and hit an end table, knocking over a lamp and breaking it.

> *Authoritarian parent* "You know better. I warned you and warned you. Each of you go to your own room and stay there. You are not coming out until I say so." (End of story.)

Permissive parent: *(Sigh.)* "Oh my, you two need something else to do on this rainy day. I know you are bored, and didn't mean to do this, but you must think of some better way to play together." (No further consequences).

Authoritative parent: "Jeff and Marty, I am angry at both of you. You know better than this—you know we have a firm rule about not running and roughhousing in the house. Look at what you have done here and you will see why we have this rule. First of all, you need to unplug the lamp, take it out to the garage, and clean up the mess that is left. When you finish, go to your rooms. I will be in there in a little while and we will talk about this, and about what you need to do to make up for it."

What did each approach accomplish?

Our **Permissive** parent may well have flinched in horror when the lamp went over, but this parent believes deeply in the magic of love and acceptance. The problem is that with this approach, little will be learned from this episode. The parent is kind and understanding, but there is little reason to expect that the same situation later will not produce the same behavior. He or she may distract the boys by finding another activity, and that may work for a while. The broken lamp itself may slow things down for a while too, but when boredom sets in again, we can expect to see the same activity creep back.

Our **Authoritarian** parent, on the other hand, takes care of demandingness. The children are reprimanded and sent to their rooms immediately, so the behavior does come to an end and does have consequences. It does not, however, become part of a larger discussion about rules and responsibilities. The act is wrong because it made Mom or Dad mad, and they are being punished because they made Mom or Dad mad. End of story, as we noted above. If this is the way things generally go in this household, it may have a positive effect on the boys' behavior in the presence of the parents, but will not do much for their behavior in less controlled situations, nor for their long-term respect for others.

The *Authoritative* parent takes it a step further. The children have to deal with the mess they made immediately, and are told immediately that they have displeased the parent by doing something that they had been told many times not to do. They are reminded right away that there is a standing rule that they violated, and that this outcome shows that there is a good reason for the rule. Without further discussion, they have to clean things up and then go to their rooms. **Lastly,** this parent will talk to them (but later, not at that moment) about what led to this problem, what they should do differently, and probably, how they can make restitution for the lamp. It is important to note that there is a little verbal commentary immediately, so they can think about what happened, but without an opportunity to argue. Most of the parent-child discussion will happen after they have received a clean-up/time-out punishment. Having to clean up the mess they made also illustrates a good principle, namely that natural consequences are highly effective ways of making a lesson stick.

What about the Unengaged parent? Even this parent will probably react, since the activity is right in the parent's face and highly annoying. The children may be physically punished, berated, sent to separate rooms, or sent outside, depending on the parent's mood at the moment. Whatever occurs, however, will have little or nothing to do with teaching any lessons about behavior. The clearest thing about this style of parenting is that it is what Baumrind calls "non-contingent." That is, the punishment will depend on the parent's mood, the amount of annoyance factor, etc., and very little on whether the child's behavior was knowingly, intentionally bad. A toddler might be punished as severely as a 12-year-old. A child who was carefully carrying the lamp and tripped might be punished as much as the two rough-housers. If the lamp was old and not valued, or the parent was more interested in something else, there might be little or no consequence at all.

Outcomes Found for These Parenting Styles

A great many children have now been studied using these four parenting styles as predictors of behavior. Baumrind's Family Socialization and Developmental Competence Project has followed hundreds of children from preschool age to high school and many, many studies have been conducted by other researchers over the last three decades.

Authoritative families The general findings indicate that the Authoritative style has the best overall results. A recent child development text[9] gives the following outcome description: "Children of authoritative parents fare best. They generally are independent, friendly with their peers, self-assertive, and cooperative. They have strong motivation to achieve, and they are typically successful and likable. Furthermore, children whose parents engage in aspects of the authoritative style related to supportive [responsive] parenting— which encompasses parental warmth, proactive teaching, calm discussion during disciplinary episodes, and interest and involvement in children's peer activities—show better adjustment and are [better] protected from the consequences of later adversity."

Authoritarian families The general outcome here is found to be much less ideal than that of the Authoritative family. At the preschool level, children raised with this parenting style were found to be more dependent on their parents. There was some difference by gender in these early studies with girls having low goals for themselves and withdrawing easily when frustrated, while boys showed more hostility and negative behaviors. At later ages, they are found to be relatively law-abiding and generally academically competent, but not outstanding.

---

[9] Feldman, R. S. (2001). *Child development,* (2nd ed.) Upper Saddle River NJ: Prentice Hall.

Permissive families This was the biggest surprise. Rather than being highly independent, as their parents might have wished, they were rather like the children of Authoritarian families in having fewer strong goals, more dependency and, in the boys, more hostility when frustrated. At older ages, they differ more, in that they have been found (as a group) to be less socially responsible and more likely to be involved in drug abuse. Like those from Authoritarian families, they are typically academically competent but less accomplished than children from Authoritative families.

Non-engaged families Not surprisingly, this parenting style has predicted the poorest outcomes in study after study over the years, with lower grades in school, more indications of personal stress and maladjustment, and higher rates of delinquent behaviors.

What this means for you as the parent.

The Authoritative style is a very solid approach. You can't go wrong by using this as a general model to follow throughout your parenting years. In the next two chapters we will look in more detail at the various ways you can practice responsiveness and demandingness in good parenting. After those chapters, we will go on to think about parenting in the "real world"—parenting that must make adjustments to this model to fit your own child, and your own, human, self. Real parents and real children bring their own unique characters into the mix. A very gentle parent will always struggle with demandingness, for example. A strong minded and highly structured parent will struggle with the need to stop and just be responsive to the child where she is. That is the nature of human life, and it is very important to begin to see how who we are affects what we do.

A final note here

The results for the various parenting styles may involve a second truth that is less obvious than the parent practices. It is reasonable to assume that the style itself is responsible for a substantial part of the outcome, but not all of it. We can make a good guess that Authoritative parents, for example, are relatively warm but firm, and strong on consistency and logical reasoning, in part because of the temperament they inherited. Assuming heredity has power, it is likely that their children are somewhat like them, and therefore often respond well to this approach.

Chapter 3

Being a Loving and Responsive Parent
What is involved?

Overview

As we have seen, responsiveness includes everything that parents do to express love for the child, soothe and comfort the child, aid him or her in learning new things, and in general, respond to current needs. In this broad sense it includes actions that anticipate those needs, such as maintaining a safe environment in which the young child can play and move about freely, and providing a comfortable time and place for the older child to study. At its best, responsiveness is a quality of mind and heart—really being present for your child when your attention is needed. It sounds simple, but in practice it is hard work.

Responsiveness includes at least four related gifts from you to your child.

Gift One. Simplest is the gift of *warmth and intimacy*.

This is what we all think of first with the word *love*. It is that joy in the presence of the child—in the very shape of his face, the sound of her delighted laugh, that makes us eager to touch and hug and talk with our little ones. This is a gift from the heart that develops with each passing moment from birth forward. For some parents it is immediate and passionate. For others it grows more gently over time. In either case it is the natural emotion that provides the foundation for all the other gifts of responsiveness.

No book can teach these feelings, but you can and will grow in love, with time and rich experiences. Vital to this, your life needs to provide

time for these tender experiences. You have to make that possible. If
your daily life is a pressure cooker, something needs to be done to
reduce the chaos and provide carefree moments. If circumstances do
not permit this, then you have the more difficult task of learning to
shut everything out very quickly and be completely with your child, in
whatever time is available. Regardless of the activities that take place
at these times, you need to be present with all your heart and mind.
This is how your son learns to believe he is safe and cared for, and
your daughter learns that she is deeply valued. These are the moments
in which you build a lifetime of mutual love. It is vital for your
child's development; it is vital for your own growth as a parent. You
have to make the time for love to grow.

Gift Two. **The second responsiveness gift is that of** *active parent*
learning.

The first part of this gift is truly *getting to know your child*. Taking
time to know the real child you have rather than the theoretical child
you have imagined, is an enormous and lifelong compliment that you
pay to her. It is a quality that will maximize your ability to listen and
show caring for your child's achievements, struggles, hopes and fears.

Observing and interacting at the very start of life The psychiatrist
and author, Dr. Stanley Greenspan, talks a lot about this.[10] He
describes what he calls "floor time", so named because much of it is
done on the child's level on the floor. In the beginning it may be the
simplest of two way conversations. Mom or dad speaks to baby,
looks for a bodily response in return, comments on something baby
might be looking at, and so on. This might be followed by a little
rocking and talking, not to quiet crying but just for the pleasure of it.
The most important feature is that the parent tries to follow the child's
responses. If rocking seems pleasurable, comment on baby's smile or
wiggle. If it is not, let your child down on a soft blanket and see if
this is her preference. The point is that you are the observer and

---

[10] Greenspan, S. (2000). *Building Healthy Minds*. New York: Da Capo Press.

28

responder, following your child's lead, and just soaking up your child's reactions to the world.

With a young baby you might notice what kinds of outside stimuli seem most pleasurable—does your child seem to love soft tones, or ignore them? Respond with interest to deeper male voices? Seem dismayed by loud noises? Watch little visual changes, or not pay much attention yet? Seem to mimic your facial expressions? Love to be touched? Hate to be uncovered in diaper changes? Awake in the crib, tucked into your arms, lying on the floor looking around—is your child very active physically, or more of a watcher? Does she shift very quickly from one mini-activity to another? Or persist rather tranquilly for a while? These are all bits of information that tell you something about what this child is doing and feeling. You certainly pick up some of this information in all the day's routine care, but it is really nice to take some time to just watch and enjoy.

Baby moving to toddler As months go on and your child becomes more able to move about and initiate play, observation in this floor-time activity merges into responsive play, with the child as leader. You are down there with whatever array of toys your child currently loves, but you are not going to suggest the game, just follow. This is the hard part. You are not there to make suggestions or dream up the fun. You are there to see what she likes, and help her to know that you are responding to her, not vice versa. You will see clearly what captures her attention, what makes him smile, what is of little interest. It is a complete role reversal for a short time. Hopefully it will be restful and rejuvenating for both of you. Then again, it may not be, and this will have much to do with your own temperament and with the other stresses on your time. (We discuss temperament differences in great detail in Parts II and III).

If such scheduled floor-time is not for you, you can still incorporate the attitude of quiet, receptive observation into breaks in the day's activity. We can't stress too much that children are all different, and are each in the process of becoming the unique person that nature designed them to be. In order to really *see* your child, you need to pause from time to time, take a deep breath, and simply absorb what is going on without wishing or expecting anything.

Observation as parent training This skill in quiet watchful waiting will be a great help to you later as your child blossoms into toddler, preschooler, and onward. This will be true in two ways. First, it will help you greatly in recognizing your child's unique temperament preferences. Does your toddler still adore being held, or wiggle away quickly? Does he spend relatively long periods of time with one plaything or bounce happily from object to object? Does she really crave having others around, and seem to love noise and activity, or is she happier in a quiet environment? These and many other differences are easy to see, when you just let yourself be the quiet observer.

Added to this is training and self-discipline in *listening with all your attention and an open mind*. When children rush in, distressed from one or another social interaction, it is just human to jump quickly to their defense, or to criticism for their bad behavior, depending on the circumstances. And yet, what is always needed first is calm, listening ear. First you need to convey that you are really attentive. Then you usually need information. What happened exactly? Why is your child angry? Distressed? What does he see as an answer? And so forth. If this child knows that you really understand, a big piece of the problem is already solved.   And way down the road, if this child has always seen you as a fair and honest listener, your difficult teenager is far more likely to still be talking to you.

The second part of this gift of learning is really getting to know yourself.

No doubt you have been doing this to some degree all your life. Becoming a parent, however, is a whole new step along the way. You have an enormous amount of control over the happiness or misery of another human being and that human being has quite an effect on your own happiness. It is a twenty-four/seven task like no other you have ever experienced, and every changing month and year will bring new challenges.

If you are a very orderly person, the environmental chaos that a new baby can produce may trigger frustrations you did not know you had. If you are very easy-going in this area, that may be less irritating, but, on the other hand, the fact that babies do not wait for you to be in the mood for a diaper change, may also demand some major changes in your moment to moment behavior. Every step of the way, parenthood offers new experiences that shake our images of ourselves as competent, full-grown adults.

Our philosophy here is that it is very helpful to come to understand the strengths and weaknesses that we all bring to the parenting task. Simply understanding this helps. Beyond that there are some ways in which we can stretch to do better, when we see what the problems are. In Part II of this book we offer a way to measure major differences in basic temperament (the building blocks of personality) and to come to understand what this means for our day to day behaviors. In Part III we offer suggestions for dealing with this in our parenting interactions, and in Parts IV and V we look at the interactions between our own temperaments and those of our children. For now, just hold the thought that a better understanding of your own feelings and behaviors is another responsiveness gift to your child.

Gift Three. **The gift of** *active teaching*—**sharing thoughts, feelings and ideas**

Talking as teaching From birth on your voice is a key way in which you express caring, concern, intimacy and enthusiasm. The author of *Dear Parent*—a guide for infants and toddlers[11], makes the provocative point that it is highly useful to speak to your infant and

---

[11] Gerber, Magda (2002). *Dear Parent: Caring for Infants.* Resources for Infant Educators: Los Angeles.

young child about each upcoming event that involves him/her. You do this even though your words have no specific meaning at the beginning. She goes on to suggest that you should allow a moment for the child's response, even though that may be only a slight wiggle or glance toward you. Thus in approaching your new baby you might say that you are going to pick him up now, and then allow a moment before doing so. It begins the human dialog, teaches that both of you are parties to the communication and gives the child, quite early, the expectation that your voice and attention means that something is about to occur. Beyond this, all of the vocal things we do with children: singing, repeating nursery rhymes, and reading stories are all a part of our web of responsiveness.

Responding to your child's activities Parents often feel that they have to constantly praise the child for his accomplishments, but that does not get to the heart of it. It is much more important that you are able to show pleasure and joy in ongoing activities when you interact with your child, than that you specifically praise them. The important thing is that you noticed and appreciated a given behavior. A big smile for the baby who stands up, or a spontaneous hug for the child who brings home a nice report card, is far more meaningful than a dozen lavish compliments. It is what is from the heart that matters. And for this to happen at the right moment, you have to have to cultivate a certain attitude of openness. That does not mean that your attention is constantly focused on your child—something that is not realistically possible—but that you are ready to respond when you are together.

Helping your child to understand others As children grow older, shared feelings on the parent side are also important. Just as it is important to be responsive to your child's feelings, it is also important to acknowledge the emotional upsets they may see in parents, friends and family. We all experience our feelings very strongly, but understanding them in ourselves and others is a complex skill.

Children need to think about what it is that makes others angry or sad, or discouraged, and they need to understand that most of the time upsets are very temporary, no matter how strongly they may be expressed. By no means do you want to turn your child into a confidant, but it is healthy to acknowledge that you are sometimes upset by events. Discussing the feelings of others with sympathy and understanding is also the beginning of sharing your sense of empathy with your child.

Clear communication about rules, reasons, and values This gift of active teaching responsiveness provides a very important support for demandingness. It has to do with teaching your child what your rules are (in calm moments) and why you have them. We are indebted to psychologist Diana Baumrind for many of the ideas here.[12] Teaching about rules may seem to have more to do with discipline (demandingness) than with responsiveness, but in the widest sense of the word it belongs here. Setting the rules and limits is certainly part of demandingness, but explaining them clearly is an act of responsiveness.

Responsiveness is really everything you do to help your child thrive and to *prevent* disciplinary crises. Making your rules and your values very clear is definitely preventative medicine. Reasoning with children in a spirit of honesty helps them, every step along the way, to learn to guide their own behaviors. Unlike the other gifts of responsiveness this only comes into play as your child grows in reasoning ability. This varies a lot from child to child, but from four or five years on you should see steady growth.

Clear communication sounds simpler than it generally is. To do this with success, you have to think it through yourself without falling back on any variation of "just because I said so." Why do you have a particular rule? What purpose does it serve? Getting straight on this in your own mind helps both parent and child in several ways. As the parent, it helps you build confidence in yourself as the rule maker and

---

[12] Baumrind, D. (1996). The discipline controversy revisited. *Family Relations* 45(4), 405-415.

it helps to keep you honest—allowing you to see when you are acting on behalf of a good rule, and when you have just let frustration get the better of you. For your child, providing you do it well and honestly, this reasoned communication helps, in the long run, to make it easier to behave and avoid unhappy consequences, and makes your rules more acceptable.

Behavioral versus dispositional compliance

An important point that Baumrind's system stresses is that you must require behavioral compliance—cooperation with your rules, but do not have to have "dispositional" compliance—that is, your child's agreement that they are the only possible rules. Your child needs to understand that you have rules that you have thought through, and intend to carry out. She doesn't always need to think that you are right, nor does he have to grow up believing that people in authority always know best. In this view you think of your child as a future "adult-in-training" At a level that is age-appropriate, the child is entitled to know why you have the rules that govern her daily life. This little trainee is also entitled to have his or her own opinions and to have you listen respectfully, *but briefly.* You need to think about this point very carefully.

Willingness to discuss your reasons in a given situation is not the same as indicating that that any particular rule is negotiable, or that discussion will go on indefinitely. There is a subtle but real difference between being willing to discuss and being willing to argue. Getting into a toe to toe argument is not healthy and it should always be clear that you are not willing to do that. At that point you have lost your unique role as the parent in charge. Making it clear, however that you expect your child to cooperate, but do not require her to be impressed with your rules if she is not, allows some mental wiggle room. When expressed in a way that the child can understand, rules with reasons provide a face-saving strategy for both the independent pre-schooler, and the rebellious 13 year old.

Responsiveness and use of reason In addition to the idea that this process helps the child accept the rules and restrictions more calmly and seriously, it also helps them see earlier in life, that rules apply to whole categories of behavior, not simply to specific acts, and are equally applicable whether the parent is present or not present. That is, it is wrong, for a host of good reasons, to take something that belongs to someone else—not just wrong if it is Billy-Bob's, or if you get caught. Such discussions also help children grow in their own use of logic and reason, particularly since they are experiencing it in an area that is very important to them.

Some further thoughts for naturally strong disciplinarians.

You may be unconvinced, wondering what purpose is served by explanations and by listening to your child's views on your actions. It is easy to see this as just another form of manipulation. If you are not going to change your decisions why bother to discuss them? There a few more reasons we can suggest, not the least of which is that it forces you to be sure you *have* reasons. ***Let's take one example***. You have an established bedtime for your child. Why? If it is eight PM, why isn't 8:30 okay? Why not be flexible if there is something the child wants to finish one night, or see on TV one night, and not another?

The honest answer is that there is nothing magic about 8 PM. You picked it because it allows enough time for the rest your child needs, and (you may want to add) gives mom and dad some evening hours for their own activities. Why isn't it flexible? This has to do with the fact that sleep comes better when you start it at the same time every night. It also has to do with the simple fact that a flexible bedtime really means a nightly discussion (argument) that you as parents do not want to have. This line of reasoning also allows you to be clear about the fact that everything is not for the benefit of your child. Parents have needs of their own and have a right to assert them. When this is part of the reason for a rule, you need to be comfortable about this and not try to hide it.

In addition, this does open the door, just a crack, to the possibility that your child may have a point in some areas. If her counterarguments expose the fact that you really have not thought through your reasons for a rule, that is a healthy thing. You don't want to be like the family that always cut both ends off the ham roast before cooking it, generation after generation, only to find that the tradition started because great, great, great grandmother didn't have a large enough pan! Also, if your discussion indicates that some further thought is needed, that may be a good thing in the long run. If one objection, for example, is that a very favored TV program is being missed, that doesn't mean that the rule should be changed, but it might mean that it would be fair to tape the program for another time.

As we noted above, we are not suggesting that you allow any discussion to degenerate into a protracted argument. A point has been made as soon as it has been stated clearly. The child who is restating it for the 2nd, 3rd, or nth time around is simply arguing, hoping to wear you down by sheer force.

Two more things to avoid in communicating about limits and rules

First, you don't want to be having this discussion with a two year old at all and not likely with a three year old, unless very precocious. That this is the *rule* is good enough at that point. Very simple explanations will also be the outer limit at ages four and five. Beyond that you need to tailor any discussions to the age and maturity of the child. Second, for any regular rule, there is no point in repeated explanations. Such simple things as tooth brushing and general grooming need to be consistent and habitual. At some time in your child's life, you may want to explain what tooth brushing does for good teeth, but beyond that it is enough to simply require it, on the basis that it is a good habit to have and something that we all do.

Where discussion becomes really important is in the great moral, ethical and behavioral questions of life. Why is it wrong to lie, to steal? When are sexual behaviors right, wrong? Why is cheating wrong? What about drug use? Early practice with your answers to simple issues like bedtime may help you to see that you need to be rock solid in understanding your own values, and your own reasons for rules and limits, as you tackle these much more difficult issues.

Gift Four: The final gift of responsiveness—providing structure.

This includes all the things you do to organize your household and the daily events that involve your child. These include providing positive family routines and a reasonably orderly home life for infants, toddlers, and school-age children. Predictable mealtimes and bedtimes are a part of this, as are times for homework and chores for older children. For the baby and toddler it means providing a safe and happy physical environment so that the child is not constantly confronted with things that are dangerous or things that are tempting no-nos.

That does not mean that things need, or even should go like clockwork. Life with children can never run with precision, and if it seems to, there are probably many precious moments that are being missed. But it does mean that life should not be chaos. Both babies and older children benefit from knowing that the people in charge are on top of things, and all is reasonably right with the world. For some parents creating structure is very easy; for others it is monumentally difficult. We discuss this in detail in Part III.

The Changing Rhythm of Responsiveness

During the first months of your child's life, responsiveness, in the simple sense of providing food, physical comfort, warm and frequent touch, close contact and lots of parent/baby conversation, will be at its maximum. This is also a period of naturally high stress for all new infants. This seems to be true across varied cultures and in non-human species also. The reason is not clear, but both measurements of stress hormones, and the simple signs of frequent crying and easy reactivity, indicate that this is so. Thus this is the time in which need for your comforting presence is greatest. It helps, somewhat, to know that this is a phase that will ease over time.

Even here, however, there need to be "spaces in your togetherness".[13] The popular idea of "baby wearing"[14]--keeping the child constantly close to you in a sling or carrier—misses the fact that even new babies need room to stretch and try out little muscles, time to look about peacefully and quietly, as well as time to sleep without being jostled and jiggled about. You need to give your child opportunities to be together with you but also to be apart. Simply laying happily on a blanket near you may be very pleasurable for many babies. Others crave much more time in your arms. These differences may signal the earliest signs of temperament preferences, but whatever the reason, wisdom suggests that you allow the newborn and the young infant to signal you about needs to be held and needs to be free. Very soon, the need for constant contact will diminish as the active baby and toddler explores the world. Your nearness and ready attention remain vital, but increasingly your child will begin to explore the world at a small and then larger distance.

As time goes on, frequent eye contact and lots of verbal interaction begin to take the place of the comfort of your lap and your arms for considerable periods of time. Throughout the toddler and preschool years, talking and listening with your full attention will remain vital. Laps will be more for sleepy times and comfort in adversity. As your child progresses into the grade school years, it will be more and more important to be sensitive about when he/she wants to talk, or is not yet ready, or is totally engrossed in something else. This is an area where all your careful and thoughtful observations will especially pay off. The better you know your child the more skillful your interactions will be as the years go by.

Recapping responsiveness

[13] Gibran, Kahlil (1970). *The Prophet.* New York: Alfred A. Knopf
[14] Sears, W., & Sears M. (2002). *The Successful Child.* New York: Little, Brown & Co.

1. The gift of warmth and intimacy
- ❖ Providing spontaneous affection to your child
- ❖ Making time for many happy moments

2. The gift of active parent learning

- ❖ Taking a great interest in your child's development at all stages
- ❖ Spending time just observing and being intimately aware of your child's feelings, interests and joys
- ❖ Learning about yourself--understanding your own strengths and weaknesses as a parent.

3. The gift of active teaching

- ❖ Speaking and reading to your child early and often
- ❖ Encouraging and actively supporting the child's education and special interests
- ❖ Sharing your own feelings wherever appropriate
- ❖ Offering clear communication on family rules, values, moral issues
- ❖ Listening and responding to your child's ideas, feelings and viewpoints

4. The gift of structure

- ❖ Providing a safe, comforting and predictable home environment

In Summary

As you can see, responsiveness covers a lot of territory, and the territory is ever changing as your child grows. Warm feelings are vital, but they are simply the beginning. What must follow are the actions you take as you express your love and caring. Noticing the new things, ideas, feelings, and interests that your child expresses, requires both a basic delight in the child, and an effortful response to these things. It requires time and attention, and a commitment to spend time in this way.

Making a sustained effort to really get to know your child, both in the beginning and as the years go by, is also a great and useful gift to your child and for yourself. Struggling to provide clear communication and logical explanations makes new demands on you, yet also adds to your own development.

Maintaining an orderly home life is a proactive, forward-looking part of caring. You are trying to shape the day so that it *will* go well, rather than simply responding to your child's distress when things don't go well. This applies equally to providing a careful environment for toddlers so that there is not constantly something they should not be doing, and to providing a regular time and appropriate space for the older child's homework. This is demanding work for you. Thus, underlying all of these gifts of responsiveness is the gift of time.

Chapter 4

Demandingness 101: Why and How Children Come to Accept our Rules.

In upcoming Chapters 5 and 6 we will get into many practical tips on how to do Demandingness well. In this chapter, however, we do something very different. First we talk about what motivates children to accept and comply with our rules. Second, we talk about what is going on in the mind and the brain of a child who is developing the self-control to do that. This is an unusual chapter in a parenting book. We spend time on it because we believe that it helps parents in their resolve to be firm, consistent, but also patient, when they can imagine how their actions interact with the natural development of self control and self-regulation in all children.

I. Why do children come to accept our rules?

In the sternest of families, the answer to <u>why</u> might be "pure fear". Here the child's good behavior is based on expectations of very bad things if caught misbehaving. This is typical of the highly authoritarian family, where responsiveness is very low and demandingness is both high and harsh.

There are a number of problems with this. One is that the odds are that the relationship of parent and child is not a lot of fun for either party. Also very important is the fact that this child would not hesitate to revel in that bad behavior if he were fairly confident of not being caught. Very little is being learned or absorbed that will help the child become a positive member of society in the long run. Such values as honesty, politeness, respect for others, etc. have only become part of the child's surface behavior (her when-you-are-looking, behavior).

That is pretty normal for a two-year-old, but for a kindergartener and school-age child it is not a great predictor for her future or of yours as her parent.

Does this mean that firm rules and appropriate punishments are not important? Not at all. Rules and consequences are the foundation for teaching children what is and is not acceptable behavior, and for helping them to become positive members of family and society. Reasonable consequences may be unwanted and unpleasant but they are not designed to be terrifying. For the child, time-outs, temporary loss of privileges or prized possessions, temporary loss of parent approval, temporary loss of on-going parent/child fun, are all unpleasant consequences. These are necessary tools in the demandingness arsenal, but not true sources of "fear" unless accompanied by strong anger, long periods of coldness and rejection, or physical abuse. What is essential is that rules and consequences be taught with great consistency and fairness, and with a minimum of anger and frustration on your part.

Is discipline really, really necessary? Well, if you have endless patience you can follow the all-responsiveness rule, and love them and let them find their own way. A few, very gentle, non-assertive children may pick up the rules just by watching and listening to you, but that is rare. For the rest, it means that most of the socializing lessons that are normally learned at home simply aren't given at all. At the best then, others—teachers and peers most of all—will teach consequences later on, and with luck your child will adapt. *At the worst, it means that your child may grow up with little sympathy or understanding of the rights of others and little self-discipline...*

Are "unpleasant consequences" really enough? Truth here—they will work better for some children than for others in changing behavior quickly, and in getting your little person to agree that your rules are good rules, and to begin to follow them voluntarily. For example, very bold children (often highly extraverted) will be less worried about consequences and more apt to do whatever comes to

mind. That doesn't mean that these strategies won't work for them. It just means that it may take longer, require more than ordinary consistency, and
involve more lapses from grace. In Part III of this book we will look at the many ways that temperament requires us to adapt our strategies to the individual child. Here we want to look at what is true in a general way. And the general answer to the question "are unpleasant consequences enough?" is that they are enough only in the right setting.

The right setting

First of all responsiveness must be working well. Perhaps the single most critical factor is the child's underlying faith in you and in your rules. A primary motivation in the long run is that children obey rules and model parent behavior because they are deeply and happily attached to them.

Think about the many things that are happening very early in a good parent-child relationship. You and your child take pleasure in being with each other and interacting with each other. You and your child each bring your own qualities of spirit and action into this relationship and soon begin to form a relationship history. Early on the child begins to learn about you--how well you respond to her needs and how smart you are about knowing what these needs are. By responding to your child's facial expressions, noises, words, you also show your child that his efforts have an effect on you, and this helps him in building a sense of his separate selfhood and power. Your child begins to learn your emotional signals and realizes that she has some ability to change them. Hey, when I smile, mom smiles. By the end of the first year most babies have a strong enough idea about emotions that they will look at mom or dad when in doubt about a situation. Should I be scared here? Well, mom's smiling so maybe not. Your kindness, and warmth and responsiveness are the basis for the child's sense of security, but that is just the beginning.

Added to that is your powerful role as the bringer of fun, new experiences, stimulation and early learning. From the early one-way conversations with baby, where parents often do the talking for both sides, to mutual chatter at age two, you are sharing emotions, responses, and simple ideas, and opening up the world of language. Reading stories, talking about stories and the way people behave in them all becomes a part of learning about the self and others.

More specifically, as your child moves into toddlerhood, conversation about the reasons for rules becomes part of the relationship background. This includes conversation that both may share about feelings that occur over discipline problems; that it can be hard, that you don't always want to do the things you should, that moms and dads get angry and frustrated too. All these ideas, expressed in a calm time, help the child to develop new insights. The point is, if things have been going well, parents are an extraordinarily important source of good things.

Researchers refer to many of the exchanges of play, of emotion, of language, of caring, as mutual reciprocity. You do good things for me and I do good things for you, and it pleases both of us. And, as it turns out, scientists are finding that mutual reciprocity is built into us, to some degree, as a biological instinct. It is part of the glue that helps relationship groups work together for survival and strength. If this has been a strong part of parent/child attachment, there it will be a positive force in demandingness struggles.

Bottom line—when your child has wonderful times with you, when your child experiences you as a major source of happiness, when your child shares budding ideas with you, from toddlerhood on, and when your child experiences you as wise and understanding and fair—she is greatly motivated to do what you ask.

Well, then, isn't it possible that this is enough?

Not really. When it comes to the first grim word "no", all of the your warm responsiveness, your fine history of being a Rock of Gibraltar in the security department, the many hours of parent/child chitchat and mutual reciprocity, will not prevent a tearful meltdown or screaming explosion. To the average child, "no" in the face of an enticing object feels like a violation of the whole parent-child joy thing.

However—and this is very important—your good relationship will make your demandingness task infinitely easier. All else being equal, it will take far fewer repetitions of the situation to bring about some compliance, will produce a return to good will sooner after a given episode, and will lead much sooner to a time when a new rule is accepted. Even more important, it is much more likely that the child in a warm relationship with parents will also come to accept the rule as something that he believes is right and good. Success in the responsiveness department is the bedrock of successful demandingness.

The rest of the "why" however, is all demandingness. You have to be very firm and very consistent, often in the face of anger and rebellion. If you haven't the patience to be both firm and consistent you will be in deep trouble. If you cannot bear to have your dear child upset and angry with you, you are in deeper trouble. If both of these are true, woe is you!

Hopefully, it will help you to look at the process as children go from little bundles of defiance to some degree of compliance. We are going to examine this in considerable detail, in the hope that seeing growth in cooperation, as a gradual but very positive process, will strengthen parent resolve. The self-control story is long and complex, but also fascinating.

How they come to accept our rules—self-control and self-regulation

Assuming that there is a warm and trusting parent/child relationship, and assuming that the parents approach demandingness in a calm, firm but thoughtful way, the question of how each child learns to accept and follow family rules has everything to do with the much broader process of self-regulation. At birth, the child has very little effect on the world that is voluntary. Movement occurs frequently, and your child can cry, sleep, and take nourishment, but most of this is automatic, reflex like. Gradually, the growing child learns to control movements, to perform purposeful actions, to get some control over emotions, to focus attention at will, and overall, to become an effective force in the world. In that process, he also comes to accept and live by at least some rules of social behavior. To really see the part that parents have to play in all this, it can be very helpful to look at the process in action.

Very Early steps in self-control The one forerunner of self control that you might see in the beginning has its start as a reflex—sucking in the absence of food or potential food. It seems intended to be calming and can be seen even before birth. Just as sucking for food will quickly become voluntary, this comfort sucking will also become your child's first resource in self-soothing—an aid to calming down and feeling better.

By two months the average child has begun look about and may clearly show interest in this, but if a feature of some object catches his eye, he is very likely to focus on one line or corner of it and become visually locked there, quite possibly ending up in distress. This is a rather dramatic example of how little self-control there is at that point.

Babies of this age gaze endlessly at parent faces, and however charming and loveable that is, it owes some credit to the fact that once started they tend to get stuck there! (Of course, the greater attraction is that mom's or dad's face moves and changes so baby isn't permanently stuck in a boring vision lock.) By four months this same child will scan the world with great pleasure and perfect ease, looking from object to object at will—all part of the natural development of self-control in the visual system.

Beyond the first early steps—self control in making things happen

As the infant matures to toddler and toddler to preschooler, very simple self-control merges into more complicated behavior that is usually called self-regulation. Now the child's actions might, for example, involve inhibiting one familiar behavior in order to do something else that is more interesting, but also more complicated. A simple and very early example of this can be seen with a 9 or 10 month old infant, in a situation where she can't quite do it at first. At this age, the child knows that objects exist even if they are covered or hidden, and will hunt for them after watching you do the hiding. At this point, let's imagine that the infant has watched you many times hide a rattle under a brown blanket. She triumphantly pulls the blanket away each time.

But now, with the brown blanket lying right there, you hide the rattle under a green blanket instead. What happens? Miss Smarty lifts up the brown blanket, even though she has seen you hide the rattle under the green one. What seems to happen here is that she has such a strong response to hunting under the brown blanket that it cancels out what she just saw with her own eyes. In effect, she is unable to inhibit her very strong response to brown blanket, in order to explore the green blanket. A couple of months later this will be very simple for her. She is able to inhibit the wrong response.

Another, rather similar situation can be provoked by placing a toy inside a transparent plastic box which is open on one side. If the child reaches in a direct line toward the toy he sees, his hand will encounter one of the transparent plastic walls. If he simply reaches to the side of the box, the toy is available. What does Smart Sam do at 9 months? He rams his little fist right into the plastic side that is directly in front of him. Even if he is a little off in his reach and touches the toy around the side of the box, he will pull back and aim straight toward the toy again, through the plastic wall.. At 12 months, however, Sam will easily reach around and get the toy. The problem, again, was that his little brain was not yet able to stop his first impulse (to reach straight forward) in order to do the smarter thing and reach around.

Lessons in self-control are by no means finished, though, just because smart Samantha can lift up green blanket B or Sam can reach around the plastic wall.

Here is a good example. We can take a nice bright little group of three year olds and put them in a sort of Simon Says game with some built-in conflict. We present simple commands through a stuffed bear and a stuffed elephant, who can say such things as "Simon says clap your hands." The trick is that the child is to do whatever the bear says, and not do whatever the elephant says. At age three to three years and four months, this is virtually impossible to do. Three-year-olds do what the elephant says as often as not, and do it just as rapidly as they do with the bear's commands. Even though they can tell you what they are supposed to do, they can not effectively do it.

At age four, there is a seeming brain miracle, with nearly all children now able to follow the bear and ignore the elephant very well. In this experiment the behavior of children who are just beginning to get control of this is particularly fascinating. When the elephant spoke they would sit on their hands or place them between their knees, physically restraining themselves from acting. The child's desire to be effective, and the brain's rapid growth and change combine to produce all these improvements in a very short time.[15]

---

[15] These tasks are taken from Posner, M, and Rothbart, M. K. (2007) *Educating the Human Brain*. Washington DC: American Psychological Association. They are found in Chapter Four, charmingly entitled *A Mind of One's Own*.

Lessons we can learn from this

What we have described above, are tasks that require thought, understanding, and memory, but also require the ability to inhibit behaviors that don't work. At one year, as we saw, extremely simple conflicts between finding and reaching for things, begin to be mastered. For more complex tasks, development proceeds step by step, depending on how strong the conflict is, how much memory is required, how long attention has to be focused, and so forth. As we saw in the *Simon Says* task, a lot changes just between ages 3 and 4. By age seven children are found to be well on their way to adult abilities in many laboratory tasks that measure a need to control conflicting impulses, but this will vary greatly from child to child. Good control requires good brain development, including increases in the ability to focus attention for longer and longer periods of time, to shift attention from one area to another as needed, and to hold a good amount of material in working (conscious) memory. All of these things improve with age and with *experience and practice.*

How control of emotion and behavior differ from control of simple actions

We have spent some time on the child's developing ability to control physical actions because this is easy to test and to understand, but most of the skills needed here are also necessary for controlling emotion and controlling social behavior. At every stage, increasing levels of brain maturity are needed in order to remember what happened in the past, in order to try something new, and in order to stop repeating old ways that don't work. Brain readiness is essential, but so is repeated experience.

The difference, however, is this: In physical tasks that are naturally interesting to the child, parents really do not have a big role. They certainly need to provide materials and opportunities but the child pretty much takes care of business from there. Good control of emotion and of socially desirable behaviors is more complicated. The same brain resources are needed, but the natural consequences of doing (a) versus doing (b) are not as clear. Here the parent needs to step in, both as guide and as a source of (hopefully) unvarying consequences.

Learning to get control of emotions

Here we are talking about the ability to calm down when we need to, and to control emotional impulses when giving in to them would produce unhappy consequences, whether having a tantrum at age three or punching out an irritating friend at age eight. Calming emotions down is the more common direction, though both we and our children do also learn strategies to lift our emotions up when depressed or bored.

Steps in this process

1. Self-soothing in infancy. As we noted earlier thumb-sucking seems to be the earliest form of deliberate action here. It seems to act to reduce unpleasant emotional arousal. In children at or beyond the crawling stage it can also include movements such as rocking, especially when going to sleep.

2. Early sensory and movement experiences. Later in the first year of life infants find that they can have some effect on mood by their own actions. This includes moving around, reaching for interesting things, and interesting people, and watching ongoing activities. Reaching for interesting people often includes using other mechanisms such as gestures, noises or even crying to accomplish this.

3. The use of distraction. Taking your attention off of what is bothering you, or even the fact that you are bothered, is a surprisingly early strategy. Children can be seen as early as four months and perhaps sooner, purposefully glancing away from something that seems frightening.

This is especially clear when the fear of strangers begins to loom around 9 months. Babies are frequently seen looking frantically away from the stranger who wants to make nice with them. The fact that distraction is a species-wide strategy, can be seen from the behavior of Kelsey—our favorite family Lab. Kelsey was trained as a pup to wait for a treat placed on her paw. She is able to do this, but always manages the misery by looking away!

Mothers and other caretakers do a lot to teach the child about the uses of distraction. As soon as a child is able to be attentive, parents can be seen showing interesting things to fussy babies, pointing things out, talking about them, or rattling objects if appropriate. As children grow older they develop their own distraction techniques. At the end of this chapter we will talk about a great study on self-control and distraction techniques in four year olds.

4. Other techniques. As adults we often avoid situations that would upset us—whether by simply not participating, or (more positively) by preparing in ways that avoid a problem—we turn in that paper, get that report out on time at work, etc. Where this won't work, (or we just did not do it) we may actively try to change the situation—have a tantrum, argue, manipulate, or try to negotiate. Children too learn to avoid and alter unhappy outcomes. It is part of the parent job to show them how to cope with aversive situations effectively.

The bottom line here From infancy onward children seek to control emotions in ways that help them to feel better, and they develop ways of doing just that. The drive for this is innate in a very general way. We all simply want to feel better. However, both the specific moods your child may strive for, and the methods he may use as he grows older, will depend on the consequences that occur in day to day living, and the positive help they receive from parents. If out-of-control emotions are allowed to produce faster or better rewards than careful self-regulation, control lessons may be learned very poorly.

Learning to control socially regulated behaviors

Along with the need to do things effectively, and keep yourself on an even emotional keel, is the need to mesh your behavior with the demands of the world. We can call this many things—socialization (a neutral sounding word), obedience or compliance (more off-putting to some parents) or *our* favorite—becoming an effective social person. For most children, and most people, this is hard. It probably requires the most deliberate effort of the three aspects of self-regulation, (understanding and memory, ability to inhibit, and emotional control) . It asks the child to do this, not for her own immediate goal, but because others require it.

For young children there is always the tempting possibility that it may not be needed. Maybe if we just yell loud enough, and often enough, the royal red carpet will just roll out and we will be able to do as we please. At least in the wider world this is never going to happen.

Fortunately, children generally wise up to this fairly early. And equally fortunately, the same resources that they put to use to be increasingly effective in their physical efforts, and increasingly in control of their emotional tipping points, are also available here. The same brain mechanism that allows the one-year-old to inhibit reaching for the toy through the plastic box wall, will go to work to help the two year old to refrain from a no-no, at least while mean mom is watching, and the three year old to do some simple positive actions.

Why does the one year old stop pushing her fist into the box? It is partly because her brain matures enough to give her insight into a better solution, but also because she learns over and over again that the first solution does not work. Teaching that similar lesson about social behavior is the duty of the parent. It is the heart of demandingness.

Steps in becoming an effective social person

1. The earliest response to commands. Between 9 and 12 months of age, at the point where children are crawling rapidly and walking, are beginning to understand the words of others, and are becoming more and more clear about the fact that they are their own little force in the world, they also begin to respond to parent words of command. There is no self-control yet. Turn your back or even stop saying "no" and it is all forgotten, but they do begin to respond momentarily to a voiced command.

2. The earliest beginning of self-control. Many months later, as much as age two years for some children, you see something new. The child may avoid doing some of the most forbidden things even without a word spoken, at least in your presence. At this point children show some ability to delay an action—to wait until someone says it is okay, such as waiting to get down from chair or out of a door. To get this far the child has needed considerable growth in memory, in order to keep in mind that something is forbidden. Children need increased language abilities in order to consciously think about these matters, and they need a strong sense of what is usually called "object permanence", a knowledge that things, and people, and therefore people's rules, exist even when they are not present. All this takes developmental time.

3. The development of self-regulation. Where self-control by definition is mainly seen as inhibition, as not doing the wrong things when anyone is looking, self-regulation goes beyond this, and is the property of *preschoolers and up.* The ability to not do *forbidden* things is possible now even when quite alone. This, in turn, requires the ability to foresee consequences and be impressed by them. From this point on, changes are gradual as the child begins to plan ahead, and do things now, for later benefit.
The development of emotional control strategies is certainly a good part of this. Speech also becomes a part of the self-regulation strategy

set. At ages three to four it is common to see children warning themselves out loud (No, Mustn't touch, Mommy be mad, etc.) By age six this is rarely seen, but a sort of silent speech continues as children use language internally to direct themselves. If this seems surprising, ask yourself whether you ever mentally remind yourself of things, or call yourself an idiot for making a silly mistake. Language then, both in understanding what others are asking, and in thinking about your own behavior, is another critical piece in self-regulation.

4. The refinement of self-regulation—beginning to anticipate. In time, the child begins to use more complicated strategies, and begins to anticipate problems and plan ahead. The six year old child who finishes a little homework before dinner, so that (a) he won't be in trouble in school tomorrow, and (b) he can watch a favorite TV program tonight, has moved a long way ahead in self-regulation both of his life and of his present and future emotions.

The bottom line again. Just as the transparent plastic wall taught the lesson over and over again that plan A (reaching for a toy through the plastic wall) would not work, just so, you as parent have to serve the same purpose. With firmness and great consistency, you take the place of the transparent wall, saying plan A (ignoring the family rules) won't work. The lesson for Samantha--perhaps needing to be repeated many times—is that, Samantha, you have to find another way to have fun and be happy.

Building it all into the brain

We assume when a child is learning something that the information is simply being "memorized in some mysterious way. Neuroscientists would tell you, though, that every learning experience makes changes in the structure and activity of the child's brain. Most are minute events, but over the days and weeks and years the brain changes to reflect everything that has happened. Centers in your child's brain that provide for self-control, ability to plan for the future, and ability to sacrifice now for long term goals, are developed both through genetic programs and through the kind of experiences that happen throughout childhood and onward, for a lifetime. The areas for self control and self-regulation are essentially a wilderness of growing neurons at birth. That wilderness is gradually replaced with a vital control center. This center can weigh (shown in a classic experiment), having one marshmallow now or two if you are willing to wait 15 minutes in four year olds, and long hours of dedicated study versus no college, for the teenager. The areas are sometimes referred to as the brain's "executive" center. They are located in the frontal lobes of the brain and develop slowly but steadily over childhood and adolescence. It is an awesome thought that your daily parenting is helping to build self-control structures for a lifetime

Lessons from all of this

In increasingly complex situations, the effective child learns to say no to one impulse and yes to another. With this, sophisticated language skills become necessary. Increasing abilities for memory storage are needed in order to retain the lessons of yesterday. All of these skills are needed in one package for the self-regulation that is involved in becoming a social person. Sam has to be able to inhibit his first impulse to pull up a chair and reach for that cookie package on the kitchen table. Samantha has to resist her first impulse to see what would happen if she pressed all the buttons on the TV remote at once. Both have to learn to take a deep breath when mom or dad say "no" to something totally fascinating, and they need to learn how to turn to something else, instead of turning to a tantrum. For this to happen, at each stage and with each temptation, Sam and Samantha have to be ready developmentally, meaning that their brains have to have made the necessary connections. However, that is only part of the story.

They get there by growing and maturing, but they also get there because:

❖ Appropriate demands are made at each step along the way.
❖ These demands are clear-cut and predictable.

❖ The demands are made by people the child loves, respects and believes in.
❖ These demands are made as isolated conflicts in a generally cheery day.

Things that work against this process

Excessive demands. Many of the obstacles to growing a sunny and cooperative child are just the flip side of what helps. Both excessive demands and a lack of demands will slow and complicate the process. By excessive demands we mean both that you are asking more of your child than this child is truly capable of at a given age, and that you have imposed so many rules that daily life becomes a minefield of 'nos".

Clearly you cannot walk out of the room and expect a 12-18 month old child to behave as if you were breathing over him. And frankly, you can't expect to take a 2 ½ to 3 year old to the supermarket and walk down the toy or candy aisle, saying no to all temptations, without provoking something close to mutiny. Those situations require good parent management skills.
Beyond that, however you have to really know your child to know what her current state of readiness is. As we will discuss in great detail in Parts II and III of this book, temperament makes a remarkable difference in how two children of the same age will behave. For example, strongly extraverted children are generally bolder, more drawn to new experiences, and less daunted by your potential anger than are strongly introverted children. Put a pair of such opposite children in the same situation and you will see very different behavior. So, a very important strategy is to really know your child, and know what is reasonable and possible for that child.

The quantity of demands The second part of "excessive" demands is included in the statement that demands (and rules) should be "isolated conflicts in a generally cheerful day". As a child matures you do naturally add new expectations, but this should occur gradually, and only as the simpler demands become a matter of habit. Try to imagine your own life if you walked into work every day to be greeted with a seemingly endless recital of the things you must do and not do. Hopefully, most of what you do has become accepted practice and no one has to remind you on a daily basis. Equally hopefully, if you slip and *get* a painful reminder, it is a rare occasion, and not the central part of your day—or week. Your child needs the same. In the ideal child world, seeing mom and dad should invoke a generally happy feeling, not a sense of doom on the way.

The toddler's special problems Children between the ages of two and three years develop a remarkably strong sense of autonomy. It is all part of their developing sense of self and goes right along with endless repetitions of "It's mine", "Me do it" and just plain "No". It is quite possible that only the teen years produce a greater period of rebelliousness. That is exactly why tantrums tend to peak around the third year.

This is a natural and healthy growth in the child's realization that she has a separate self, and her growing sense of independence. At the same time, these are the new expectations of a very small child who is far from seeing the big picture. Unchecked, the demands of this new "self" would have parents spinning like tops to meet the child's new wishes and desires. The answer lies in making necessary demands (we go to bed when it is time to go to bed, sit at the table during meals, brush our teeth, etc.), but *only* necessary demands. We all need to be very clear with ourselves about the things that are and are not critically important. A "No" blip line is an interesting way to think about it. Imagine a day in the child's life as a line, bumbling along fairly evenly, with generally interesting happenings along the way. Each "no" is a spike or blip along the line.

Graph 1—Family A
(/ is one blip)

7AM   7PM

In this ideal day, this child (family A) is able choose what he will play with, what he will do, who he will talk to, etc. most of the time without causing problems. Every now and then a trouble blip pops up with a "no" and then things calm down again. (In the middle, the first blip didn't work very well and led to a couple more).

Graph 2—Family B

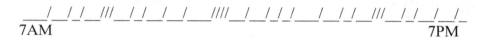

7AM   7PM

Here we have as many repetitions of "no", "stop that", "go to your room" as we have good moments. The child would be miserable, the parents would be miserable and most importantly, it would be very hard for the child to see that there are simple things he could do that would make things better. There is no happy background to contrast with the trouble moments. This child is probably emotionally upset and hardly even listening most of the time, and is learning nothing. *The day in Graph 1* is perhaps too good to be true for the average parent and child, but it is a model to keep in the back of your mind and work toward. It is based on having a minimal number of things that require a "no", but doing that firmly. It is also based on a child who is, by some combination of personality and family effectiveness, pretty happy and disposed to cooperate.

Is the day in graph 2 ever normal? There will be days like this. If a child is sick and feeling miserable, much of the fussing and crying may have little to do with her usual behavior or normal willingness to follow a few rules. Sometimes, also, this may be a darkest before dawn period. A strong-willed toddler who thinks he wants to defy all rules as a new way of life, may have some days like this at his very worst, just before accepting that tantrums are not working, and not all that much fun. If so, that is a signal to be calm and hang in there. When this is a typical pattern, however, it should not be thought of as normal.

The opposite demandingness error—caving in

Here you are, essentially, trying to please the new little Emperor of the house by not making demands. Reasons for this are varied. If your child is spirited and ready to have a tantrum at the drop of a "no" it may just seem too hard. What you need to know here is that not getting things under control is much, much harder in the long run. Other reasons tend to be more philosophic. You believe you will crush her spirit, ruin her budding self-esteem, destroy her trust in you, and tear a rent in the mother/child bond.

This is just not true. We would venture to guess that the totally undisciplined child is the one who loses the most trust and respect for a parent. What you need to see is that by thoughtfully and effectively making demands on your child for social behavior, you are teaching a vital life-lesson.

None of us are simply autonomous. We have large areas of life where we feel in control and make important choices for ourselves, but we do this in a social context, knowing where the boundaries lie. Most of us pay our taxes, honor red lights, accept our family obligations, and work for a living. All of these requirements mean that we need a lot of self-regulation and impulse inhibition to live a successful life. The last thing you want for your child is the idea that only his own needs matter.

Again, why social self-regulation is so much more complex

For just a moment, let's go back to our one year old and the toy in the transparent box. Part of the reason that she has now solved this problem has to do with maturation in brain centers. But the important second reason is that she saw over and over that her strategy was not working. Human brains are problem solving machines and they go to plan B eventually when plan A continually fails. The nice thing about tasks of this kind is that they have natural consequences.

How social learning differs. The more difficult thing about social learning is that other people provide the consequences, with all the trouble and emotion that goes with that. Where a lesson in social cooperation must be learned in the early years, it is the parent who must provide it. The answer to a child who is consciously, deliberately, throwing tantrums to gain some advantage must be that it doesn't work, ever. Each blip in the family day-line, when it is done calmly and effectively, is saying to your child, over here you have freedom and autonomy, over there you do not.

Why social learning is so hard. This is a tough lesson for a three year old. Here you are, you have learned to walk and talk, you remember yesterday pretty darned well, and you have very clear feelings about what you want, and what you like and don't like—even if those feelings change minute to minute. And now these so-called dear parents want to stop you? We'll see about that. So you cry, or scream or just wait until a back is turned and do what you wanted to do anyway. And then they catch up to you and put you in toddler lockdown. And you think—"you want screaming—you'll see screaming!"

But, if your parents are good at all at this, you will find that no tantrum and no defiance will bring you anything that you want. It is that life-lesson again. The can-do parts of the three year old brain have gotten ahead of the self-regulation parts in this situation. It is a major parental task in life to make it clear that these tactics won't work. You are the force that will help them to find a plan B eventually for situations where the answer is "no".

And for the parent

Demandingness is hard work too. As a parent, you have to understand and accept the fact that this is hard work. You need to balance an understanding of how your child feels at this early point with the fact that she urgently needs to learn some things about the limits of her power. Having sympathy for the dilemma, you want to teach these limits slowly in terms of the number of rules you set up, but very consistently. Hopefully there will be no possibility that the three year old brain might be remembering past times when you gave up and gave in.

You want to teach it as calmly as possible. Out of control emotion is the enemy here for both child and parent. No child learns much in the midst of an adrenaline surge. Think of any quarrel you have had, at work or at home. If you ever came around to thinking that the other person had a point, it was certainly not in the midst of battle. The parent, too, is likely to be less effective the angrier he or she is.

Good demandingness asks the child to grow and mature. Much of the time it stays just a hairs-breadth ahead of what the child is ready to do, and says "come on—grow a little more—behave a little better. Find your plan B." Often, over time, plan B becomes not asking for things where you know the rule will be "No", and looking instead for other things to do or be interested in. With older children, plan B may become talking an issue over with mom and dad. Some rules are hasty and may genuinely need to be rethought. There is nothing wrong with having this discussion in a calm moment. Nevertheless, a major role of all good parents is to stand as the social consequence for truly unacceptable behavior. If you could only do responsiveness or demandingness, responsiveness would be more profoundly necessary to the child's well being, but every child needs a great deal of both to grow up strong, happy and socially effective.

In closing: Two stories from the laboratory

One marshmallow or two: A classic study on early self-regulation

A group of four-year-olds, studied at Stanford University, were led into a separate room, one by one.[16] There sat a gorgeous gooey marshmallow, in plain sight. Their choices were either to eat that marshmallow now, or to wait until the researcher ran an errand—a span of fifteen minutes. They were told that if they waited they could have two marshmallows. Interestingly, two-thirds of these remarkable four year olds waited the entire time, while the rest gobbled the marshmallow-in-the-hand, so to speak, immediately.

Those who waited did all sorts of things to make it more tolerable. Some covered their eyes or put their heads down. Others hummed, sang, or talked to themselves. Clearly this group understood both temptation and a variety of ways to combat it.

Even more interesting, though, is the follow-up for these children at age 17. The two-marshmallow group turned out to have significantly better high school grades and college SATs than the one-marshmallow group. Choosing the two marshmallows with a wait was a better predictor of academic success than childhood IQ, measured at the same age as the marshmallow test. Even more amazing is a later finding that marshmallow behavior at age four was remarkably predictive of the quality of organization and self-regulation when these children were 30 year old adults.

A tale (and some tails) from the rat laboratory.

Some years ago, an animal researcher found that young rat pups that have been handled regularly by humans, grew up to be calmer and more together as adults. This was surprising, as young rats find this

---

[16] Shoda, Y., Mischel, W. & Peake, P. (1990) Predicting adolescent cognitive andself-regulatory competencies from preschool delay of gratification. *Developmental Psychology, 26* (6), 978-86.

handling to be stressful. Not only were they less afraid of being handled later, and more open and exploratory in a variety of lab tasks, but they even produced lower levels of stress hormones. The researchers' first idea was simply that early stress was good for you--a little like a vaccination!

Eventually a better explanation turned up. It was more complicated and a lot less flattering to humans. The mothers of handled pups licked them much more vigorously after each handling--presumably to get rid of that nasty human smell! And--it turned out that this maternal licking, at a critical point in the young pups' life, strengthened their entire stress-resistance system.[17] Following up on this they found that rat moms varied a lot in their normal patterns of licking the young, and this, in itself, was a major influence on later stress responses. The curious researchers cross-fostered pups from low licking moms to high licking moms, and vice versa. It turned out that resistance to stress was not simply something you inherited from mom, or grandma, but highly dependent on your mom's willingness to lick your little body from end to end, vigorously and often!

However, that is not quite the end of the story. When all the reams of analysis were done, it seemed that the very best recipe for a calm stable adulthood involved both the early stressor of frequent handling, and the comforting post-handling licking sessions from mom. What we have here is a pattern of a mild challenge or demand, followed by a reassuring cuddle, and repeated again and again over a long period of development. A little demandingness, a little responsiveness. A little responsiveness, a little demandingness. ***There is something to be learned here!***

---

[17] Sapolsky, R. M. (1998). *Why Zebras Don't Get Ulcers*. New York: Freeman.

Parenting by Temperament

Chapter 5

Demandingness 201: Getting Started

The early learning that toddlers do for themselves is mostly pure fun. As we have noted, there are many behaviors and many kinds of learning that are so deeply embedded in the human brain that every child learns them without help and without any external incentive. Crawling, walking, talking and exploring new things, are all examples of this.

What comes later is more effortful, and sometimes more bitter-sweet. Not only do mom and dad stop Sam from doing neat things, but soon they begin to make him do things he would never have volunteered for. Put away toys? Brush those teeth every night? Pretty soon—do homework? Mow the lawn? Whoa there. What's all this?

All these things may seem like fun to try when they are new and your child is in the mood, but day in and day out, chores are chores, and homework is homework—not high on the child excitement list.

Schoolwork as an example A behavior like learning to read, as opposed to learning to talk, requires much more recently developed areas of the brain. It is not something that will be learned without effort. For most children, it will not be learned well without external demands from parents, teachers and society. A few natural puzzle solvers virtually teach themselves to read, but this truly is the exception. Most children need to work at it and then need to keep working at it if they are to become really skillful. The same is true for math and for all studies that require the young person to systematically store information. The problem is that the brain is maximally ready to acquire all this new knowledge long before the child is able to see why it is important.

Aren't there natural rewards here? There certainly are, but the gap between performance today and that natural reward may be too distant to motivate today's activities. Reading can bring a world of pleasure of its own, but this requires that skillfulness be acquired first. The gap between formal learning and reward, for most children, requires that parents and teachers step up to demand, praise and reward effort.

Social behavior as a different example

Becoming a good member of your family, neighborhood and social world is also anything but easy. Consideration for others requires over and over again that you give up some of your immediate wishes in order to do your share of work, to take no more than your share of family resources, to modify your behavior for the comfort of others, and on and on.

There are some children who seem to learn to do this pretty easily, but most of us struggle with it throughout our lives. For young children it is extremely difficult. They learn at first because we insist on these basic behaviors, reward them for sharing and showing consideration, and because we offer increasingly unpleasant consequences for antisocial behavior. But anyone who says this is easy or inevitable just hasn't really gotten to know a two-year old—or an eight year old.

And sometimes, it is a pretty gray area. Far removed from the joys of learning to walk and talk, much of cooperative behavior lies in a murky area that involves deciding what is fair and agreeing on compromises. Parents ask you to stay at the table until everyone is finished, but some family members talk and talk and never seem to finish. Is that fair? It is a complicated dance even for simple issues. If you, as an adult, stop to think about the quarrels you have had with close friends and family, don't most of them come down to what is or isn't fair and kind to both parties?

If we are still arguing over this at 30 it should be no surprise that it is a long slow process for children. In these difficult areas--balancing our own desires and our responsibility to others--it is a lifetime struggle for everyone. If we have been taught well, we know that we can't have everything we want in a given moment, and we learn to find alternative ways to pursue happiness and meet goals without harming ourselves or others. Teaching this lesson must be one overarching goal of good parenting.

What about natural consequences for all of this?

This is a part of the problem. Falling down is a natural consequence of being unable to balance yourself at 10 months. Having everyone around you walking while you crawl is a natural consequence of not having walking skills. Nature rules here and failure just spurs you on. Your toddler has a natural drive for getting good things—the same drive that sends him headlong toward some gorgeous but breakable object.

That drive can certainly spur him to persist past obstacles if there is a good reason (e.g. I get a smile and a hug and a bedtime book after I brush my teeth), but unlike the baby crawling toward a visible and fascinating destination, these links require much more external motivation for a long time. Life eventually gives out many natural consequences for failing to learn self discipline and self-regulation— but they are a long way down the road, and children are insulated from most of these consequences in the first years of life. Parents feed them and clothe them, buy them toys and entertainment, and generally comfort them, even when it is their own behavior that has made them miserable.

Think of the fable of the Ant and the Grasshopper, in which the ant toiled all summer laying away food for winter, while the grasshopper played and chirped. All children know the grasshopper skills— playing in the sun, and looking for things to feel happy and excited about. The ant skills—storing up food for tomorrow, next week, or next year are learned only slowly and with help. Similarly, other human skills, whether brushing your teeth so that they will remain

67

healthy, learning things because they will be useful tomorrow (though they may not be deeply interesting today), or saving for that rainy day, are not built into the young brain. Instead, both parents and society demand these things of children as they grow. Demandingness teams up with experience (and with brain growth) to produce the mature adult who can both plan for the future and take pleasure in today.

Nature and nurture together Nature has provided a very effective brain center for self-regulation, as we saw in the last chapter, but in the area of social behavior and goal setting, parents have to provide the incentives for a long time. One of the most important things that good parents do is to set up very clear consequences, and make them happen consistently—the royal road to your child's eventual self-regulation.

Successful demandingness requires that you ask for behavior that is appropriate for your child, considering age, developmental stages and temperament. To demand more than your child can successfully do is to invite failure, frustration and unhappiness. To demand less is to invite your child to linger in behavior that has really been outgrown. Finding the balance is an art, but one that caring parents master remarkably well.

And so: Each parent/child dispute deals with a single thing that you are insisting that your child must do or must not do, but it is good to keep in the back of your mind that you are always teaching a very broad life lesson. If you are consistent and patient your child will slowly get the message that we have many choices in life but are always limited by the fact that choices have consequences for ourselves and for others. This is the heart of all that you are doing in this area. In the end, life itself will deliver the real consequences if the lesson isn't learned, but parents exist to protect children from this until they are old enough to protect themselves.

The major components of demandingness

❖ Establishing clear expectations for learning and development

❖ Establishing realistic behavioral limits and appropriate social consequences
❖ Confronting your child's misbehaviors as needed
❖ Consistently monitoring your child, knowing when rules are kept and rules are broken, and knowing how your child is developing
❖ Maintaining consistent, contingent discipline—applying the rules and consequences very promptly and regularly

Notice that these are not the soft and gentle words of responsiveness.—clear expectations, realistic limits, appropriate consequences, confronting, monitoring, and consistent, contingent discipline. This is all effortful, and often painful. At times it will call for all the self-discipline *you* have accumulated over the years.

We use Baumrind's term demandingness here because we see it as broader than the image parents usually have of discipline. It is different mainly in including things that may not come to mind with the word 'discipline'. Most of all demandingness means that you have thought through several very important things. First, at a given age, and with your unique child, what negative behaviors do you wish to say "no" to, and what positive behaviors do you want to foster and teach?

Second, of these, how well do you and your spouse or other caretaker agree and how will you handle the areas where you do not agree? Third, what are your reasons for your rules and limits in each case? Fourth, what actions do you intend to take to see that these things happen? This all adds up to using reason, logic and careful planning, plus a good understanding of your child's capabilities at any given moment.

Discipline—a core demandingness skill

According to the dictionary definition, to discipline is to teach. Disciplines are bodies of knowledge, and disciples are learners. For the parent the life lessons to be taught through discipline and the larger term, demandingness, are threefold—that there are things we cannot do because they interfere with the needs and rights of others, that there are things we must do for our own long-range well being, whether they interest us or not at a given moment, and finally, that our own actions have predictable consequences.

Every responsiveness act of caring, every heartfelt hug, teaches that the child is cared for and safe. The demandingness lessons are those on the other side—the need for respect for others and for the gradual growth of self-regulation. If you truly think of discipline as teaching these lessons, then you realize that the real goal is effectiveness. It is not simply keeping the peace at the moment; it is also not simply showing your child who is boss in any given situation. It is teaching these life lessons in a way that will help your child to be happier as both child and adult, and a better member of the human community. In practice, it is both science and art.

Doing Discipline and Demandingness: First and foremost--have a plan.

An informal survey on AOL in 2006 indicated that 40% of all parents who responded gave no advance thought to how they would discipline. Evidently they simply responded to situations as they occurred. Unless you are just incredibly talented at this by nature, this is not the best way to do demandingness. This area needs serious planning.

Knowing what behaviors you really want to insist upon.

These need to be,
❖ Appropriate for the age of your child
❖ Appropriate for the maturity of your child
❖ Appropriate for the temperament and interests of the child
❖ Appropriate for the many different situations where problems arise.

70

***Knowing how to work out differences with your spouse or other
primary caretaker***

The two of you need to try very hard to be in agreement with about
the *behaviors to be insisted on.* It is very difficult to get the results you
want if you don't share values here. In later chapters we will talk a lot
about the truth that people with very different temperaments may also
have quite different ideas about discipline and demandingness. Here
we can only say that you should try to find some common ground that
you can both agree on, even if this is less than ideal. It is consistency
that is critical to being effective in this area, and there can be no
consistency without a common baseline agreement.

It is less critical that you both use the same exact consequences; as
long as you both agree on the behaviors you are working toward.
Fathers may find that a loud commanding voice is enough, while
mothers may need to rely on time-outs or removal of the offender.
The important thing is that the consequences bring the behavior to a
halt.

Knowing what your reasons are for your rules.

These do not have to be perfect. They just need to be genuine and
meaningful to you. Many rules have an arbitrary side to them.
Bedtime may be 7 PM in your house and 8 PM or even 9 PM for a
neighbor. It is perfectly okay for your reasons to include both what is
best for your child and what is best for you as parent. What matters is
that you are clear about your reasons, and could talk about them if
asked.

Similarly, you might insist on the same times on the weekend and the
neighbors may not, reasoning that everyone can sleep in on weekends.
Their children (and the parents) may be easy sleepers and fine with a
fluctuating schedule, while your family may not adjust that well. That
is really all the reason you need, but you should be aware of it.

Knowing how you want to handle misbehaviors

- ❖ Your warning signals,
- ❖ Consequences that fit the "crime" wherever possible
- ❖ Consequences that step up in seriousness as needed (what the business world calls "progressive discipline")
- ❖ Modifications you are willing to plan for, in a tired, hungry, strung-out child.

Especially for first time parents, your plan will develop as your child develops and begins to show new and more independent behaviors, both good and bad. This is natural, but when a problem behavior is repeated again and again and needs to be dealt with, it signals you that it is time for some advance planning.

How discipline and demandingness begin and grow

In the earliest stages Perhaps the simplest and truest thing that can be said about demandingness and discipline is that the process is easiest if it is there is a strategy in place from the very beginning. Well before they reach the age when saying "no" to you becomes a part of their growing sense of identity, (typically somewhere around two years, but some precocious little souls start even sooner) young children need to become used to responding to simple requests.

They need to stop a behavior when you say *no,* come to you when asked, and sit still or stand still, at least briefly, when asked. That they willingly stop in response to "no" doesn't mean, at this age, that they won't repeat the same action later. It does mean that they respond to you on the spot, and that is important.

Agreeing to be dressed and undressed is a very early battleground for some children, however. If so, your best bet is to try to chat with them cheerfully during the process, "okay, here's where your right arm goes, etc. etc.", but not allow negativity to slow you down or to destroy your own cool.

72

What is extremely important from the beginning is *that the child's behavior not succeed in changing your behavior.* Children do not begin fussing over such basics as getting dressed for any reason other than they don't want to be bothered, but if the fuss has an interesting outcome they can certainly learn to fuss purposefully.

In these early actions you are trying to accomplish two things.

First to establish a simple habit of obedience. You are the parent, you are in charge, and there will be less conflict if the child is used to this fact. For some of you the very phrase "habit of obedience" will raise *red flags.* If it does, please consider that the intent is not at all to raise children to adulthood who are submissive, or blindly obedient to authority. A good demandingness plan is designed to help in getting behavioral compliance in young children and, hopefully, voluntary compliance in older children. It is designed, most of all to show a bright line between those behaviors that are harmless and therefore freely available, and those that are potentially harmful to the self or to others, and therefore ruled out by the adults in charge. Think, too, how useful your own "habit of obedience" is with respect to stopping for red lights, even when you are daydreaming about other things. *Two-year- olds are not adults, nor are they deeply rational,* nor automatically ready to act in their own real best interests or in the best interests of others. They are babies who greatly need adult control until they achieve some maturity.

There may be some rare children who are so temperamentally gentle that they are easily over-controlled, but this is truly rare. Most will storm through toddlerhood, adolescence, and adulthood with plenty of fire and willpower. (Middle childhood is often the calm between two storms). If you do chance to have that very rare and gently submissive child, you will soon know it, and need only the lightest tone to get compliance. In this as in other things, your child's temperament will be a powerful guide for you, as we discuss in later chapters.

If, however, you have a child who is anywhere from average to very strong in assertiveness, establishing that simple "habit of obedience" before toddlerhood takes over, will be an invaluable aid. If this does not seem obvious, think about trying to enforce a time-out period with a child who has never been willing to stand still or sit still or come to you when asked. You have a nice little corner area arranged, and you say the appropriate words, but your little culprit simply walks away.

Now what? The answer is that you will either start now to teach that simple habit of obedience, or you will have to abandon time-outs as a strategy. The third possibility is that you will truly lose your temper and (A) physically restrain the child or (B) resort to spanking. Physical restraint has a very big downside in that it tends to turn discipline into a potentially exciting wrestling match, at least for the child. A two swat spanking is probably not the disaster it is portrayed as, if done very rarely, but as a regular strategy it is not an answer.

Something to think about Feeling ambivalent about demandingness generally means that you will apply some of the strategies, somewhat, but not all of them wholeheartedly. If so, the effect will likely be to make you less effective and quite likely this will produce more, rather than less conflict. If you are wrestling with your feelings about this, the best approach is to keep the number of rules minimal, but enforce those you have with great firmness and consistency. Efficiency in this helps your child to see early, and beyond any reasonable doubt, what you are asking. This, in turn, helps her to develop self-regulation in this area much more easily.

Your second purpose in early stages of discipline

From the beginning you are working to forge links from the child's actions to some simple consequences. For that reason, firm and noticeable removal is better than distraction when the child is old enough to understand the connection. Distraction fuzzes up the meaning of the situation. That is fine when that is what you want—to save the moment (or the vase) by diverting a very young, or a very tired and frazzled child to something else. When the intent is discipline—learning something—distraction will not help.

Generally, when your requests are simple, calm and cheerful, most of them should just become part of the rhythm of daily life. With most children during this period, it is the lure of fascinating but forbidden objects or activities that are likely to cause the most trouble. Within the second year, your "no" is successful if it works for the moment. That the child might return to a forbidden activity after a time does not mean that they have failed to respond to "no". It does mean that you need to think about your next level strategy.

At that moment, the very young child probably needs to be separated from
the object or situation of attraction. This needs another firm *no* and your removal actions. Again, for the very young child who cannot yet make a connection, you may simply want to change location and distract attention. However, by two or even earlier, if the activity is a definite no-no, it is fine for the child to know that she is being firmly and purposefully removed. (This does not mean that you need to do it in anger—simply with determination.)

Something to be aware of for yourself—one of the motives that keeps us using distraction long past the appropriate age, is that discipline is much harder, more energy consuming, and less joyful for all if the child rebels. But at the point where discipline as teaching begins, putting it off is just pushing the problem into the future, and probably making it harder to cope with later. Your darling does need to learn to accept your "no", and early is genuinely better than later.

More on planning
_____

Also part of your very early planning, is deciding where you want to teach "no" and where it is better for all concerned to put many irresistible objects out or reach or out of sight. Our own philosophy at every level is to keep it simple. Light cords, and stove controls are danger areas that must be shown to be off limits very early. Antique vases are up to you, but it is important to realize that too many forbidden objects offer two problems. They require a great many unpleasant *no*s and they make the child's task of understanding what is forbidden and what is not, more difficult.

Where you must say *no,* insist on it, but don't turn the whole house into a minefield. Your child must learn to obey your *no*, both because some things are dangerous, and because you and your child will not always be at home and you will need to control behavior in that situation. At the same time, be always aware that children are often sorely tempted, and need your help in self control, and in finding safe but exciting things to do.

What you can be very sure of is that sometime after 18 months and generally before age two, children begin to resist your requests, not only because they want something, or want something not to be happening, but also because they are increasingly interested in themselves as actors in their own lives who can say *no.*

From this point on your responses become critically important. Some writers have suggested that toddlerhood and adolescence have much in common. In both stages there are amazingly rapid changes in brain structure and in newfound abilities, and a remarkable ability to lose control. The toddler now toddles, literally and can reach all sorts of fascinating and dangerous places. Language skills are growing rapidly, and the idea that she has choices, and the ability to make choices, is also growing. In adolescence, cleverness and thinking power seem to outstrip emotional control for a time with similar results.

Unfortunately for the toddler, all this power is bedazzling. The budding self that can make choices is also overwhelmed by this, and by the inability to stick with a choice, once made. Just try taking a two year old to the supermarket, and stopping at a candy display. He wants—this—no that—no this one—and no matter what choice is made, something else will look better a moment later. Similarly the power to actually say *no* may be intoxicating, but also rather terrifying when the beloved parent reacts badly. Trying to do something new that just won't work—putting that shoestring into the hole—can lead to all consuming, utter frustration. And so, there is a meltdown.

Once the tantrum spiral starts there is no control—toddler is just gone, gone, gone. Any parent who understands this will try very hard to interrupt the process before it starts. For this there are many good responsiveness tricks that may help in advance, but the pure, hard, cold, fact is that preventative measures can do just so much, and sooner or later they fail.

When they do, you are faced with the fact that above all else, tantrums must not work in bringing the little actor either what was originally wanted, or any amount of secondary attention from you. Even a grown-up getting upset and yelling means that this little actor has produced some effect. He may well be noticing between screams that you are getting pretty red in the face yourself, and footnote that to test again later. So, truly now you need a plan. In the next Chapter we look at demandingness and at discipline techniques in greater detail and with more emphasis on the years from toddler-hood on up.

Parenting by Temperament

Chapter 6

Demandingness 301: Specific Discipline Tips and Strategies

A general plan:

The basic strategy This simply means that you approach any discipline action with a series of consequences that increase in seriousness as the problem continues. A simple *No* comes first. You may find it very helpful to have some standard phrase with this rather than just the word. "Oh-oh, that's a no-no" or "whoops, trouble coming" are simple examples. Either can be said initially in a fairly calm and friendly voice (unless a rock is headed toward the TV or some other equally catastrophic possibility that requires the sharpest and loudest of NOs).

A virtue here is that either of these phrases can be said without initial anger, which is good. A second advantage is that because it is calm, but is a signal of trouble to come, the child is likely to begin to use the phrase as an early step in self-regulation. (He may, of course, say it and then choose to ignore himself, but still--!) Just make it simple, but much the same each time.

If and when that is not effective, firmly stopping the child and giving very simple reasons (including the upcoming more serious consequence) comes second. If this fails, as it well may, it is time for other enforcement. Time-out is the most obvious, but other actions may depend on the circumstances (e.g. for the 18 month child throwing dishes and food, the meal may simply be over).

Time-out, in turn may need a further back-up for children who do not comply voluntarily with the time-out. Depending on parent philosophy this might be a brief isolation in a separate room or (if you feel comfortable with this) a very brief "two swat" spanking. Generally speaking, isolation is the better choice. What seems to happen in either case is that the more severe measures act to make the child increasingly responsive to the less severe measures, so that time-outs are effective alone, and, with luck, eventually reasoning and even just "No" become effective.

The sequence model depends on consistency for its effectiveness. Each step along the way must signal that tougher things are coming if there is no compliance. Consistency, however, begins with your demandingness pre-planning. You need to think through what you will and will not permit, and what positive actions you will insist on, and what the consequences are going to be when things go wrong at each point in your child's life. As we have said many times, in doing this you want to think about your own reasons for your rules, why they are important (and in some cases, *whether* they are really important.) Parents need to negotiate all of this together, and find workable compromises where they don't naturally agree.

Again, if you think of discipline as teaching, you can see that firmly enforcing a limited number of rules is going to be more successful than being erratic about enforcing a whole world of rules. (The obvious exception is where behavior is dangerous, whether physically or emotionally. There you need all the rules that security requires.) When you are clear about the rules you want to enforce, you need to be as firm and consistent as you are humanly capable of being. This is truly critical. The greater the consistency early on, the fewer the repeat episodes will be. That is also part of the value of the sequential approach. It signals that a now familiar set of events is going to unfold, but preventing the next step is always within the child's control.

Ages and stages in discipline

80

There is usually a big difference in dealing with your two year old versus your three year old here. At two you still want to think carefully as to whether your child is just too tired and strung out to cope at all. This is especially likely if it is late in the day or just before a meal. A little time in your lap or some other distraction (not a treat though, as that teaches a different lesson) may be the best strategy to try, along with an early bedtime.

By two and a half or three, defiance and tantrum behavior will have taken on a purposeful character and will need to be treated that way. At three, if the child is taken to her room and told to stay ***but does not,*** the answer has to be a shut door for a very short period. If the door is opened then it must be a locked door—similarly briefly. You need to carry this out and remain quiet (although staying nearby for the child's safety). She needs to know that you will time the time-out and won't start this until the fuss is over. With the average child it is unlikely that you will struggle with this level of defiance, but you do need to know what you will do if it occurs.

Further thoughts

Above all, do not let the steps in your discipline sequence bog down in argument. Once you have moved beyond the first verbal steps, you want to move quickly to the consequence phase of your sequence, without allowing room for argument. Kids are good—very good -- at noticing when consequences can be delayed by words ("No fair!" "You're a bad mom", "No, it isn't Timmy's"). Once that starts, like a tantrum, it can spiral out of control. You find yourself arguing back, the child comes up with a new plea, and you are off and running. It can happen all too easily.

The same reasoning holds for physically holding or restraining a child during time-outs. Your angry attention may not be what your child would prefer, but it is still attention, and far better than being ignored. The child who is acting out needs to do it alone in order to calm down and in order to discover how little fun that is. If your child seems to want to talk about it after things have calmed down, this is fine, as long as it is a low key, non-blaming discussion for all.

Misbehavior in public especially needs advance thought. When you first begin to take a toddler or preschooler out in public, (shopping, meals, etc.) you really need to know what you plan to do if tantrums or other rebellion break out. Children figure out remarkably early that you will hate disruption and hate to make it worse by taking a strong stand in a public place.

The best advice for new parents, especially, is to regard these first ventures out as a training exercise. Be prepared to say no to unreasonable demands, and be prepared to follow up with a trip to the car, and if that fails, a return home. When eating out, and with more than the one offending toddler involved, it may even make sense to take two cars, so that one parent can take the little trouble-maker home without ruining the outing for everyone.

Discipline with older children

The sequence: Here you may or may not be able to start with the gentle warning *no*. If things are beginning to unravel in front of you, you can certainly start there, but often it begins with something that has already happened—chores undone, homework, neglected, misbehavior at school, and so forth. In those cases, the important thing is that your rules and their consequences have been thoroughly discussed in advance, so that the more serious consequences are the next step.

More often here, your sequencing will be in terms of stronger consequences for each repetition of the same problem behavior. If the consequences are in the area of grounding, or loss of privileges, for example, repeat offenses would seriously extend the time of this.

Grounding: its uses and problems

Where withdrawal of privileges or household grounding is the primary consequence, you need to be particularly honest with yourself. It is very common to react to a serious misbehavior with a strong punishment—"you are grounded for a month, young lady!"-- but have second thoughts as time goes by. Your anger or shock ebbs, your child is sorry, and well behaved, and then some unexpected event comes along. Your child's friends have a party, or relatives come in from out of town and want to do things, or dad comes home in a great mood on a Friday night and wants to take everyone out. It feels kind and warm hearted to let the little dear one back into the world of fun. But—unless the circumstances are extraordinary—it is a mistake. If you have not said that there could be any exceptions, then the right answer is—"sorry, you're grounded".

If you think ahead about the grounding period, it is possible, and perhaps wise, exclude certain specific events when the grounding is given. A major game that the child is to play in, or a major end of the year event at school are examples. Unexpected visits by relatives could be handled by exempting the time that they are there, and adding it on at the end (you would want to give your child a choice in that) but it should be clear that this is because it is a major event that could not be predicted.

The point is—your child is paying great attention to this. Her first reaction, if you make an exception after the grounding period has started, will of course be happiness and gratitude toward you, but the second reaction will be a much more sophisticated recognition that you caved, and, perhaps, these punishments are not to be taken seriously.

Grounding specifics

The first instance of grounding for a specific behavior should be brief but thorough. Three days may be a good start, if you do it well.

To tell your child he is grounded at home, but then allow the Internet, TV, IPod etc. won't really do it. All communication devices have to go. If TV is in the general family areas, your child will need to go to his room when it is on. Any breaking of these rules just adds more days. The whole idea is to make this period of time aversive. And that accomplishes two things. One is that hopefully your son, Sammy, will think twice before getting in the same trouble again. And two is that it makes it clear that you have the power to enforce your rules—a fact that has its uses beyond the current situation.

Like the situation that fewer rules, consistently enforced, are a better teaching tool, a shorter length of grounding or loss of privileges that is rigidly enforced, is far more effective than a monumental punishment that gets canceled. The thoroughness with which a punishment is carried out also conveys its own message. It not only says that you are serious and will follow through (very important as we have said many times), but it also sends the message that this is an issue that matters to you. That makes it a little more likely that your child will think about your rules and reasons—perhaps even internalizing them, at least a little.

Discussions during discipline with an older child

Where it is best to avoid all discussion with a two year old during a discipline sequence, the situation may be more complex with an older child. If the particular problem has never occurred before, you may need to discuss why you think the behavior was a wrong choice. If it is something you did not personally witness, you may need to explore the truth of the matter. For school-aged children this is an appropriate first step. It is useful to state your reasoning here, and it is appropriate to listen to what you child wants to say in return, in a disciplinary encounter. But, at this time, the critically important word is "briefly". Unless you are convinced that you don't have a clear picture of what happened, any further discussion should wait until the consequences have been accepted and carried out.

When Samantha is arguing with you after having misbehaved, she is trying to get out of the current situation, not exchange deep philosophic views. This is not the time to discuss any rule changes. Tell her she is welcome to discuss this further after the current punishment is over, but not now.

Prolonged discussions at this time generally take one of two forms, depending on the child's temperament. A child who is strong on verbal logic will try to convince you that you have a bad rule, and will muster every possible argument to prove it to you. If very assertive, this child may go on to anger or sarcasm if you will allow it, and if there are chinks in your armor. This is where thinking your rules through thoroughly in advance, is a huge boost to your own strength and confidence. The answer to any argument for change in your established rules should be that you will not discuss this now. Your basic approach should be that ***today's rules hold for today's problem.***

The child who is more into feelings and emotions will have other possible agendas. One is simply to go on talking about what happened, emphasizing how much she didn't understand the situation, or was pressured by others, or was simply feeling so sad, angry, scared, (you name it) that she just didn't think. This is an early effort at trying out victim-hood.

A second approach, sometimes linked with the first, is to show how very sorry she is, how much she wishes it had never happened, how sure she is she will never do it again, even that you are right, your rule is good, etc. Tears are a good add-on here. Consciously or not, your child is trying to win your sympathy, show heart-melting levels of contrition, and come out with a clean record. There is no doubt an element of truth here, but over time you will see purposeful strategy too. Your answer here is also "later" for further discussion. Once the bare facts appear clear, the conversation has to end, and the planned consequences need to begin.

Good tactics at all ages

Sound like you mean it! This can be a little tricky. You do not want to escalate to out of control anger with any child, but some parents, in order to indicate that they are calm and in control, end up sounding like they are emotionally uninvolved, or interviewing for remakes of a happy 1950s sitcom. That is okay for your initial warning to a young toddler (Oh-oh, that's a no-no"), but for the child who is old enough to know that she just did something on the forbidden list, you need a little more firmness.

A very gentle voice will sound to the child as if the problem is no more vital than items you want to add to the grocery list. It certainly will not be attention getting. So what you want is a sort of calm, controlled passion. It has to sound like it matters to you, or all the talking and reasoning in the world will not be effective. And, realistically, it also has to *actually* matter to you in order to sound like it matters. If you do not have any deep conviction about the rule you are trying to enforce, you really need a long talk with yourself. Why then are you doing what you are doing? If you do have conviction, be sure it rings in your voice.

Never reward whining

We generally think of whining as the domain of small children. By and large it is, but school-age children do it too, although the style changes a little. You say no to a snack shortly before dinner and the three year old whines, screams or falls on the floor in a tantrum. I'm hungry!!!

Your ten year old will have developed more style. This may involve coming at the same position from several persuasive angles. "Gee mom, I got home so late today that I missed mid-afternoon snack time," "Gee dad, coach made us do a zillion laps at soccer, and I am just starving." "Gosh, mom, I gave away half my lunch to a friend who forgot his. I hardly had anything for myself." (This one is particularly touching). Or, "I don't know what's the matter with me, but I feel week and shaky. Maybe just a small cookie?" (Especially good for pushing mom buttons.)

From your logical child "You know me, mom. I'm always on the move. A snack won't spoil my appetite." At fourteen, the approach may change to criticism, sarcasm, etc. "You treat me like a baby." "I'm old enough to know when I need to eat." "What are you, the family food Nazi?" etc., etc. All these approaches are forms of whining though. They are a continuing attempt to get you to change your mind.

So, what's wrong with that? Well, everything. When whining in any of its forms is successful, it teaches, once again, that you are not serious about what you say, and/or that whatever seriousness you have can be destroyed by persistence. If this happens with any frequency it has ripple effects on all your other attempts to keep order and enforce the limits you have decided on. Even more to the point, successful whining strengthens whining behavior. Worst of all, it often teaches that it takes a lot of persistence but it works in the end.

Why you may be rewarding persistence in spite of yourself

One of the best examples of this powerful effect can be seen in the animal laboratory. In a common learning experiment, a young and hungry rat is given a metal bar in her cage which, if pressed, will produce a food pellet. At first it is all accidental, but eventually she gets the connection and begins pressing at amazing rates of speed. Once the connection is well established, she can be coaxed to keep on pressing even if only one in fifty or one in one hundred presses produces food. And—our young rat will show the greatest persistence if she is trained on a varied schedule (one time ten presses will do it, next time one, third time, fifty.) ***The lesson learned is that there is just no predicting when the reward will come, but if you just keep doing it, and doing it, it will come eventually.***

It is the same effect when a parent trains a child in persistent whining for an unpredictable reward! As parent, you may hold out for a long time on some days, only giving in at the end of your patience. On other days you may collapse early. You tell yourself you have done a better job on the days when you were slow to give in, but, in fact, that is not true. Overall you are teaching the worst possible lesson--just keep trying—there is no way to tell when the reward is coming, but eventually you will hit the jackpot. What you are doing here is turning your child into an endurance champion.

Using responsiveness alternatives in these situations This whole scenario is just no fun. Most of all it is no fun for the parent and for the rest of the family listening to this, but even the child is not having a terrific time. Most situations that produce this type of behavior are fairly predictable. What you can do on the responsiveness side is to try to plan in advance for any alternatives to "No", that are acceptable. For the child wheedling for sweets, chips, sodas, it may be possible to say that there is fruit available, or that the salad for dinner is made and can be eaten now, if your child prefers. This does no nutritional harm and may be a reasonable compromise. If the snack has to be really appealing to be desirable, hunger is not really the problem.

If tempting toys or snacks in the supermarket or mall are a major issue, what is and is not possible can be decided in advance, as an end of the shopping trip purchase, if that fits your budget. What is critically important, here as in all other issues, is that you are totally clear about what is possible and what is not, and very consistent in carrying this out. If this does not produce a good outcome, a younger child probably just shouldn't be there, if at all possible. A child who is old enough to grasp the situation should be told that mall privileges will be lost after any bad trip, and not restored for a while.

Timing and tempo both at home and away

Generally speaking, punishment should be prompt—ideally, immediate. The child who is starting a world-class tantrum in the supermarket should get the 1-2-3 sequence--1. (Command)--"Stop" 2. (Brief reasoning)-- "You are disturbing others in the store and I can't let you do that. If you don't quiet down immediately, we are going out and you are not coming back." 3 (Brief wait and then action)--Pick up the child and go outside. If you are alone and this means abandoning your shopping basket you will just have to do that. There needs to be as little attention and payoff for this behavior as possible. Threatening some later punishment is not an answer for a young child for whom time has little meaning. The behavior and your action need to be closely tied. *Continuing to threaten and struggle is disastrous. It totally blurs the lesson, suggests that the child has power and you are helpless.*

Is delayed punishment ever appropriate? In more complex situations—the child is older, the behavior has ethical or moral aspects—there may be good reasons to delay a decision on what the exact consequences will be. You may want time to think about it or to talk with your co-parent--but something needs to happen immediately.

You may want to state your position on the behavior briefly, listen carefully, but again, briefly, to the child's explanation, and then send her to her room for the moment to do some thinking. When you have gathered your thoughts it will be time enough to finish the discussion and lay out any serious consequences, but some reaction is needed immediately, to make it clear that the issue is important and is not going to slide by.

Selecting the best consequences

Appropriate to the crime. Staying with the theme that the primary point of discipline is to teach life lessons and make lasting changes in behavior, it is very fitting that wherever possible, the punishment should fit the crime. A good example can be seen where something has been broken because of rough handling/horse-play, or harmed because a job wasn't done (e.g. plants were not watered). Restitution is very appropriate here. Not only should the child pay for it (or part of it, depending on age) but also should be involved in buying/replacing the item.

It is harder to find natural-seeming consequences for toddlers, but certainly a time-out for tantrum behavior is a rational consequence since what the child needs most is to calm down and be quiet. Losing out on a family outing is often a very good consequence for chores or homework not done. Many times this takes thought, but there is no harm in telling an older child that you will announce the consequence when you have had time to think about it, as long as you are very clear that it is coming. (That gives them time to think about it too!)

A good fit for this child. Complicating things a little, the more the consequences are tailored to work well for your unique and specific child, the more effective they will be. Telling your little Introvert that he or she is grounded from all social events for a month may not really be a blow to the heart. This would be especially true if this child is free to use the computer, read an exciting book, etc. The same grounding rules might grab your Extravert's attention dramatically. When you put together both logical cause-and-effect consequences, and child-specific consequences, there is plenty to think about.

A Family Example

Mike, the oldest sibling in our family, wanted to learn to play the guitar when he was about nine, and a friend wanted to join him, so mom, the family guitarist at that time, started to give lessons to both boys. Great fun—but practice every day—that was something else. It dwindled and dwindled for Mike, until little was being learned, while the friend dutifully forged ahead. The end result was that cruel mom said "No practice? Then no lessons." Mike had to listen in another room on lesson day, while his buddy got better and better.

It worked. After a few weeks, Mike forced himself to practice and soon outdid his pal. With more formal lessons later and a lifetime of voluntary practice, he became an accomplished guitarist. Joy in the skill provided the lasting motivation, but good demandingness consequences got the process going. Was "no practice, no lesson" the right consequence? Well, it was for Mike. Daily nagging produced nothing; he wasn't very disciplined, hated to be shut off by himself to practice, and just tuned the nagging out. On the other hand, he loved music, and had a competitive streak, so this set of consequences did the trick. You really have to know each child. (And we will really get into that in upcoming chapters!)

Rules and Limits should also fit the child's maturity and temperament.

Are your rules really appropriate for this child's age, understanding, and temperament? For example, say that you are expecting "A" or "Excellent" grades from your second grader. You need to be sure of a couple of things. Is this child capable of this performance at some reasonable level of effort? You want to see what the teacher thinks, see how hard or easy any homework is for the child, and so forth. You want to look at the child's temperament and natural interests. Does this child, by nature, want to excel in this area, or is that *your* dream? That does not mean that you have no standards here, but rather that you take your child into consideration when you establish them.

For a different sort of example, you require your happy-go-lucky child to make her own bed. Fine, but are you asking obsessively for the child-equivalent of hospital-bed corners? Is what she does ever good enough, or is there always that disappointed little sigh coming from you? You must have rules and requirements but you can certainly tailor the details to your child's own nature and maturity, and you should.

Other things that help: Monitoring, family organization, parent as role model.

Monitoring When your child knows that *you know* what he or she is doing, and knows that there are real consequences for misbehaviors and undone assignments, that child is much more likely to start getting things done before trouble strikes. The same is true for doing things that are forbidden. Much of the child's ability to resist temptation comes from awareness that parents are keeping track and do have a pretty good idea of where each child is and what he or she is doing. We have gone through a period where this aspect of parenting has sometimes been downplayed as invasive or untrusting, but a great deal of research today points to it as hard, sometimes painful, but very necessary work.

Parents have much more control over preventing exposure to harmful influences while their children are young and at home. This job becomes more of a challenge as the child experiences the larger world and becomes more independent in daily activities. By the time adolescence is reached, the parent's direct control decreases significantly. Nevertheless, the adolescent is not an adult. She may hate your continued involvement in her life, but may still be very much in need of it. Control becomes subtle now, and success is much based on the strong family bonds that were established over the years and a long history of consistent and successful rules and limits in earlier years.

Family and household organization Fitting into this like a hand to a glove, is maintaining a reasonably organized household. The more there are fairly regular times for chores, homework, meals, bedtime, etc., the more likely it is that the child comes to anticipate and fit into the routine without constant reminders. At the same time, it is much easier to keep track of your child's activities if they do happen in a predictable framework. Both of these factors have been shown to promote self-regulation and a general attitude of planfulness in growing children.

The parent as role model Being a good model is important in two ways. Most directly, children tend to model the behavior they see every day. This is far more vivid and influential than your verbal recitations about values. Young children may do what you say because they wish to avoid trouble, but ultimately they are most likely to make your values their own if they see them every day in action and see that the results are positive. Equally important is the fact that they will be much more likely to accept your rules and consequences if they perceive your honesty and fairness, and this can't happen if your rules and your own behavior are miles apart. Family problems will occur, all parents lose their cool from time to time, and sainthood is not expected, but the genuineness of your efforts matters tremendously.

A Last Few General Principles (Some repetitions here, but that can't hurt!)

❖ *Don't have any more rules and limits than you really believe you must have.* Your child needs to breath and feel like an independent person as much as is compatible with being a positive member of the household community. And your child needs to learn, above all, that the rules you have, are to be obeyed. This goes best if you don't have an overwhelming number of them.

❖ *Don't have any _fewer_ rules and limits than you really need.* If you are constantly irritated by noise, mess, commotion and general disruption by your child, you may be being much too tolerant. In part, this is another temperament issue. If you are accepting behavior that is just *not* acceptable for you, the outcome will not be good. You will be tense and inwardly angry, and this will have bad effects on the happy responsiveness side of your parent/child relationship. Your rules and limits really do need a lot of thought.

❖ *Choose your consequences wisely and with determination.* Never threaten a consequence that you cannot or will not carry out. "If you don't stop this I am just going to leave you at the

93

store" is simply silly, as you cannot carry it out. "If you don't watch out, I am going to ground you for a year" is equally silly. You will never do it, and would go mad if you tried. Plan ahead for what is reasonable and then carry that out absolutely. If you say grounded for a week, it is a week, not just four days because "you have been so good about this." If you say no TV for X days, it is no TV, with no exceptions for a favorite program or a big game. However warm and loving it feels to relent, you are just teaching your watching child not to take you seriously next time.

❖ *Demand only what you can actually get control over.* You can insist that your child go to bed; you cannot force him to go to sleep. You can insist that a child in the midst of a tantrum go away and not have it in front of you, but just saying "stop crying" won't get you far. Eating wholesome meals is an important issue for most parents, but you can't directly make your child eat. You can insist on good behavior at the table or removal as a consequence of acting up. You can, and truly should, insist on no dessert and no after-dinner snacks when the meal has been snubbed! Appetite is your friend here. Understanding where compliance is and isn't possible, is another area where forethought and planning is very helpful.

❖ *What you say you will do, you really must do.* This consistency rule is the heart of effective demandingness. Realize that your child is always torn between wanting to do exactly what she wants to do, and wanting two things that conflict with this--a warm and loving bond with you and no bad consequences. In the long run, your affection and esteem are all important, but in the short run, and especially if the child is angry—her top deterrent is avoiding bad consequences. If that is to work, you need a clear history of meaning what you say and doing what you say you will do.

❖ *Be open to discussion about rules in calm times.* It is a very important part of demandingness that your rules and limits be well thought out, clear in your own mind, and communicated as needed, to your child. There are many reasons for this, but perhaps most important is that it keeps you honest. To discuss them you have to have rules that are defensible in your own mind. Whether or not they will impress your child is a separate matter! The second very good reason is that in the long run, it helps your child to internalize your values when you explain them freely and clearly, and when you are willing to hear your child's view also.

❖ ***Be ready to put a cap on discussion when it becomes angry or repetitive.*** The down side of any discussion about rules is that your child is always motivated to get rid of your restrictions and rules, and ever ready to give it a try. It is good to be willing to discuss a rule the first time that the rule comes up and the child asks "Why, can't I-----? ". It is good to briefly talk about the broken rule after an incident is over, provided your child feels up to it (don't use this time to browbeat an already sad child, though.) However, in each case you also have to be wary of having the original discussion degenerate into an endless argument.

❖ When you have explained yourself as clearly as you can, and given your child a chance to say his/her piece, it is time to stop. If your child has raised a point you think needs further thought, say so, and agree to talk again later. If not, remind her that rules are ultimately up to parents. End of discussion.

The top rules for all the years—Be clear, consistent, and prompt in follow-through; be as fair as is humanly possible; know your child and yourself. Be sure that each day has far more fun than fury.

The changing rhythm of demandingness

In the beginning In the years from two to three and even four, large parts of the child's motivation consist of trying to assert and reassert that "you're not the boss of me"! Other parts, of course, are much more specifically related to things the child wants to do and is not permitted, or does not want to do, but is expected to do. Generally fierce conflict peaks around age three and begins to decline as the child's self-regulation skills increase.

Middle childhood This period, corresponding to the early grades, is normally a pretty happy time for both child and parent. The basic rules have been learned, and there is usually a big drop off in conflict as pure power struggle. Apparently you are the "boss" for the present, and anyhow, other things are more interesting. Conflict will continue over current wants and needs, but not so much over control for control's sake.

If either side of authoritative parenting has gone badly, however, this may not be the case. The child who does not feel both loved and respected, who has not deeply bonded to you is a child who lacks a major reason to obey you. For some children that may be reflected in constant anger, fighting, and disrespect for your authority.

On the other hand, the child who is well cared for and loved, but ineffectively disciplined, may also continue to break all the rules. If you threaten over and over again but rarely follow through, if you respond to rule breaking with a serious punishment but let it lapse out of pity or boredom, or simply react to misbehavior with sad eyes and solemn words but no action, a child with any spirit will test the limits forever. You have failed to make it clear that you _are_ "the boss of him".

And then there is adolescence. Even after the best and most peaceful of middle childhoods the dormant power struggle usually re-emerges here. At this point you may find yourself with a very tall, very bright and articulate three year old, ready to fight to the death to have her way, even if she has no idea what that might be. We have known for a long time that rapidly changing hormones play a part in this, and brain science is now revealing even more incredible changes that are occurring in the adolescent brain.

These rapid shifts contribute to the storm and stress of adolescence for all young people. It will be greater with some temperaments than others—a fact you have no control over. But it will also be far more tempestuous in the adolescent who did not form a strong relationship with you through responsiveness, and the adolescent who never came to terms with your authority in earlier years through successful demandingness. Throughout your child's development, every good action you take is laying the groundwork for a more peaceful future, and a happier young person.

Troubleshooting when demandingness strategies are not working

Are you blowing the discipline basics?—A quick checklist

- ❖ You have no clear system of rules and limits and enforcements?
- ❖ You are inconsistent in your rules, limits and enforcements?
- ❖ You have no clear set of reasons for the rules and limits that you have?
- ❖ Your demands are excessive for this child's age, understanding, abilities?
- ❖ You start out all right but weaken, shorten or cancel consequences?
- ❖ You let yourself get bogged down in discussion during a discipline session?
- ❖ You find confronting and monitoring just exhausting and tend to just hope for the best.
- ❖ Your own life is chaotic—little is predictable or on schedule for you or the family?
- ❖ You postpone action until later—after dinner, when mom/dad come home etc.?
- ❖ You erratically give in to whining?
- ❖ Your philosophy is do as I say, not as I do?

If the answer to one or more of the above is a resounding YES, you already know that you have work to do. In Parts II and III of this book we help you to understand not only your child's temperament but your own, and in Parts IV and V. we offer ideas and tips for working with temperament related problems.

Are there problems on the responsiveness side?

❖ Is there chronic ill will in the air between you? No matter how much you love your small one, some temperament clashes require a lot of work and thought. If you are extremely organized, and your child is of the extremely happy-go-lucky temperament, it is always going to be hard work to find a middle road between you. If you are a strong logical thinker and have an inner sense of disappointment about your "wimpy" emotional child—he will know that and feel rejected, even unloved. The same is true if you have very deep emotional responses and see your logical thinker child as too cold and impersonal. These and other differences can bring a chronic edge to the parent-child bond. Bridging the gap is your job as the parent and grown-up. (Again, the rest of this book is designed to help you do that).

❖ Are you just too busy for optimal responsiveness? Many of us, especially those who were just born to "get things done", like to think we can do everything if we just organize well enough. When it comes to responsive parenting, that is simply not true. You need actual time, as well as a sense of time and space, in order to stop and listen and watch and respond. If you have committed your self, your child, or both of you to obligations and activities 24/7, it may be that you both need most of all some tranquil time together

Are there too many discipline blips in your day?

In Chapter Four we graphed possible timelines for a day where discipline problems were a remarkably small part of each day (A), and one in which these blips came thick and fast all day long(B).

(A) ____/_____/_____/ _____//_____/

As we noted there, the day shown in (A) is unusually peaceful, and perhaps too much to hope for on a regular basis, but (B) is at the other extreme. If these discipline encounters disturbed the peace for an average of 10 minutes each, that would total to five and one/half hours of disruption and unhappiness out of a 12 hour waking day. Parent/child relationships and pleasure in each other's company would be severely down. In addition, the child would have a hard time finding anything that she could do that would not be a source of trouble.

Getting a handle on this   If you sense that your days might be closer to (B) than (A), a useful step would be to try to record the daily parent/child interactions for a week or so. If you make brief notes about the time, the issue, and the underlying cause (if you see one), it could help in trying to pinpoint the problems. These might be any of the problems we have discussed here, from poor demandingness strategies to responsiveness problems, but noting them down would help to make it clearer to you.

Sometimes it is as simple as carrying on old bad habits, just reflexively saying no, or scolding without really considering whether it is necessary. Recording these events for a week is time consuming, but definitely worth a try.

Is there a more serious problem that needs attention?

If your child is having frequent and troublesome problems in school or at home, or is chronically sad or anxious, or chronically angry beyond what seems normal to you, it may be time to look for a good counselor or therapist. ***When all your best efforts do not seem to be enough, finding professional help is clearly the next step.***

This is true for yourself also. If there is deep marital conflict, or long lasting depression, if everything seems just too hard, this is the time to reach out for a lifeline.

Part II

The Idea of Preferences and the Meaurement of Preferences

Overview

In part I we have taken a good look at the authoritative parenting system. We are confident that this is the best general approach to parenting that you will find. At this point you might be thinking "fine, let's just do it" and wondering why we are heading in a new direction here in part II. Or you might be thinking, a little more skeptically "well, if this is such a good system, why doesn't everyone just do it, and why doesn't it work perfectly for everyone?"

Logically, this suggests that everyone within reach of this book should soon be parenting wonderfully well. That has never happened as the result of any book in the history of publishing. **And why not?** We tried to suggest in Part I that children bring their own genetic gifts (and shortcomings) into the world. That is one very important reason that you cannot simply apply a good system and get perfectly predictable results. Every child is a unique experience in parenting, and the same exact approach may produce remarkably different results with different children.

Equally important, and equally true is the fact that every parent has come into the world with her own and his own genetic gifts and shortcomings. These have been stretched and polished with a lifetime of experience but these qualities are still unique to each individual.

We differ enormously from each other, and it isn't simply because our mothers before us didn't have the ideal parenting system. We are highly organized and loving it, totally disorganized and loving it.

People oriented, task oriented. Dreamy or down to earth. Highly social and self-assertive, reserved and hesitant. Much of that came in our gene package. These different qualities affect how we live, our choice in mates, in work, in friends, and certainly how we parent. They affect the things that resonate with us in any parenting philosophy, and they affect our ability to carry out even the strategies that speak to us most clearly.

The same is true for our children. They come with tendencies that make demandingness easy in some areas, hard in others. Some are more responsive to us, some less, depending on their own uniqueness. Some come with temperament preferences that are so strong that they need our help in developing skills in less preferred areas. The very extraverted child who seems incapable of doing anything alone is an example, as is the very introverted child who hates social settings.

Any approach to parenting that does not take all of this into account will simply fail many children and many parents. If both you and your child fit a sort of golden mean in in all your preferences (neither highly extraverted nor highly introverted, neither extremely organized nor terribly disorganized, neither very dreamy or extremely matter of fact, etc., then following the very good advice in Chapter 1-6, just as it is, should go very well for you.

If, however, you and/or the child you parent do have clear to strong preferences in some areas, then you need to take the next step, and look at these preferences and their effects on your parent/child interactions. In our experience, that golden-mean child or parent is far more often the exception than the rule. We believe that the great majority of our readers will benefit significantly from examining these temperament differences and then going on to think about applying this knowledge to responsiveness and demandingness.

In later sections of this book we will return to practical parenting advice that will help you to adapt the basic principles of responsiveness and demandingness to fit your own preference strengths and weaknesses, and the genetic push and pull that your child brings into the world. In *Part II, (and in Part III)*however, we need to take time out to look at the preferences themselves—the inborn qualities that are the bedrock of what is generally called personality. Personality is best defined as the sum of these inborn qualities plus your own life-long experiences, but the foundation for this is given by your natural temperament preferences

Parenting by Temperament

Chapter 7

Every Child is Unique

Your child's developmental plan

Just as your infant comes into the world with the skills, drives and motivations common to all human children, he also brings a developmental plan for himself that is entirely his own. Research indicates that about 50% of adult personality comes from gene-based differences in temperament.[18] Recognizing these differences in your child will give you a great advantage in making the most of both responsiveness and demandingness. The same is true for you, as the unique parent. It is one thing to see a best possible way to parent; it is quite another to make the ideal method fit with the real you. Your own individual temperament pushes and pulls you in ways that you may not fully recognize. In this chapter we will talk about temperament differences in children. Later we will look at parent temperament and how it may affect all that you do.

Some early differences you might see in your child.

In the beginning it's confusing. The first two or three months of life are pretty hard to judge. Some babies are cheery from the start, some are rather quiet, and some seem to be pretty mad about the whole thing much of the time. But, this is a very tumultuous time. As we noted before, stress hormones shoot up in newborns at the slightest provocation, and that can be pretty disturbing. New parents are unsure of themselves, tired and sometimes not parenting brilliantly yet. And then there is colic for some infants, disturbed sleep patterns

---

[18] Bouchard, T. J. (1994). Genes, Environment and Personality. *Science* 264 p 1700-1701.

for others, problems with formula for yet another set. You really can't make much of this in the early weeks.

IMPORTANT NOTE: To keep this story clear and simple we are describing extremes in the baby and toddler behaviors below. If your child falls closer to the middle, that is also normal and unsurprising.

By three months.

As things begin to calm down around the third month, the most distinctive difference may be in how much your child smiles, grins and giggles. The big smiler may also be a very noisy babbler. As he gets better and better control over muscles, this same child is likely to be pretty active and eager to meet the world. At the other extreme are babies who are quiet and rather serious, giving you a big smile as a special treat, but not tossing these out routinely. Such babies have sometimes been described as "old souls", serious about the world from day one.

Another distinction is among babies who are very cuddly, who just melt right into your arms and seem to be in heaven, and those sometimes can take it or leave it. The cuddlers are often happy to be passed from person to person in the early months, love prolonged contact, may virtually purr over being touched, sung to, etc. At the opposite extreme are those who cuddle rather briefly, and are soon looking around for something else to see, hear, and react to. As they grow older and more independent, such children may accept your hug briefly and then squirm and wiggle to get down and do things.

Interestingly, these two sets of differences may come mixed and matched. We can find smiley cuddlers and serious cuddlers, smiley non-cuddlers and serious non-cuddlers. By about age four we can begin to measure these differences and make some predictions about each child's future behavior.

By three years.

If your first observations were accurate, we can now see quite a bit more in the behavior of these children. The early big smilers are likely to be outgoing and friendly, noisy and active. As toddlers they are apt to be bored quickly without some company. It is likely that the classic "fear of strangers" period was relatively short and mild, and it is very probable that they will adjust pretty easily to their introduction to nursery school. They generally enjoy having a fair amount of chaos and activity at home, and are rarely upset by it.

The more serious babies are now showing you something else. Chances are, they had a significant struggle with the *fear of strangers* period, and may not yet have accepted preschool or other group activities without complaint. At the least they tend to watch a group quietly from the sidelines for quite a while before venturing in. Long periods of group activity, even household chaos, are likely to be tiring, where the same activity might rev our little giggler up.

If there is going to be a tantrum-like meltdown for this child, it is likely to occur when there has been too much chaos (from their perspective) and too little quiet time. If your big smiler is going to have a tantrum it is more likely to be over something he really wanted to do that you did not allow. *Reserved* is a word that may come to mind as you watch your serious toddler, just as *bold* may now be a good fit for your smiley toddler.

Our cuddlers are likely to be demonstratively affectionate, and gentle souls overall. By three they may already be showing signs of their ability to empathize with others. They may get upset if another child is crying or hurt, and even go so far as to seek help at that tender age. In the family setting you may find that they become tearful if there are voices raised in anger. Disciplining or criticizing them may lead quickly to emotional meltdowns.

Non-cuddler babies may now seem to be a cooler, but calmer breed. At the extreme they can be children who quickly wipe off smeary kisses from overly-enthusiastic aunts, and are choosey as to who they want to hug and be hugged by. They might do something practical to help another child in distress, but they would be much less likely to be upset by that child's tears. As they grow older and more verbal, you may find that you need to remind them that *not* everything that is thought needs to be said—a nice way of saying that they can be outspoken and overly frank

Mix and match again. It may seem logical that smiley toddlers would be cuddly toddlers and serious toddlers would be non-cuddlers, but the fact is that we come in marvelous combinations, so that this can go either way. The one thing that is very clear is that the more serious toddler (and adult!) reserves her many or few hugs and kisses for family and very close friends, where the smiley toddler is willing to disperse them (however few or many) widely.

Head in the clouds, feet on the ground

Some of us have our eyes on the road directly in front of us, and keep a close eye on street signs and passing traffic. On a trip we have our route clearly in mind. When we tell someone about the trip later it is likely to be in detail and in pretty good chronological order. We are practical, and pretty much assume everyone else should be also.

Others are dreamier and more in love with what we can imagine. At our worst, a practical spouse may have to remind us that we just missed a turn-off on our trip while we were fantasizing about how much fun it would be to be at our destination. If we describe it later we will probably sail by all the practical details, and talk about what the outing meant to us, or what the most interesting thing was that we learned from it.

These differences are certainly not evident in your three month old, and hard to see at three years or even four. However, if you are sensitive to the signs you may begin to form an opinion about whether you have a daydreamer or a down to earth toddler, even in the first years. All children ask a million questions over the years, but if you pay attention to the ones where they seem to want serious answers, you may see a difference.

Your dreamer may ask many more "why" questions, and these may have an increasingly abstract quality. Not "why do we have to have peas again" or "why is daddy mad", but "why do things die", or "what makes it rain on some days and not others". Your practical toddler is more likely to ask you equally challenging questions about how things work or how the picture gets into the TV set.

The more practical child may talk a great deal about what she is doing right now, or what she is excited about right now. The more dreamy child is more likely to begin to muse on what she will do when she grows up or gets "big". Their choice of favorite stories may also reflect this difference, with dreamers enjoying stories full of make-believe, and practicals relishing stories about real life adventures. Even earlier, you may see some differences in everyday play behavior. In the bathtub, baby practicals of all ages may delight in the sensations more, splashing and playing endlessly with the water and their water toys. As they get older, dreamers are more likely to turn even their soap bars into dragons or speedboats, and/or to begin telling stories about them. The little practical child may delight more in interesting sensations. Running through puddles, squeezing gooey clay, looking at textures, making simple but realistic structures of all sorts, is especially pleasing.

The dreamer, playing in the sandbox, is more likely to get carried away with some story about what might be happening, than with the details of her creation. Lastly, it is highly unlikely that your practical child will ever have an imaginary friend, while your dreamer might at some point. All children do all of these things, but different temperaments are likely to emphasize one group of activities over another.

Structure-lovers and freedom-lovers

This is yet another area where people can differ radically from one another. It is particularly hard for people at one extreme of this to make any sense of the person at the opposite extreme. *Some of us are at our very best* and our most comfortable when life is extremely orderly and predictable. If so, we will work very hard to keep it that way. The person with an immaculate home, car waxed to the nth, clear desk, empty in-basket, garage tools that fit the motto "a place for everything and everything in its place", and a state of the art scheduling calendar, really does love structure and organization.

At the other extreme is a free-spirit who is somewhere between indifferent and hostile to orderliness. If we could force that free-spirit (perhaps as a reality show participant!) to spend most of every day maintaining the structure-lover's order, it would be cruel and unusual punishment. This free spirit would not only *not* do it well, she would absolutely hate it.

The motto here is close to an old fifties song "Don't fence me in." She wants to wake up in the morning and think, "well, what do I feel most like doing today?" And if she changes her mind after a couple of cups of coffee, she would like to be free to do that too. Chaos is comfortable, plans can be easily changed, and life is a daily adventure.

This is perhaps the hardest thing to see in a very young child, since no child, by definition, is ever very orderly. However, if your toddler has a favorite plate and really insists on it, or likes his part of the table set always the same way, he might be a budding order-lover. It is too much to imagine a three year old tidying her room regularly, but if she seems to like it when things are done up neatly, if she arranges toys or stuffed animals in a particular way, she might be an order lover. If he seems totally content when all his toys are absolutely everywhere, he might be an up and coming free spirit. If he revels in having muddy clothes, or at least is blissfully unconcerned about it, a free spirit may be developing.

A child who is upset when clothes get dirty (and not because that will bring down parental wrath) is signaling concerns about order. The small person who can, when asked, lead you directly to his shoes, or even *your* car keys, has a future as structured soul, where the child who loses gloves, jackets, small toys, with surprising frequency, may have a promising future as a free spirit.

Told to do some one thing—"put this teddy in your room", or "wash your hands for supper"-- your future structure lover is likely to do this fairly efficiently, where your little free-spirit is much more likely to start out all right, but get distracted along the way and be found busily doing something else when you go looking for her.

Lastly, if your toddler has been really looking forward to a Saturday activity, and plans change, it is the order-lover who is likely to be the most frustrated and unhappy, while the free-spirit is more likely to complain a little but soon go off fairly happily to do something else.

Each temperament preference will present its own strengths and weaknesses in demandingness situations, but the free-spirit can present some unique challenges. The below is one family example.

Trying to discipline Mike.

For many children, time-out periods where they must remain quietly in their room are effective discipline tools. It's a revered strategy, with a positive track record in many homes. But, there are certain children who are really not fazed by this, however much they protest momentarily. As a result, they may gain little from the experience. In our family, the oldest sib, Michael, was one of those. At around age four Mike went through a period of fascination with water and hoses. Regardless of stern warnings, let out to play in the yard he would soon have the water running and muck and water everywhere.

Putting him in a corner of the living room was useless, as he soon adjusted and began chattering happily or counting his fingers and toes, or just peeking at the general family commotion. So, step two was off to the bedroom, door closed. The designated time would go by, but there was no sad voice asking "is it time yet?" When he simply never reappeared, one of us would go to rescue him, only to find that he had found something else fascinating to do, and was completely oblivious. This was a little boy who really didn't mind playing alone, and had the ability to make something interesting happen with whatever props came to hand!

Some interesting combinations

The child who is both practical and in love with good order Should your toddler fit both of these descriptions, many aspects of parenting will seem remarkably easy. There is something about this combination that leads to an exceptional love not only of orderliness, but of doing things the "right" way. As they grow they seem most comfortable and secure in a world where things happen in a highly predictable and clear fashion. For that reason, they tend to accept rules and limits remarkably well and be respectful of authority. They are likely to be tidy with their own possessions, and as they move along in school they may become very good about motivating themselves for chores and homework, being on time, and just generally being organized.

The dreamy and free-spirited child Here is the flip side of what we just described. It is not hard to imagine that this child is maximally oblivious to orderliness. Between the happy indifference of the freedom loving tendency, and the fascination with things of the imagination of the dreamy child, the everyday world of following directions, heeding rules, putting things away, and knowing where things are, is really not on the radar. This child will often delight you with spontaneous joy in the moment, but parenting may be much like the expression "herding cats.

Interlude: Taking the Temperament Measures

Preliminary Information

Temperament Sorters—our measurement questionnaires Adult temperament has been measured for many years in the well-known Myers Briggs Type Indicator[19], and later in the Keirsey Temperament Sorter[20]. More recently we created our own Harkey-Jourgensen Sorters for both adults and children, for the use of our readers. These instruments have been developed in a University setting, through scientific research on hundreds of children and their families, and separately on several hundred adults. Results have shown high reliability. As long as you answer carefully and thoughtfully, your results should indicate your genuine impressions of your child's temperament and your own. This, in turn, will help you to begin "parenting by temperament".

Instruments Included on Our Website

Harkey-Jourgensen Early Childhood Temperament Sorter (Ages 4-8)
Harkey-Jourgensen Middle Childhood Temperament Sorter (Ages 9-12)
Harkey-Jourgensen Adult Temperament Sorter

Why the term Sorter? We use this term because what you are doing as you take our questionnaires is sorting individual behaviors that you already recognize into meaningful categories. This will become clearer later, but that is the reason for using that name.

---

[19] Myers, I. B., McCaulley, M. H., Quenk, N.L. & Hammer, A. L. (1998). _MBTI Manual, 3rd Ed._ Palo Alto: Consulting Psychologists Press.

[20] Keirsey, D. (1998). _Please Understand Me II: Temperament, Character, Intelligence._ Del Mar: Prometheus Nemesis Book Company.

Infants and toddlers Although there are early indications of preferences and temperament in toddlers, there are not enough unique behaviors in that age group to make a measurement Sorter possible. Your best estimate would be to look carefully at the behaviors described for young children in chapter 7

For children above the age of 12 Again we have no formal instrument for that age group. However, up to about age 14, the 9-12 sorters should give you a reasonable estimate. At fifteen or older, it will depend on the teen-ager's maturity, but it may work well to let them take the Adult Sorter on their own.

All questions are intended to measure normal behaviors. The Sorters do not include questions about extremes of anxiety, depression or other behaviors that go beyond everyday expectations. If you have concerns about these areas they are best explored with other scales, and preferably with the help of a counselor or therapist.

Go for it Now!

Go to www.parentingbytemperament.com.AboutourSorters.html This brings you directly to a page with links to the sorters Each one should take about 20-25 minutes. At the end you will receive several pages of feedback on your results which you can print out (see print command at top of first page of feedback). At the end of the feedback pages you can return to take another Sorter. Be sure to keep these results to refer to later.

Part III

The Four Major Preference Pairs

The Preferences

These are literally preferred ways of thinking and behaving. In our system and those seen in the Myers-Briggs (MBTI) and in the Keirsey Sorters, there are four paired sets of these preferred behaviors, as you have just seen in the last chapter.

These are **Extraversion/Introversion** which corresponds to the more smiley or more serious child we described in Chapter 7; **Sensing/Intuition** which corresponds to the practical versus dreamy child; Feeling/**Thinking** which comes closest to the cuddly/less-cuddly child, and **Judging/Perceiving**, which is the category for the structure-loving or freedom-loving behaviors.

Some of these names may seem pretty strange and even off-putting, but there is a long history and a long research tradition behind them, so we are sticking with them throughout this book. Each preference pair will be presented and described separately in the next four chapters (Chs 8-11).

In each chapter we separately describe the typical child and the typical adult in each pair of preferences (for example the Extraverted child compared to the Introverted child). Each chapter also has a summary table for both children and adults, comparing the ways in which the two different preferences affect what we focus on, how we prefer to act, and what our possible strengths and weaknesses may be.

Not better—just different. Each preference offers its owner unique strengths and unique problems. This is very important in understanding ourselves, our children and spouses, and the conflicts that arise between us. There is no preference or temperament that is the "good" preference, unless you first ask "good for what?" For example, we note in the next section that the Introvert is typically less sociable, but more reflective than the Extravert, while the Extravert is more active, and more social but less reflective, and often more impulsive. Because of this we each have particular strengths to contribute to family and to society, and weaknesses in areas where others do better. Accepting this is a very important part of growing up at any age

And so--

These next chapters should give you a good feeling for your own preferences and (if age 4 and up) for those of your child or children. If you and your significant other both take the adult sorter, you will find your similarities and differences to be interesting and useful also. Whether this information surprises you or confirms what you thought all along, it will give you a great start in thinking about the relationship of temperament to parenting. Part IV introduces you to the temperament combinations, and V and VI of this book deal with all the practical applications of preferences and temperament to love and discipline—responsiveness and demandingness.

Remember, as you read these descriptions, that they are based on strong preferences. With milder preferences you will see the same behaviors but to a lesser degree.

Finally, for the younger age group, or in any case where the child preference is slight, it makes worlds of sense to take the Sorters again after a year or more has passed. Four-year old results can be very helpful, but they do usually get stronger and clearer as the child gets older

Chapter 8

Buzz and Hum or Peace and Quiet:
The Extraversion or Introversion Preference Pair

When Introversion and Extraversion come to mind, you probably
think mainly of differences in sociability. That is certainly part of it,
but not the whole picture. Your most preferred source of stimulation,
and the most preferred direction for spending your energy, tends to be
either out toward the world or in toward your own mental activity.
Strong Introverts tend to look inward first for ideas, projects, even
excitement, and feel frustrated when the outside world is constantly
intruding on their thoughts. They share their inner world with family
and close friends, but it is inward first, outward only when ready to
share. Most daily experiences are taken in and reflected on before any
actions are taken in the outside world.

Extraverts tend to turn outward first for all types of stimulation.
Being with
others, getting input from others, responding to outside events as they
happen—all of these things get their juices going. They tend to focus
on the words and actions of others and act/react quickly to what is
going on. Any reflection will be most likely to happen only when
events are over, and outside stimulation is minimal.

A fascinating research finding helps to explain this.[21] In this study,
Introverts were found to have higher overall brain activation than
Extraverts while doing a series of tasks. This is not a matter of
smartness, but of the level of arousal. It is rather like the Introvert
brain is on two cups of coffee from the starting gate. From there it is

---

[21] Wilson, M. A. & Languis, M. L. (1989). Differences in brain electrical activity
patterns between introverted and extraverted adults. *Journal of Psychological Type*,
18, 14-23.

not hard to understand why the Extravert seeks outside stimulation—to get that two-coffee buzz-- while the introvert finds a lot of noise, chaos, crowds of people, too much—revving him or her up to the unpleasant four-cup buzz.

Looking at behaviors—the Extraverted or Introverted child

In Action. Extraverted children, like the "smiley" baby and toddler, tend to smile more, and certainly talk more. Introverts are more reserved and adapt to new group situations more slowly and cautiously. Being with others that they enjoy tends to leave Extraverts revved up and excited. Introverts, after a long period of socializing with friends are more likely to feel spent and long for quiet time. Similarly, Extraverts are generally more physically active. They move about more, and love seeing things happen and to make things happen.

The Introvert speaks more quietly and even plays more quietly as a rule. This child will prefer to play with just one or perhaps two children at a time, and tends to make very close friends, but slowly. With those friends the typical Introvert may be willing to share many personal confidences, but does not do so at all with acquaintances.

The Extravert delights in group play, and in having a wide variety of different friends, and is pretty relaxed about sharing feelings with most of these. The two preference types may be most different when it comes to working and playing alone. Even as young children, Introverts can be quite content with this for long stretches of time, finding the quiet, uninterrupted time enjoyable. Most Extraverts will become distinctly restless in the same setting, and look around for company very quickly.

Extraversion/Introversion and learning experiences

In learning situations the Extravert seems to learn through talking things out, where the Introvert prefers some space and quiet to think.

For that reason, Extraverts are more likely to relish group learning activities in class than are Introverts. Small Introverts in the classroom are good listeners and observers, but are not often heard from for two reasons. One is that they are often somewhat shy about speaking out, but the other reason simply goes back to the fact that they take ideas in and reflect on them before they are ready to say anything. By the time they know what they want to say, the topic has often moved on. Extraverts simply love to talk, and in class may often raise their hands before they have any idea of what they want to say. They tend to make it up as they go along—sometimes well, and sometimes just ridiculously.

Their natural Interests, and the sort of environment that seems most comfortable, both fit right in with other Introvert/Extravert differences. Extraverts are more likely to have a wide variety of interests, but not delve deeply into any one of them for long. Introverts are much more likely to develop a few interests in considerable depth. Noise, excitement, and things happening are the preferred Extravert world, where the Introvert wants calm and quiet. Broadly, Extraverts tend to be more bold, and daring, while Introverts tend to be more cautious and less willing to venture into new experiences without testing the waters.

The Good and the Bad

A very important point to recognize is that each side of a preference pair, especially where the preference is very strong, has its good points or strengths, and its drawbacks or weaknesses. Americans are particularly likely to assume that Extraversion is more desirable, but it is not that simple. The Extravert will certainly have an easier time in the social world and may more often be found in leadership roles— clearly a strength. However, this child is likely to maintain friendships on a cheerful but superficial level. If the preference is very strong, there may be real problems when it is necessary to study or work alone. The highly Extraverted child may also be more impulsive is good for safety or parent peace of mind, and you are more likely to hear from teachers that they are somewhat disruptive in class.

The Introverted child, in some surprising ways, is more capable of being independent. They are more content with their own company and are more likely to develop a depth of interest in particular areas that keeps them motivated and busy. In terms of grades and related achievements, they are likely (all else being equal) to outdo the Extravert.

Below are summaries for both Extraverted and Introverted children. They are written for children who have these qualities strongly. Your child might be similar or might show only some of these qualities, depending on strength of preference.

The Strongly Extraverted Child—A Summary

Prefers

Activity, action, noise, exitement
Socializing with many friends
Variety in friends and activities
Talking and communicating
Talking while playing and learning
Learning and working in groups
Sharing emotions and feelings

Strengths

Often leader of the pack
Makes friends easily
Active, enthusiastic group member
Plays well with a variety of children

Weaknesses

Often impulsive
May not invest in close, personal friendships
May be bored and restless when alone
Can be overly bold and incautious in actions

The Strongly Introverted Child—A Summary

Prefers

A calm, controlled, quiet environment
Playing with one or two close friends
Pursuing special interests and favorite things
Talking and playing rather quietly
Quietly reflecting
Often likes to work on tasks alone
Being private about feelings

Strengths

Talent for independent work and play
Develops close friendships
Devoted and loyal to best friends
Excellent listening skills, highly focused

Weaknesses

Hesitant about new experiences
May have a hard time making new friends
        and fitting in to new environments
May find long social activities tiring
May be overly cautious

Looking at behaviors—the Extraverted or Introverted Adult and Parent

In Action. Introverts and Extraverts in work groups paint a picture that is rather like these two preference types in the classroom, except that adult strategies are added. The Extravert dominates the conversation in a committee meeting, while the Introvert is thinking about it. Each may resent the behavior of the other, and with some good cause. A talkative Extravert may find out later that his Introvert opponent in some group decision is now complaining about the decision, sending e-mails, talking to one or two friends, even re-raising the issue at a later date. Mr. Extravert's strongest feeling is "well, why didn't you say so at the time"? Ms. Introvert resents the fact that the Extravert hogged the discussion, and in her opinion, really hadn't thought the issues out, or at best, used the group's time by thinking them out while talking. Both have a point.

In an office setting it is the Extravert who will wander in and out of a work cubicle—perhaps driving Introverted co-workers to distraction. She is likely to have her office door wide open and the space often full of co-workers, while the Introvert will long to shut the door entirely and have space to think.

Paralleling the interest differences in children, Extraverts are somewhat more likely to have a wide range of interests, while Introverts are more likely to have specialized and highly prized interest areas and hobbies that they develop in depth.

The Goods and the Bads

In general, the Extraverted adult is high in interpersonal skills. He is adept at making friends, expresses feelings easily, may be a very good leader, is an effective participant in work groups, and a generally pleasant person to be around. On the downside, working alone may make him restless and unproductive, and if the preference is very strong, there may be impulsiveness and overconfidence at times, leading to unwise decisions.

The Introvert will likely be more focused, may have developed better in-depth skills and knowledge, may be better at building life-long close friendships, and may be a better independent worker. On the downside, this individual will struggle more making new friends, especially when jobs and living locations change, will struggle more making his or her viewpoint understood in group meetings, and may never come to love large meetings and large parties.

When preferences conflict

When paired as husband and wife, and especially if the Extravert is a stay-at-home mom, there can be substantial conflict. Imagine the Introvert husband coming home after a full day of intermingling with co-workers, bosses, clients, etc. He longs for some total down time. Meanwhile, Extravert wife has saved up things to talk about all day long, and is ready to burst into conversation the moment the door opens. What fun that will be! Similarly, she will long to go out with friends as many evenings as possible, where he might choose never, under the circumstances. Temperament differences need a great deal of understanding and compromise.

Parenting interactions

The highly Extraverted parent may create more stress for an Introverted child than would be true if these roles were reversed. This parent naturally enjoys lots of company in the house, and lots of outings with friends and family—making it hard for the little Introvert to find peace and quiet.

The reverse situation is more easily handled by the Extraverted child who can soon enough seek sociability outside the home environment. Extravert-Extravert combinations should generally be sheer fun for all. Introvert-Introvert combinations will be very comfortable, but here it is possible for the child to be too protected from social situations. Like table manners, social skills do need to be learned and practiced, whether or not they fit in with your preference.

Strong preference differences can also easily lead to parent friction over child-raising. Imagine a highly Introverted dad, highly Extraverted mom and a very Introverted child. He might have great rapport with the child, while she is constantly concerned about a lack of outgoing behavior, and constantly trying to force a resentful child into all sorts of social activities. She is practically ready to take their child to a therapist while he is convinced that everything would be perfect if she would just calm down. Unless they understand these differences, they are in for a lot of stress—and so is the child.

The Strongly Extraverted Adult—A Summary

Prefers

Focusing on the outside world
Activity and action—busy chaotic enviroments
Variety of friends and social settings—large parties
Wide variety of interests and activities
Talking! --talking out ideas, feelings, small talk
Social interactions because they are energizing

Strengths

Can be a very good leader in appropriate areas
Effective in groups, generates ideas quickly
Relates well to many different people
Takes an interest in many different things

Weaknesses

May be impulsive
May act, speak, before thinking through

May be restless, unproductive working alone
Can be overconfident, underestimate problems

Parenting by Temperament

Chapter 9

Facts and Details or Ideas and Theories: The Sensing or Intuitive Preference Pair

Overview

Now we are looking at something that is more subtle and less noticeable in everyday interactions than Introversion or Extraversion. This pair of preferences concerns our most comfortable ways of thinking about things. Intuitives just naturally love to connect the dots, creating a mental picture of the way events or ideas seem to go together. Like other preferences, this is very natural, and really not learned behavior for the true Intuitive. Sensors, on the other hand, are very impatient with that sort of dreamy meandering (as they would see it). They are fascinated with the factual and actual, and will spend a great deal of time storing up information that the Intuitive might easily just gloss over.

Sensors attack problems methodically in step by step fashion, while Intuitives like to try to imagine what might be possible and leap into it at the nearest starting point. This is true whether dealing with daily work or political philosophies. Where Sensors are acutely focused on the present moment, Intuitives may be fascinated with stories of the past, and certainly are forever looking to the future. Where Sensors store many details of past experiences and rely on these when a new problem comes up, Intuitives tend to have an optimistic faith in new ideas, believing that better solutions can always be found if you just keep looking.

Looking at behaviors—the Sensing or Intuitive child

In Action. Our practical toddler is likely to grow up to be a Sensor, and our dreamy toddler to grow up to be an Intuitive. Sensors just relish and delight in things that have actual presence in the world— things that can be seen, heard, touched, measured and weighed. They love developing skill with all sorts of materials and all sorts of tools, from skis, skateboards and bicycles to hammers and stethoscopes. And they love all the intricate details about these things. They are the baseball fans who know every statistic on dozens and dozens of players, or the budding teenager who not only follows the popular rock and hip hop stars, but knows their producers, salaries, and real names! When a classic Sensor comes back from a trip you are likely to hear amazing details about it, and often in strict chronological order. By some estimates about 73% of the American population are Sensors in some degree. They are the practical doers that keep the world running.

A another family story with Mike

> When Mike, our oldest, was about 13, his seven year old brother, Scott got an elaborate tinker-toy set (the Legos of his day). Big brother was simply astounded by the complex designs that little brother was soon making. He finally had to ask him how in the world he did this, and Scott gave him a "you're an idiot" look, and said "It's easy. I just did it like the pictures that came with the box." This had truly never occurred to Mike, the dreamer, who made all his own creations from scratch.

A hallmark of Sensing children will be their far greater interest in stories that involve real people and real-world events. It is the Intuitive that will delight most in fairy tales in early childhood. Later this may show up in greater interest in science fiction, mystery stories, or in stories set in ancient times. Even in playing make-believe games the Sensor is more likely to want to be a fireman or doctor, or other

128

real-life hero, while the Intuitive child may delight in pretending she has just come to earth from Planet X.

Sensing/Intuition and learning experiences

In school work, it is typically the Sensor who gets the arithmetic facts down cold, and the spelling words right. The Intuitive, who may also know these things, or may not, having been thinking of other things when multiplication was the topic, tends to zip through instructions and make careless mistakes. On the other hand, given an open-ended writing project, the Intuitive may shine, while the Sensor, grumbles about the "stupid"assignment and just plods through it. For this reason, the early grades are often a Sensor's delight, while the Intuitive comes into her own in later grades where topics are more theoretical.

Related to this, the Sensor is often most comfortable in a structured classroom, while the Intuitive loves projects that challenge him to "use your imagination." Sensors take great pride in their storehouse of knowledge, while Intuitives take more delight in their flashes of originality. When each is asked to describe a story read in class, the Sensor is much more likely to give accurate details, while the Intuitive jumps over this to tell you what she thinks the point of it all might be. Finally, although there is no clear research evidence on this, we tend to think that the Sensor, with his skills focus, and here-and-now attitude, is a little more likely to take well to athletics.

The Good and the Bad

As with all the preference pairs, there are both strengths and weaknesses here. The most obvious strengths are seen in the different learning styles, with Sensors absorbing important factual details that Intuitives skip over, and Intuitives seeing meanings and connections that Sensors really don't want to deal with. On the downside, the Sensor may tend to resist new ideas or experiences because the familiar is so comfortable, and at times will be wrong in doing so. (A lot will depend here on another preference pair—Judging/Perceiving). The Intuitive will welcome these new experiences with delight, but at times may go off the deep end over ideas that just don't fit the real world.

Each will benefit from building strengths on the non-preferred side and both will benefit from learning to respect the opposite preference and work well with others of that preference.

The Sensing Child—A Summary

Prefers

What is real and can be touched, seen, etc.
The present—what is happening right now
Realistic stories—here and now adventures
Knowing how things work, how to do things
Using what they have learned to do things
Polishing existing skills

Strengths

Attentive to details
Strong memory for detail
Values and relies on stored knowledge
Accurate in following instructions
Develops strong skills areas

Weaknesses

May struggle wih abstract theories
Resists new methods that conflict with
        established skills
Frustrated by vague/ loose instructions
Bothered if change disrupts known methods

The Intuitive Child—A Summary

Prefers

Things that can be imagined,
What will happen in the future
The "why" of things
Understanding the meaning of what is learned
Having new/novel ideas
Fantasy, imaginary stories of past/future

Strengths

Perceptive about meanings and ideas
Enthusiastic about learning new ways to do things
Loves finding new ideas
Good at generating creative ideas

Weaknesses

May be poor about attention to details
May be poor at following instructions
May neglect polishing existing skills
Easily bored by routine and structure

Looking at behaviors—the Sensing or Intuitive adult and parent.

In Action. Grown up Sensors and Intuitors are simply more of the same unique people that they began to be in childhood. If they have a facility for writing, Sensors are far more likely to produce technical manuals or factual biographies than novels, while the Intuitive adult in this area might be the novelist or someone writing theoretical non-fiction. If they have an interest in medicine, Sensors are far more likely to become physicians than medical researchers, and the reverse might be true for Intuitives.

The Good and the Bad

In a committee meeting, Sensors want the facts laid out clearly in order to make a decision, while Intuitives want to think about all the possible outcomes that the decision might produce. Both are strengths, but need to be combined for good decision making. Unfortunately, strong Sensors and strong Intuitives are slow to admit that they each have only part of the solution. Sensors will also use recent experience and that storehouse of knowledge to aid in this, while Intuitives will always assume that this situation may be subtly different from the past and want to analyze that. If preferences are strong, each is quite likely to be impatient with the other's style and find it hard to reach a consensus. Organizational experts often work with groups on just this sort of conflict. These same differences, of course will also play out in close personal relationships.

In addition to differences in thinking style, there are also some differences in work style. Because Intuitives are most intrigued and most motivated by what is new, they tend to work very hard in developing new ideas and new projects, but lag and drag somewhat when it becomes routine. As a result, their work pattern often shows an erratic boom and bust pattern that is not true for the Sensor.

When preferences conflict

Husbands and wives who differ strongly here will have their problems. Unlike the Extraversion/Introversion difference, trying to agree on mutual activities is not such a great source of conflict, but truly understanding one another may be a greater problem. Most of us are not in the habit of thinking of people as Sensing or Intuitive. As a result, when we find ourselves understanding events and working toward solutions in very different ways, it is easy to think that the other person is just being incredibly unreasonable (or even a touch stupid!). When you do learn about these preferences, you may still wish that your significant other would be more like you, but at least you begin to understand it. Like other differences, this one is not just going away and will not change because you wish it would, or because you try to bully your partner into enlightenment.

Parenting interactions

For parents, a parent/child difference in these preferences will mainly present practical problems in the area of schoolwork. The Sensing parent may fail to understand why her otherwise bright Intuitive child often makes so many careless errors, or just zones out on routine rote learning.

The Intuitive parent may be impatient or even critical when her Sensing child wants to do things methodically and does not show flights of imagination. It is also very important as children grow older, that parents be able to recognize and accept the child's differing interests and differing learning styles, and not try to steer him or her into career paths that will not reward natural strengths. Outside of academic areas, these differences generally will not present conflicts or discipline problems. If they are not understood and truly accepted, however, they can certainly reduce the child's sense of being seen and loved for the person she is.

The Sensing Adult—A Summary

Prefers

Facts and data—useful information
The real far more than the possible
The present far more than the future
 Enjoys perfecting skills and using them
Enjoys interacting with the physical world

Strengths

Highly observant of events and details
Strong memory for events and details
Strong respect for experience
Reliable—rarely makes errors of fact
Acts efficiently on known information

Weaknesses

Doesn't appreciate theoretical issues
May not see "the forest for the trees"
Dislikes having to use new methods for
        familiar tasks
Little interest in future possibilities

****

The Intuitive Adult—A Summary

Prefers

What can be dreamed/imagined
The future over the past or present
The possible
Theories, ideas, novel concepts
Connections and patterns
Thinking in intuitive leaps

Strengths

Ability to see connections--the big picture
Optimistic belief in the power of ideas
Optimistic belief in the future
Strong intellectual interests
Originality—creativity

Weaknesses

May ignore facts chasing exciting theories
May be a poor and inaccurate observer
Dislikes routine tasks, may do them poorly
May neglect past experience

Parenting by Temperament

Chapter 10

Mercy or Fairness in Decision Making:
The Thinking or Feeling Preference Pair

Overview

The core of this set of preferences takes us back to the cuddler/non cuddler difference. Feeling children are intensely motivated by their need for others and their closeness to others. All human beings share this need, but we do differ in its driving force.

The names for these two preferences refer to the ways we use them in making decisions. In resolving problems, many of us are more moved by our interpersonal values and by the impact of decisions on individuals and relationships. Others tend to rely more on what they see as logic and fairness. As adults, this is the primary distinction, but in children we may see it most clearly in the Feeling child's concern for being liked and respected by others, and his reciprocal concern for others, and the Thinking child's greater focus on activities, ideas, and projects. A common expression for this in the business world is being more *people oriented* or more *task oriented.* It would probably not seem surprising to most readers that about 56% of men score as Thinkers while about 75% of women score as Feelers.

Looking at Behaviors—the Thinking or Feeling Child.

In Action. The young Feeler will show an early interest in making friends and, if also Extraverted, may be ahead of his age in being interested in being popular. Especially within the family, this child is highly motivated to please others. At school you will hear her mention new friends with delight. Being liked by the teacher is an important theme also, and will make a great deal of difference in happiness and hard work in the classroom. It will also become clear that quarrelsome and aggressive peers are not high on the friendship list, and again, especially at home, this child will be disturbed by adult anger or unhappiness. For this reason, and because empathy develops very naturally in this child, she is quite likely to be a peacemaker in the family and on the playground.

The Thinking child may also be very sociable, if Extraverted, but the strong concern about being liked is much reduced here. Instead, reliance on fairness is a key behavior, as is a great pride in being competent. A strongly Thinking child is likely to be unusually frank, sometimes to the point of pain, because opinions are usually not tailored to fit the feelings of others. Reason, fairness and logic are the decision-making tools, not the reactions of others. On the positive side, this means that you know where you stand with this young person, whether or not that pleases you. However, others, especially those with a strong Feeling preference, may see this as coldness or unkindness.

To see this difference, think of a situation in which a child is choosing classmates to work on a project. The Feeler is very likely to choose friends, not wanting to hurt feelings, while the Thinker will try hard to pick people for talent. Our Thinker may create hard feelings right at the start, when a good sports buddy is not chosen because the Thinker doesn't see him as an asset here. The Feeler is likely to bring in her friends regardless of talent and keep things calm. Chances are, however, the Thinker's project will go better, and perhaps with less conflict in the long run, based on the ability of the people chosen. Which is better? Well, your answer to that will depend on your own preference!

The Good and the Bad

Strengths for the Feeling child include concern for others, insight into the feelings of others, and a talent for smoothing over conflicts that increases with age. Generally, this child will put a high value on relationships and will become skillful in maintaining them. The downside, however, is likely to be an excessive dependence on the good will and approval of others that may interfere with standing up for the self, when there is a conflict. The problem with people-pleasing arises both when varied friends want different things from this child, and when the child, herself, disagrees with friends. If the Feeling preference is very strong this child needs help in the developing years, in strengthening Thinking skills and broad skills in self-assertion. Where such assertion is felt as extremely painful there is a temptation to carry tactfulness to the point of dishonesty, and to learn some manipulative strategies to meet needs without direct conflict.

The Thinking child brings good analytic problem-solving skills to the world, and a refreshing candor when dealing with others, and generally has minimal problems with self-assertion. The downside of things for the Thinker may include excessive focus on accomplishment, and a lack of sensitivity to the feelings and needs of others. Strong Thinkers do need to be helped to develop skills on their non-preferred (Feeling) side as they grow older. This is something that will not be second nature to them. They will need to see the logical importance of this and work at it like any other mental task, but improvement can be made.

The following summarizes the qualities found in Thinking and Feeling children.

The Thinking Child—A Summary

Prefers

Fairness and justice
Knowing what is logical and true
Being competent, being right
Accomplishing goals
Respect for abilities more than niceness

Strengths

Just and fair toward others
Good at communicating about fairness
Good at problem solving
Good at keeping calm under stress

Weaknesses

May not consider needs/feelings of others
May be too blunt in communicating
May seem critical and cool to others

****

The Feeling Child

Prefers

Happy, harmonious relationships
Pleasing others
Understanding feelings of others
Warm friendships
Being well liked

Strengths

Kindness, consideration
Natural empathy
Insight about own and other feelings
Often a good peacemaker

Weaknesses

Problems standing up for self
May be overly influenced by others
Ssometimes emotionally controlling

Looking at behaviors—The Thinking or Feeling Adult and Parent.

In Action. Thinking and Feeling differences can be seen everywhere you look in the adult world, and they show up most clearly in the decision-making process. Here we quote an example from our earlier *Raising CuddleBugs* books:

> *Let's take, for example, a very serious problem--the decision to place an unwilling elderly parent in an assisted-living facility of some kind. The parent does not want to go and may well be less happy there than in a family home of many years. Let us say that this person shows early signs of Alzheimer's or other dementia, and is at a point where he or she may be some danger to self in living alone, or even a danger to others (leaving gas burning, starting a fire, etc.). The Thinker sees that the new living situation would be protective, and that this will have to be done sooner or later, since the problem will only worsen. The Feeler is acutely conscious of the parent's sadness and wants only to shelter him or her from the severe unhappiness of this move. Both understand each other's argument perfectly well, but logic will be more compelling for the Thinker and emotion for the Feeler.*

The issue is not that the Thinker is without inner compassion, nor that the Feeler thinks less well or is less capable of logical analysis. You can see in this situation that there are good arguments on both sides of this problem, but each party is more deeply compelled by the arguments that are natural to their preference style.

Once you become aware of this fundamental difference you can see it everywhere in the decisions human beings make and the arguments they advance for those decisions. Is it true that war never solved anything, or that some wars are just and necessary? Should illegal immigrants be welcomed into society or should they be sent home because they came illegally? Is it rigorous phonics instruction that

141

helps children best learn to read, or is it a whole-language approach, stressing the enjoyment of stories? The list is endless.

The Goods and the Bads

So much here, in terms of strengths and weaknesses, depends on the situation the Thinker or Feeler is in. When the important thing is to see an emotionally difficult task through to completion, it is often the Thinker who will best get it done, where the Feeler will be too enmeshed in concern for others to make hard decisions effectively. If you must fight a war—get a Thinker. In deciding whether a war is necessary, listen hard to a Feeler! If you must lay off personnel, get a Thinker to make the decisions, but get a good Feeler to help employees cope with the decision.

Strong Thinkers tend to give too little consideration to the emotions involved in all situations. They tend to be too frank, too blunt, too unsparing of others. They can certainly do better, but they need to learn that they should. Feelers, on the other hand, may be overwhelmed by their life-long desire for harmony with others. At best, they may sacrifice their own needs and desires, in the service of peace. At worst, they may learn to meet these needs through manipulation of the feelings of others—not a pretty picture.

Just as the Thinker needs to learn empathy and respect for others, the Feeler often needs to learn some quiet self-assertion and personal integrity.

When Preferences Conflict.

It is our experience that strong Thinker/Feeler differences trigger the greatest anger between spouses and partners in the interpersonal world, and probably the greatest conflict between partisan groups in the wider world. A great deal of understanding is needed here. If strong Thinkers and strong Feelers can see that each preference is invaluable in different situations, and come to appreciate that, they have made a good start. If each one can then see the downside of their own preference behavior, they are farther along the road to understanding. In any close relationship a great deal of compromise is needed, and depth of understanding is the place to lay the ground work.

Parenting Interactions

Among other problems, a highly Feeling parent may long for greater closeness and bonding with a highly Thinking child, and a highly Feeling child with a strong Thinker parent may easily feel unloved. Disciplining the highly Feeling child can be problematic. A strong Thinker approach may very easily trigger emotional meltdowns, for example. On the other hand, with a strongly Feeling parent it may be very hard to carry through on discipline, as we will discuss in a later chapter.

Parents who have a great deal of trouble in their personal relationships, revolving around Thinking/Feeling differences, are very likely to take this out into the parenting arena. She is too soft, he is cruelly harsh. Sometimes there may be truth in that, and that needs to be dealt with, drawing on both patience and determination. Often, however, the biggest problem is that the parents are working out these differences in their own relationship, during their arguments over parenting. We discuss this further in our chapter—*When Moms and Dads Disagree.*

The below summarizes the Thinker/Feeler differences for adults. The contrast "Fairness over mercy" versus "Mercy over fairness" may be the core example. When you think about it carefully it is easy to see problems in either approach, taken to extremes.

The Thinking Adult—A Summary

Prefers

Reason and logical analysis

Parenting by Temperament

Fairness over mercy
Honesty over the soft answer
Knowing what is true
Good ideas and effective actions
Being competent and effective

Strengths

Can be tough when this is needed
Makes a strong effort to be fair
Stands up for principles
Logical and forceful when disagreeing
Articulates reasons for decisions well

Weaknesses

Too business like/lacking sociability
May be unaware of feelings of others
May come across as critical—too blunt
May seem emotionally distant and cold

****
The Feeling Adult—A Summary

Prefers

Harmony/minimizing conflict
Liking and respect of others
Warm relationships
Personal values in decision making
Mercy over fairness
Soft answers over blunt truth

Strengths

Tact and diplomacy

Protective of needs/feelings of others
Makes strong effort to be considerate
Good at fostering group cohesion
Gives a soft answer in disagreeing

Weaknesses

May be too much influenced by others
May tend to ignore unpleasant facts
Trouble making decisions clear
Sometimes can be emotionally manipulative

Parenting by Temperament

Chapter 11

How You Structure Your Day, Week, Life: The Judging or Perceiving Preference Pair

Overview

This is the final set of preferences, and takes us back to the structure-loving child and the freedom-loving child. The Judger is our structured child. The name comes from the idea that children and adults with this preference like to make decisions and have things set, so that they can make plans around them. Perceivers (our freedom-loving child and adult) like to keep options open, since a better plan may always turn up, or new information might change the tentative decision at any moment. Thus they spend far more time looking at everything (Perceiving) and much less time making decisions, and plans based on decisions.

At bottom this is fundamentally a comfort issue. Judgers feel most relaxed and comfortable with a well organized room, a well planned day and a well planned life. Perceivers are most happy and comfortable when they are free to do whatever is most interesting at this very moment, and are not irrevocably bound to any long range schedule.

If two people at the extremes of these two preferences were looking at each other, the Judger would (rightly) see that the Perceiver is never very neat, has tons of unfinished projects and just generally seems disorganized. She would thank God she is not one of those. The Perceiver would look at the Judger and see an excess of seriousness, rigid adherence to plans, a lack of willingness to romp through life and enjoy the moment. He would thank God he is not one of those. From their own perspectives, each would be right. It may be one of the most fascinating aspects of temperament, that we really do love our own preferences, no matter how unappealing they may seem to someone else!

Looking at Behaviors—the Judging or Perceiving child

Of all the preference pairs, Judging/Perceiving may be the most obvious in everyday behavior. Judgers are increasingly neat as they get older. They generally tend to their chores with a minimum of prompting, and again, increasingly with age, take on the responsibility for getting school work done in a timely manner. They feel a sense of pleasure when they complete a project or assignment. If Judging is very strong they may be all too ready to make pronouncements on what the right or wrong thing to do is, in a given situation. In that sense, some Judgers can be critical of others. Because they plan their days well (and in considerable detail), they are also likely to grumble, or worse when plans are changed by others.

A typical young Perceiver has a terrible time completing the simplest task. On the way to brushing teeth for the night there may be a half-dozen interesting things that pull her away. What did they just say on TV? What is my brother looking at on his computer? Whoa, look at this Indian-head penny on the rug. Wonder who dropped it? Well, here I am in the bathroom. Look at my hair. What if I gelled it till it stood straight up? Tooth-brushing may never happen without further parent attention.

An interesting quality found in Perceivers is that they are often very good at getting things done at the last minute under great pressure. Many of them have had a lot of practice over the years; no doubt that is part of it. However, there is something about finally having an impressive deadline that seems to get the juices going. Chores dangle and drag on, but if there is a real outside deadline with real consequences (no trip to Disneyland for you young man) the Perceiver can sometimes work miracles.

Judging, Perceiving and Learning Experiences

Like chores and other duties, Perceiver homework is inevitably postponed to the last moment, and parents need to be very mindful and on guard about that. On the other hand when that last moment arrives, a very good product sometimes emerges—but, like everything else in the Perceiver world, this is unpredictable. Inattentiveness in class is sometimes another Perceiver fault.

Judgers generally have a much smoother road in school. Research indicates that the Judging preference predominates among teachers, so that may also make a difference in teacher/student compatibility. This would favor the Judger child and make life a little harder for the Perceiver—even though they do need to know about getting organized.

The Good and the Bad

Perceivers are spontaneous, highly adaptable, and easily able to adjust to change, and with all of this, pretty tolerant of others (non-judgmental). On the down side, Perceiver life has a lot of chaos, lateness, missed deadlines, and people lining up to complain about these things. Judgers typically are organized, dependable and productive, and rarely yelled at. But—they may miss some of the spontaneous joy of life, and may be hard on others who do not share their diligence and planfulness.

Perceivers clearly need to be helped to build a few Judger skills, and learn to bring a small amount of organization into their lives. Judgers especially need to see that other life-styles have their own merits, so that they will hold back on criticism of others. They also need to learn to let go when plans have to be changed. It has even been suggested that parents may need to schedule some free play time into their school-age Judger's life so that they will take it!

These qualities are summarized next.

The Judging Child—A Summary

Prefers

Neatness and order
Planning ahead in work and play
Knowing what will happen next
Getting things decided
Getting things completed

Strengths

Well organized and tidy
Can make choices and stick with them
Gets things done
Predictable, dependable, reliable

Weaknesses

May sometimes make hasty choices
May be upset by unexpected changes
May unfairly resist change
Wanting order, may seem bossy or rigid

****

The Perceiving Child—A Summary

Prefers

Happy enjoyment of the here and now
Going with the flow of events
Curiosity about everything
Seeking variety and stimulation
Living with cheerful chaos

Strengths

Relaxed, easy to be with
Ponders all sides of a decision
Good at big, last-minute efforts
Flexible, adaptable, open to change

Weaknesses

May postpone, drag out, making choices
May be bored by and resist routine tasks
May resist demands for school/home tasks
May have problems finishing things

Looking at behaviors—the Judging or Perceiving Adult and Parent.

In Action In this area adults will differ from children in three main ways. First, Judging, as skill in organization, may be more complete in the adult than in the child, where playfulness still competes with order and structure. Second, the strongly Perceiving adult has been scolded and punished throughout development, both by parents and by life. As an adult she has either made some useful adjustments or now has more serious problems.

The third change, with adulthood, complements the first two; these characteristics are now applied in more serious situations. The Judger or Perceiver generally has become an employee or employer, and perhaps a spouse and/or parent. Certainly, the best overall adjustment the Perceiver could make would be the growth of a few organizational skills. To some degree, life insists on it. In the work world, a very useful adjustment is finding an employment situation that capitalizes on the Perceiver's love of freedom and ability to produce at the last moment. If the Perceiver is imaginative and creative, jobs in writing, art and graphic design, computer programming on the creative end, and other similar work, may provide a more comfortable environment. Emergency services such as Fire, or Paramedic may also fit the Perceiver temperament. Certainly, if a strong Perceiver has stumbled into accounting as a life work, she should consider running to the nearest exit!

The Goods and the Bads

Judgers make great contributions to getting the work of the world done. They are dependable, predictable and effective. The most common problem for the adult Judger, if the preference is strong, is the temptation to be controlling of others, and/or critical of others. In the workplace, the strong Judger as boss may be a micromanager. As an employee he may be (just below the surface) very critical of a poorly organized employer. On a personal level, when you have very clear plans for your daily, weekly and yearly life, it is obvious that you can't carry this out easily unless others in your life cooperate. This leads very naturally into the temptation to try to maximize the cooperation of others by any means available. In a strong Judger, this is not a loveable trait.

Obviously, the happy-go-lucky Perceiver is often fun to be around. Naturally non-judgmental and always in search of whatever is interesting or exciting, this is usually a very up-beat companion. In the strong form, though, this is also the undependable employee, spouse, or partner, the last person to make it to a meeting, get a project done on time, and so forth. If the Perceiver has not learned some coping skills she may also be someone who started but never finished college, has had multiple jobs, and is employed at a job that is well below her natural abilities.

When Preferences Conflict

In terms of relationships, much will depend on the match of temperaments. Certainly a strong Perceiver-strong Judger pair are going to have a lot to negotiate simply because these preferences

152

involve so many events in daily life. This combination can be highly volatile, with the Judger wanting order and predictability, and quite ready to press for this, while the Perceiver desperately wants freedom from this stress. If the Judger also lapses into criticism and self-righteousness, the combination can be lethal. The situation cries out for understanding and compromise.

Two very strong Judgers? Well, on the surface this would sound like an easy pairing, but that may not be true. Remember that each one now wants to structure the hourly, daily and weekly activities. If their interests are very similar this may work out nicely. If not, these two determined people also have a lot to negotiate. One thing that this suggests about life choices is that very strong Judgers who pair off with other very strong Judgers should be sure that their goals, interests, hobbies, etc. are highly compatible.

Two Perceivers may have a wonderfully spontaneous time together. We just have to hope that they can afford to hire household help, and perhaps personal assistants, to keep things going.

Parenting Interactions

Finally, as parents, these preferences also come into play. The Perceiver parent is generally a lot of fun for young children, having a lasting sense of playfulness. He is also more able than the Judger to drop whatever he is doing to attend to a child's needs or give immediate comfort. Obviously, for the Judger there is always work to be done, and a checklist to check off!

On the downside of the Perceiver parent, children need a fair amount of structure in the home to help them in learning to regulate themselves and get things done, and they are unlikely to get this from the strong Perceiver parent. The Judger child needs it less, but may feel chronically anxious in a really unstructured environment. The Perceiver child won't miss it but may need this structure much more in the long run in order to develop some organizational skills. The

Perceiver parent often falls short here, and may be even less talented at consistently enforcing rules. This can be a serious shortcoming— particularly if it is true of both parents. The Judger parent will be much better at rule enforcement, and much better at providing a structured household.

Problems between Judger parents and Perceiver children will mainly fall in the area of excessive expectations for organized behavior. With Judger children this will go better, but as the little Judger grows older there may still be surprising conflicts over plans and schedules.

With a changeable Perceiver parent, raising a Judger child may seem easy most of the time, but when this parent feels like turning plans upside down at the last moment, the resistance and distress may be surprising. Finally, the combination of strong Perceiver parent and strong Perceiver child will feel easy and fun, but there may be real problems in giving the little Perceiver some necessary Judger skills.

The Judging Adult   A Summary

Prefers

Being organized-- plans, schedules, lists
Making firm decisions/getting closure
Bringing projects to completion
Being clear about opinions, positions
Being able to predict what will happen next

Strengths

Disciplined and efficient
Decisive
Dependable, predictable
Maintains an orderly environment
Comfortable in advising others

<u>Weaknesses</u>
lMay make decisions too quickly
May be inflexible-- unwilling to reconsider
Frustrated by constant change
May seem too controlling of others

Parenting by Temperament

Part IV

The Critically Important Temperaments

About the Temperaments

There are four sets of preferences that combine to produce particularly strong personal styles. These pairs are Sensing and Perceiving (SP), Sensing and Judging (SJ), Intuition and Feeling (NF), and Intuition and Thinking (NT). Each of these temperament pairs will be discussed separately in Chapters 12-15. There you will find that two strong preferences together sometimes increase the effect of each one alone, but in other cases tone down the effect of each one alone.

For example, Sensing and Perceiving each increase the person's tendency to live in the present moment, so Sensor-Perceivers (SP) are especially likely to experience life in a happy-go-lucky way. Sensor-Judgers are also very aware of the present moment but feel in constant need to get as much accomplished in that moment as possible. They are anything but happy-go-lucky.

We have given our own names to each of the four temperaments, hoping to make them memorable for you. As you will see, SPs are Masters of the Moment, SJs are Keepers of the Flame, NFs are Humanity's Champions, and NTs are Passionate Achievers. Hopefully these labels will be helpful as you read through the descriptions.

Types

Finally, unique differences can be identified even further by looking at every possible combination of the person's four chosen preferences.

For example, Extraversion, Sensing, Thinking, Judging preferences would create the type ESTJ, where Introversion, Intuitive, Feeling, Perceiving preferences could combine to create the type INFP (where N stands for Intuition). This leads to 16 separate possible combinations or types.

In our earlier books Raising CuddleBugs and BraveHearts— Volumes I & II, we described parent and child situations for all 16 possible types, but found that there was a great deal of overlap in parenting style between types with similar temperament cores, so we have put our main focus here on preferences and temperaments. However, at the end of each temperament chapter (Chapters 12-15) we will give you brief descriptions of the types that are related to that temperament. (For example, the SP temperament is a part of the following four types: ESFP, ESTP, ISFP, and ISTP). You will see that each complete type has varying effects on the basic temperament.

Things to know.

Why temperament matters. All the preferences, temperaments and types that we discuss in this book are visible in both adults and children. They are descriptions of normal differences, and determine much of our individuality. Although we can learn to behave in non-preferred ways where the situation requires it, these are "non-preferred ways", and cost us in effort and self-control. You will find it tremendously helpful to look at your children, yourself, and perhaps your spouse, in this way. It can unlock the door to warmer, more positive relationships, more effective discipline, and greater family harmony.

Chapter 12

Masters of the Moment (SPs)
The Sensing <u>and</u> Perceiving Temperament Group

Looking at preference combinations

The last four chapters each described the actions of one set of preferences. Now for the next four chapters we will look at some powerful combinations of preferences—Sensing and Perceiving together (SPs), Sensing and Judging together (SJs), Intuition and Feeling together (NFs), and Intuition and Thinking together (NTs).

The SP Child

Focus on What is Happening Here and Now. Both Sensing and Perceiving have an intense here-and-now quality about them. The Sensor is concerned with real and tangible things, and on what can be seen happening right now. Sensors have a fascination with how things work—whether that be conquering a video game or fitting together bicycle parts. They enjoy becoming really good at something and then being able to use that skill. The Perceiver comes to the here-and-now with a slightly different focus. Perceivers are endlessly curious and just enjoy seeing what will happen next. "Next," however, really means immediately next—not next week, month, or year! Put those together and you have a child whose whole focus is on this moment. This moment-to-moment focus is the result both of the blending of the SP temperament with the greater here-and-now-ness of all children. This is likely to lead to plenty of parent-child stressors over schoolwork, homework, chores and other everyday demands. On the other hand, it produces a special ability to be absorbed and happy in the moment—a great asset for both parent and child.

Focus on Applied Skills and Applied Knowledge. For the SP child, there will typically be a great interest in hands-on learning, in skills learning, and in acquiring and storing a great deal of information. Strong powers of observation and memory are common for the young SP. If talented in one of those directions, they may become very skillful in art, music, and/or sports and other physical activities. There is substantially less interest among this temperament group in traditional academic learning, whether literature, history, higher mathematics or the theoretical sciences.

Love of Change and Variety The present moment is fascinating as long as new things keep turning up. This means that the opposite— repetitive sameness—is often experienced as aversive. Before you assume that this is simply a quality of childhood, you should recall that other preferences may produce a very different outcome, even in young children. The strongly Judging child, for example, often loves predictability and structure.

On Freedom from Restraint This follows directly from the previous love of novelty. Routine demands, rules, regulations—all the trappings of organized adult life—are the enemy. They are limiting, and boring, and to be avoided wherever and whenever possible.

The Goods and Bads

These follow logically from what we have described. The SP child will show a great ability to enjoy life, will be a pleasure to be with most of the time, and will be accepting of others. The obvious downside is the trouble this child may have in being at least a little organized, getting the minimal required things done, and working toward some future goals. If the strong SP preference is combined with strong Extraversion, this child may also be something of a daredevil and risk-taker.

The adult SP: Love of tools, aversion to rules!

Maturity brings some hard-learned lessons about the fact that work is inescapable, some things really do have to be done on time, and life cannot be totally fun. Just the same, the adult SP is a close cousin to the child. The Sensor delight in making things, and great pleasure in skillful performances remains coupled with the Perceiver passion for the unexpected. The adult SP is intensely practical in interests, here and now in focus and--at least in bursts and spurts—very active and productive.

We use the term "tools" here to emphasize that the SP likes to do things, and enjoys practicing and improving techniques of many kinds. Tools may be literally that—from bats to hammers to cardiac resuscitators—or may be more figurative—techniques for running workshops, getting group cooperation, etc. In either case, however, they will intrigue the SP as long as they present challenge and require skillful performance. The Perceiving preference brings to this a strong inner wish to be able to live according to the Perceiver's own timetable and work methods. We use "aversion to rules" to note that this individual will resist structure and routine.

In addition to the focus on the here and now, it is very clear in adults that just as SPs do not spend much time on past or future, they also spend little time or thought on things that are purely theoretical. Things that can be seen, touched and otherwise directly experienced have the greatest appeal. This can range from a profit and loss report to a beautiful painting; from a superbly played baseball game to a gourmet meal. What is truly unlikely is a strong SP devoting hours and days to questions of philosophy and/or life's meaning.

Related to the desire to live in the present and to deal with concrete, tangible materials, is the focus on practical utility. The SP's questions in experiencing something new are always along the lines of "What is this good for?", "What can it do?" or "How might this bring pleasure to my life?"

Special Strengths

Spontaneity, flexibility, tolerance Both the here and now quality of the Sensor, and the Perceiver's love of change contribute to a temperament structure that is easy and open. A change in plans is much more likely to be welcomed than fought. Minor catastrophes are not likely to rattle the SP. Suggestions from others are generally received well—unless they are focused on regimenting the SP! Perhaps most important, this freedom-loving person is very willing to tolerate a wide range of differences in others, and is not often critical or judgmental.

High levels of accuracy in recall In any area that is of interest, the SP adult is typically a champion at noticing and recalling information. This comes especially from the Sensing preference, which keeps the individual focused on the present, but the Perceiver's habit of scanning for new events also seems to strengthen this. Because of this, the SP is a particularly good source of reliable and accurate factual information.

Special talent for practical troubleshooting All of the other strengths and areas of focus for the SP seem to come together here. If there is a problem to be solved, our SP will feel free to try any idea that comes to mind, unconcerned about what other people do, what is usually done, or what the rulebook says. This gives the SP special strength in situations where there is no rule to fall back on. Given an emergency, whether a gushing water pipe or a financial crisis, the SP tends to stay cool, take in all the relevant facts, and look for innovative ways to solve the problem. Typically, this is a good person to have on your side, whether fighting a fire or meeting a medical emergency.

Potential Weaknesses

Lack of interest in needed future planning. As is often the case, the other side of a temperament strength may be a weakness. Not everyone needs to take the long, long view of life, but a very strong SP may carry this to the point of failing to look far enough ahead to keep life in order. Completing an educational program, boring or not, keeping track of finances to avoid problems, saving a little money, etc. are all simple forms of future planning.

Most SPs make their way through these minor minefields adequately, but some do not, yielding too much to the impulses of the moment. Completing needed education can be a particular problem, since much of high school and college work stresses theory, and this is often a turn-off. SPs are wise to choose their life-work very carefully, with their temperament preferences in mind, and then plow through the classroom work that is needed—but no more than that!

Too much resistance to structure and routine If the adult SP has not absorbed life's lessons about duty and obligation, the delight in the moment can lead to resistance to rules and regulations that simply goes too far. Like it or not, the world is bigger than any one of us. It is hard to escape the minimal requirements for school and work deadlines, productivity, and punctuality. Similarly, we all make promises and incur obligations to others that have to be reasonably met if we wish to hang onto our friends and loved ones. For the strong SP who has never come to terms with this, it can be a major life problem.

The SP Parent

All the strengths and problems described separately for the Sensor parent and the Perceiver parent really combine here. The SP parent is likely to take great joy in the playful life of children, and indeed can sometimes be more like one of the children than like a strong, firm parent. Much depends on what lessons the SP has gained from life along the way. If not much has rubbed off in the way of accepting the need for some self-discipline, then much of parenting will be a hard row to hoe. Two SP parents together are a potential recipe for chaos, unless they gain some understanding of strengths that they need to develop. It is the demandingness tasks that will come hardest, from consistent rules and consequences to monitoring the child's whereabouts. Responsiveness will be an area of strength, with the exception of providing a structured home environment. This, again, will be a struggle.

Looking at the four types that share the SP temperament

In each person the SP core will be found combined with either the Extraverted or Introverted preference and the Feeling or Thinking Preference. These combinations affect the core in various ways, sometimes bringing out the strongest form of SP (see the ESTP), sometimes producing a quieter form (see the ISFP), and sometimes having more subtle actions

A recap of the SP descriptions tells us that all SPs have a heightened zest for living in the moment, a love of skillful performance and action, a very practical take on life, exceptional memory for factual information, and a passionate desire to be free of schedules, timetables, rules and restraints.

Below are the differences found in individual types as a result of the added preferences.

The ESFP—Extraverted, Sensing, **Feeling**, Perceiving: Most social and outgoing of all SPs Most fascinated with and easily distracted by the outside world. Happiest working in people services. Sympathetic, tactful and non-confrontational.

The ESTP-- Extraverted, Sensing, **Thinking,** Perceiving: More guided by Thinker logic, and somewhat less distractible as a result. Most adventurous of the four SPs. Sociable but not as warm and tactful as ESFPs. Often the life of the party. Most likely of all types to defy rules.

ISFP—Introverted, Sensing, **Feeling,** Perceiving: Introversion, Feeling and Perceiving join here to produce an SP who is exceptionally sensitive and gentle, but reserved with casual friends. Like the ESFP, ISFPs tend toward people-services as a career. Dislike rules and routine, but tend to suffer in silence.

ISTP—Introverted, Sensing, **Thinking**, Perceiving: This SP makes exceptionally good use of observation skills and practical information, using the Thinking function to organize this well for problem solving and troubleshooting. Reserved but self confident, capable of confrontation if needed

Parenting by Temperament

Chapter 13

Keepers of the Flame (SJs) The Sensing *and* Judging Temperament Group

The SJ temperament, when contrasted with the SP of the last chapter is an outstanding example of the way that one preference may influence another. SPs tend to be light-hearted and fun-loving. Strong SJs, in contrast, are serious, and exceptionally responsible in their daily lives.

The SJ child

Overall. The Sensing preference means that these children are practical, are focused on what is real and concrete and are more interested in what is happening now than in dreaming about the future. SJ children pay close attention to the physical world around them. They seek to make sense of what they can touch, taste, hear, feel, and see. The addition of Judging means that SJ children appreciate structure and routines and are generally happiest when they know what to expect. Although all children wish to be free to explore and play at will, SJ children prefer to know the boundaries of what they can and cannot do. Once rules and routines are clear to an SJ child, he or she is typically more comfortable and cooperative. Disorder and unpredictability create stress and resistance in the SJ, as do new experiences in general. However, once new experiences are familiar and part of the regular routine, the SJ child often embraces them. Parents can expect some initial negativity and a "warm-up" period when these children encounter new things.

Getting things done. The term "worker bee" is a great way to describe the growing SJ child. This child is usually busy learning how to do things and focused on the real world around them. SJ adults are typically hard-working and self-disciplined. As young SJ children, you will likely notice a strong determination to persist when learning something that interests them or while completing a task. SJ children will want to finish what they start, from finger-painting projects to bedtime routines, and may resist unexpected interruptions. They are practical, hands-on learners, and typically persist in learning and completing tasks. From learning how to tie their shoes to completing homework and chores, SJ children seem driven to get it done.

On Hows More than Whys SJ children want to learn how to do things and work hard to do them well and correctly. Although all children will ask questions about why things are the way they are, including SJs, these Sensor-Judgers will spend much more time learning how to do things than questioning and wondering why. As they grow, both Sensing and Judging lead them to be more likely to read and follow directions than to experiment. As adults, SJs rely heavily on their past experience, as well as the experience of others, for what works well and how to do things successfully. As children they generally trust the knowledge and experience of those in authority—their parents, teachers and coaches, and experts more generally.

On Belonging One of the strong underlying characteristics of the SJ temperament is the desire to belong to groups. Of the four temperaments (NTs, SJs, NFs and SPs), SJs typically have the greatest desire to be an accepted member of a group whether it be the family, classroom, team or choir. They often make excellent team players, and this is meant in the broadest sense. They want to learn their part and fulfill their responsibilities. They often happily take leadership roles. However, they see themselves as leading others according to the rules and values of their group, rather than by any unique vision of their own.

The Good and the Bad

For a parent this child can seem like a miracle to discipline. The Judging strengths seem to shine in the SJ child, so that they are generally neat and tidy with their own things, good about chores and homework and pretty compliant. They tend to do well in school, early on but show less interest in abstract and theoretical subjects, which may be reflected in some drop off in grades in later years. If there is parent/child conflict it is most likely to occur if a very strong SJ child has a very strong SP parent. Chaos and constant change is unnerving for this child, and as she grows toward puberty she may become openly critical of the SP parent. In general the tendency to see a best way to behave, and to be critical of those who don't meet the SJ's standards, is something that will require some help and advice over time.

SJ Adults—Tools, rules and stewardship

The adult SJ tends to be the mature, determined and effective person that you would predict from the young SJ. The desire to get things done now goes with an earnest sense that accomplishment is not simply pleasurable, but also necessary and important to the well-being of both self and society.

In the chapter title *we called them "Keepers of the Flame"*, because of their strong tendency to accept and fulfill responsibilities. People who share this core often display a very deep desire to keep home, family, and society running properly.
Like all Sensors, they delight in the tools that will get things done, whether these are physical tools or organizational resources like spreadsheets. Tools are their technique for managing and shaping the world around them. Since SJs are focused on what is happening here and now as opposed to the far future, they typically are attracted to tools that have practical uses. When learning new technology, they would be most interested in those applications that have a clear positive impact on everyday life.

On following tested methods. As strong Judgers, SJs typically have clear opinions and standards about how things should be done. The combined Sensing and Judging preferences result in a focus on standards, methods, and techniques that have been tried and tested successfully. Therefore, SJs have a great deal of confidence in past practices that have succeeded. SJs are typically patient with learning before doing, so long as it is practical and useful in the immediate future. There is a natural relationship here between tools and rules. Tools should be used for their intended purpose. The SJ will typically find an improper but inventive use of a tool, inventive but *improper*, and assume (often rightly) that it will produce inferior results.

On being prepared and organized. SJs constantly rely on structure, organization, checklists, and planning, in order to achieve their goals. If at the end of the day, SJs have done what they have set out to do, they are rewarded with a deep sense of satisfaction. Because they are practical and realistic, SJs naturally prepare for setbacks and have realistic views of the ups and downs of life. Taking care to prepare for that rainy day just makes good sense to them. Sorting through facts and details, coming to conclusions, and taking practical action are all driving forces for those individuals who share the SJ temperament. True to their nature, as they would not waste their own time, so would they not waste the time of others. SJs are rarely late to events.

Respect for authority/need for regard from others. SJs naturally respect authority, often assuming that the individual has earned the right to their position (from team captain to parent to boss). Therefore most SJs do not automatically question authority and will often give individuals in positions of authority the benefit of the doubt. In turn, SJs expect to be treated with respect for their own authority and may be greatly offended when this is challenged or questioned. Perhaps because SJs work persistently to develop their abilities and skills, they have a strong need to be recognized for their talents and contributions.

Like the SJ child, the adult seeks and cherishes membership in family, workplace, and community. For the SJ this is all part of having an orderly and predictable world. Knowing where they comfortably belong, and where they have particular obligations to others is satisfying and reassuring.

Strengths

Strong memory for details As a result of the facts and details focus that all SJs share, an SJ often has a strong memory for information and events. Because they seldom pass on information that they are not sure about, they tend to be exceptionally reliable.

Disciplined and dependable Because SJs tend to be disciplined and persistent in whatever they decide to do, they can be counted on to make significant
contributions to organizations, communities, and families. Combined with their factual accuracy the SJ is solidly dependable.

Decisive and action-oriented Since SJs are driven to achieve through action, they are often very decisive. This characteristic typically results in behavior that is firm, resolute, and determined. Once an SJ has reviewed information and determined a course of action, the resolve to get to the finish line can be very intense.

Natural leaders All of these qualities result in a person who is often comfortable with and highly effective in leadership positions.

Potential Weaknesses

Easily frustrated by change Unlike the SP who often thrives in chaotic situations and enjoys change and variety, the SJ has a difficult time responding to new and unexpected circumstances, and may experience anything from frustration to great stress. This can be a significant challenge for SJs in some settings.

May rush decisions The strong desire to decide and take action enables the SJ to readily achieve goals. However, this can also be a problem for SJs, since they may rush to decision-making and action with insufficient information, resulting in poor or faulty decisions. SJs may also experience frustration and even stress when action is delayed by the needs of others to continue to collect and understand information, and may be heard complaining that nothing is getting done.

Difficultly making changes Related to their preference for predictability, SJs are not fond of changing direction or method in midstream. The SJ's determined ability to achieve a particular goal is a strength that becomes a potential weakness when an accepted course of action that is now underway, requires change.

May be too controlling Finally, others (mostly people of opposing temperaments) may find very strong SJs to be somewhat over-controlling. This is much more likely if the SJ core is combined with the Thinking preference. This is often due to their powerful focus on achieving goals, and on sharing their knowledge with others. Regardless of motive, however, if friends and colleagues are frequently resentful, it is time for the SJ to do some self-analysis.

The SJ parent

This parent should be very good at demandingness tasks. Both rules and consequences can be expected to be clear and consistent, and effective monitoring should be high on the agenda. If there is a problem here it might be that rules and limits are carried to the extreme. An SP child might feel truly smothered by a strong, successful SJ parent. Nothing in the SJ temperament would interfere with responsiveness, and certainly the need for a clear, structured environment will be well taken care of. The principal problem here might be that the earnestness of the SJ (as is true of all Judgers), keeps this parent from enjoying some teachable moments and some huggable moments—all in the service of getting everything done on that list!

Looking at the Four <u>Types</u> that share the SJ temperament

For all SJs, the SJ core will be found combined with either the Extraverted or Introverted preference and the Feeling or Thinking Preference. These combinations affect the core in various ways, as you can see in the following table. However, the SJ core effects remain clear.

A recap of the SJ descriptions tells us that, dependability, self discipline, love of order, love of accomplishment, respect for tradition and authority all characterize the SJ "Keeper of the Flame". Practical, decisive and action oriented, SJs are the bedrock of organizations, communities and families. Below are the differences found in individual types as a result of the added preferences.

ESFJ—<u>Extraverted</u>, Sensing, **<u>Feeling</u>**, Judging--Extraversion and Feeling produce an SJ who enjoys exercising organizational skills in the world of people management. The ESFJ tends to be warm, sociable and tactful, and uses these assets to keep groups and interpersonal relationships running smoothly. Like all SJs they are practical and realistic.

ESTJ—<u>Extraverted</u>, Sensing, **<u>Thinking</u>**, Judging--The Thinking preference adds a strong use of logic to the SJ ability to organize information. This is the most decisive, and action-oriented of the four SJ types. ESTJs are skillful bosses, highly task-oriented and focused on outcomes. They are clear, self-confident communicators, but can be overpowering at times.

ISFJ—<u>Introverted</u>, Sensing, **<u>Feeling</u>** Judging—With Introversion and Feeling combined with the SJ core, this is the most unassuming of the SJs. They share all the love for organization and structure, and good informational skills, but are quiet and non-confrontational. Others find them hardworking reliable and considerate.

Chapter 14

Humanity's Champions (NFs)— The Intuitive _and_ Feeling Temperament Group

Intuition brings a great love of what might be possible, and Feeling contributes an intense wish for human betterment. When the two combine in the NF temperament core, it has a powerful impact on the passions and behaviors of the individual. Here the Intuitive preference and the Feeling preference seem to fuse together.

The NF child

Overall Two of the most striking characteristics of NF children are their insightfulness and their natural empathy for others. NF children seem to be born with a deep sensitivity and a very early awareness of how others feel. As they grow, NF children will express this passion in many different ways: in close and caring relationships, an unusual concern for in the suffering of others, and for many, in writing, music or art. Having close relationships with family and, later, with friends will be unusually important to these children. Success in these relationships will be vital for their sense of happiness and self- worth.

On Imagination Very early on, young NF children tend to be highly imaginative, and enjoy activities that require this, such as reading fantasy stories, playing make-believe, making up stories to share with friends and family, and possibly even having an imaginary friend. Typically they project their imagination into the future at an early age, spending considerable time dreaming about what they may do when they grow up. More than most children they also begin to wonder about the meaning of life at an early age, and tend to ask many probing questions.

Learning Much of school will come easily. We would expect that NF children are very interested in new ideas, and especially where that relates to people. For the Intuitive child, an interest in the "why" of things is likely to be especially important and to remain and intensify as they grow. It is common for school-age NF children to particularly enjoy literature, writing, and social studies. If they have any problems in school they will be in a tendency to skip over facts and jump to exciting ideas. Similarly, they may tend to skip past instructions and make what might be called "clerical errors" on tests in spite of understanding the overall ideas.

On Relationships and Acceptance NF children have a deep need for close relationships and are often very affectionate toward others. Whether they develop a large group of friends, or just one or two special friends, NF children are likely to invest a great deal of time and energy in these relationships. NF children tremendously enjoy pleasing family members and, for that reason, are often charming and engaging. As they grow, these children will want to be accepted and well liked by friends, schoolmates, teammates and teachers. Peaceful and harmonious relationships are vital to NF happiness.

The Good and the Bad

Since warm relationships are a central value for the NF, making and keeping them is a great strength. Most NF children are kind and thoughtful and well liked by others. In the family they tend to be peacemakers rather than storm-centers, and are well motivated to follow the rules and please parents. This is a truth about Feelers in general but it rises to new heights in the NF.

The down side of this may be problems in self-assertion, when personal wishes conflict with keeping the peace. A demanding friend or family member may make the NF's life miserable. It is also true, however, that this problem may drive the very strong NF to become somewhat devious with others. Precisely because they are skillful in reading and understanding the feelings of others, the NF is tempted to use these skills in finding indirect ways to get others to do what is wanted. If this child is not helped to develop a certain amount of firm self-assertion, manipulative strategies may be a great temptation.

NF Adults

Idealism as a central focus The adult NF is concerned with human dignity, rights, social values, spirituality, and ultimately, the meaning of life itself. Not all NFs are active in organizations that work for human betterment, but it is very common to find them there. They not only pursue their own vision of the ideal life, but also deeply wish to involve others in striving for a better world. They may express their concerns in a variety of ways, from journalism to art to religion to political activism.

On the uses and joys of imagination As an Intuitive, the adult NF relishes the power of imagination. They are often found looking for the patterns that can explain seemingly random facts, and projecting into the future to see what might be possible. Unlike Sensors, who focus on what is real and immediately applicable, Intuitives are much more interested in what might be possible.

The NF moves quickly through facts and details, looking for patterns and connections between surface facts and their deeper meanings. It is as if they can suddenly step back from a spider web, gaining just the right light and angle that enables them to see the pattern perfectly. But unlike other Intuitives, the patterns that captivate the NF are those that have to do with human behavior and interpersonal relationships.

On value-based decisions When making decisions, NFs will focus on their personal values and feelings in order to determine the best course of action. They will consider how the decision might affect their core values, and the personal and emotional impact it may have on themselves and on others. NFs will work hard to make decisions that are consistent with these concerns.

On relationships and harmony The NF's focus on relationships typically results in a strong drive for interpersonal harmony. In interactions with others, the NF is likely to choose tact over truthfulness, and mercy over fairness where these values conflict. This means two things: First, where the blunt truth would be hurtful to another, the NF will look for a gentle way to soften it or even avoid it. Second, where a general standard of fairness does not seem to take someone's special problems into account, an NF will always be tempted to make an exception for the individual or find some other way to help the person having the difficulty. Surprisingly, however, NFs are not necessarily uncomfortable with conflict when the focus is on helping to resolve interpersonal relationships. The NF can be very good at and drawn to resolving this type of conflict (the divorce mediator, for example). It is likely that interpersonal conflict is viewed as an opportunity for growth and development in relationships, and a better and deeper understanding of self and others.

On the search for identity and meaning The NF's search for identity is really a search for his or her uniqueness and authenticity as an individual. NFs often have a powerful need to discover what makes them distinctive as individuals and what their life's true meaning and purpose is. They are happiest when they are free to explore who they are and what they are meant to do. As a result, they sometimes pursue many different career paths and lifestyles. Learning for learning's sake is highly valued, and if it leads the NF into a new and exciting direction, all the better.

Strengths

Optimistic Many Intuitives have a great deal of confidence in their ability to understand complex problems and feel that the future hangs out there as an opportunity to promote positive change.

Insightful, enthusiastic, eager to learn Along with their special strength in seeing broad patterns themselves, they are also devoted searchers for new ideas, and new theories—from self-help to politics and philosophy. This is most true in the area of social institutions and human relationships for the NF. Learning for its own sake is energizing and fulfilling.

Diplomatic Because of their ability to recognize emotional climates and their value for harmony and relationships, NF's are often very skillful at diplomacy. If an NF must articulate a controversial viewpoint, he would take care not to hurt or anger someone in the process. NFs may take pride in their abilities to recognize and respond to the emotions and needs of others.

Caring and passionate This strength shines through in everything they do, and all their relations with others. Both in their professions and in their families and friendship networks they strive to be a force for good.

Weaknesses

May ignore important information As is true with all individuals who prefer Intuition, NFs may struggle with respecting facts. All Intuitives move quickly from specific data to patterns and connections. This can easily result in conclusions that are not supported by all of the details or facts. In addition, those who prefer Feeling may be especially tempted to ignore or downplay facts that are not consistent with their values and feelings. For the strong NF, this can be a double whammy, first moving too quickly from data to patterns and second ignoring critical information.

Can be emotionally manipulative This is not common in NFs who have developed in a positive, life-enhancing way of life. Nevertheless, NFs do have both natural skills at understanding others, and a lifetime spent in polishing these skills in the interest of avoiding conflict. In a situation where their personal needs or values seem threatened and direct confrontation seems too painful, NFs may sometimes use their exceptional abilities in this area, in order to manipulate or even cause hurt.

May lose interest and momentum when work becomes routine

Finally, just as the excitement of new ideas provides the NF with great energy and direction, as soon as the work becomes routine and repetitious, some NFs lose interest. Creativity and imagination get the juices going, and NFs do learn to live for this. Much will depend here on the Judging/Perceiving preference, with Perceiving strongly supporting a desire to work only on what is exciting, and Judging introducing greater self-discipline in this area.

The NF Parent

The typical NF is the ideally responsive parent. They are warm, caring and concerned always for the child's welfare. They are good at understanding the child's feelings and needs. Though often talented in the uses of distraction, they usually have problems with firm discipline. They may develop a good set of rules in the abstract, but enforcing these with a crying child is a whole other matter. A common strategy here may be to announce clear consequences and then withdraw these when the child's contrition and/or distress becomes painfully obvious.

Looking at the four types that share the NF temperament

In each person the NF core will be found combined with either the Extraverted or Introverted preference and the Judging or Perceiving preference. These combinations affect the core in various ways, sometimes bringing out the strongest form of NF, sometimes producing a quieter form, and sometimes having more subtle actions

A recap of the NF descriptions tells us that NFs are deeply involved in maintaining harmony with others, understanding human relationships and searching for new solutions to social and interpersonal problems. They use intuition well to understand relationship patterns. The search for meaning, both in personal life and in social, political and spiritual areas, is critically important.

Below are the differences found in individual types as a result of the added preferences.

ENFP--<u>Extraverted</u>, Intuitive, Feeling, **<u>Perceiving</u>** Extraversion adds an extra burst of energy and enthusiasm here. Highly sociable and zestful they are warmly supportive of others. They are likely to be involved in many projects as innovators and facilitators. As Perceivers they do dislike routine and may be better at generating ideas and starting projects than tying up loose ends.

ENFJ--<u>Extraverted</u>, Intuitive, Feeling, **<u>Judging</u>** The Judging preference here adds structure and organization to NF activities. Empathetic and supportive, like all NFs, with Extraversion added they do great work in consensus building, and in finding ways to organize the needs and desires of others for harmony, productivity and mutual enjoyment.

INFP—<u>Introverted</u>, Intuitive, Feeling, **<u>Perceiving</u>** Introversion brings a more reflective, less action-oriented NF. Their inner values guide decision making strongly, and when threatened may bring out surprisingly intense emotion. Reserved, they prefer working alone, but are sensitive and caring about the emotional needs of others. They honor their commitments, but struggle with routine work.

INFJ--<u>Introverted</u>, Intuitive, Feeling, **<u>Judging</u>** As reserved Introverts, INFJs spend more energy in thinking and analyzing than in networking, but they remain deeply empathetic and focused on human betterment. Compared to Extraverted NFs, they are more the visionary planner and less the networker. Compared to the INFP, INFJs are more strongly motivated to organize and implement plans.

Chapter 15

Passionate Achievers (NTs)
The Intuitive _and_ Thinking Temperament Group

The NT fuses Intuition with a strong preference for cool analytical logic. This tends to produce an individual with an exceptional drive for accomplishment, and so we call them the "passionate achievers." Depending on other preferences they may be highly organized, action oriented individuals, or they may be more internalized designers and planners. Either way, they aim to have an effect on their world. Every temperament has its share of high achievers. NTs differ only in the degree in which life seems to be focused around this.

The NT Child

From the preference for Intuition comes a child with a great delight in using imagination. From the Thinking preference this child tends, from a very early age, to decide what is good and what is true on the basis of reason and logic. The back-and-forth between these two preferences is fascinating. "I can imagine." "I can reason about whether the things I imagine could possibly be." At an age where children still passionately believe in Santa Claus, this child may first come up with the most elegant explanations about how Santa gets to every house in the world on one night, but later be one of the first to decide that this is impossible, and so is Santa.

Focusing On "Whys" Even More than "Hows." All children spend a lot of time asking "why," but in some this seems to be just interesting conversation. The NT really wants to know. Your NT child may seem old for his/her age, even precocious. It is not so much an advanced intelligence that gives this impression, but an early passion for understanding things and really being sure about what is so. Reason and imagination; imagination and reason form a spiral of growing understanding. At first, imagination may dominate, but as NTs grow older you can expect to see strong stress on logic emerging.

A joy in being Competent. An early trait that NT children share is a strong drive toward accomplishment. They want to be able to do everything that their developmental timetable makes possible. This can sometimes be seen even in infancy, in an early desire to reach things, hold things, feed themselves and so forth. In general, they are likely to be more the busy explorer and less the cuddly lovebug even as toddlers.

On Solving Problems A common, but surprising, trait in little NTs is their early interest in fixing problems when they crop up. It is not unusual to find them, even at the age of five, listening intently to an adult conversation about some family problem and chiming in with "Well, couldn't we try doing this? (or idea B? or idea C?)" This seems to be part of the package, and is seen in the adult in many forms.

A Strong Emphasis on Honesty and Fairness The NT tends to be frank and
outspoken—sometimes more than others would want. At least in part, this seems to reflect their passion for honesty in all things. All children do their best to use cries of fairness to their advantage, but NTs are generally quite sincere in trying to go by what is fair— perhaps because they are very good at reasoning about it.

De-emphasis on emotion At a remarkably early age, even young NTs can be seen struggling to suppress emotional disturbances. They often reject comfort in small injuries, or interpersonal hurts, preferring to shake it off and go on to something else. Some may be less emotional from the beginning, but many seem to work at getting unpleasant emotions under control, becoming better at it as time goes by.

The Good and the Bad
_____

There are many good traits to praise here. Young NTs often show admirable amount of honesty and fairness. They are industrious and rarely have to be goaded to take an interest in accomplishing things, though this may be somewhat scattered in a strongly Perceiving NT. Both imagination and logical thinking dominate in the NT in a productive way.

The downside of all this is a lesser degree of empathy and concern for the feelings of others. Young NTs often need help in this area. They are likely to be much too outspoken about the perceived faults of others, and need to learn, as we have said elsewhere, that "not everything that is thought needs to be spoken." With this they really need to gain some insight into the fact that not everyone values the "best" (most efficient) solution to every problem, as the most important factor. Human relationships matter too, and the NT may need help in understanding that personal needs and values should be taken into account in all actions and decisions.

The Adult NT

While Intuition gives us castles in the air, Thinking plans, organizes, and tries to improve everyday life on the ground. Where both preferences are strong, it tends to produce a remarkably effective adult who is very likely to be a leader in work and life. The strong Thinker preference anchors the Intuitive tendency, and directs it toward real world projects, while the Intuitive preference makes for a Thinker with substantial imagination.   All of the trends that are seen in the child—the strong reliance on reason, the emphasis on honesty and fairness, the desire for competence, independence, and even the tendency to keep emotion in the background, are found in fully developed form in the adult NT.

Independence. This shows itself in many ways. For example, the adult NT is impressed by good ideas wherever they may originate, but not at all by the status of the idea's owner. With a highly developed ability to reason, the NT often has remarkable confidence in his or her own judgment.

Logic based decisions. With this preference, the individual will have respect for what has been done before, and for factual information, but will not feel bound by either of these. The theme of knowing what is true, being honest with oneself and others is very strong in most NTs. They do not simply want to be logical; they want to be accurate. They don't just want to convince others that they are right; they want to be genuinely right!

On systems and how they work. Set an NT down in almost any situation and he or she will begin to look around at how things are being done, and will soon feel the urge to suggest changes and improvements (whether wanted or not). The NT is powerfully compelled toward solutions. Effectiveness and mastery are great driving forces, and are brought to bear both in problem solving and in understanding new information, and new ideas. There is a passionate need to delve in and gain a sense of clarity and mastery. As a result, these individuals are often in leadership positions in business, in science and technology and, less frequently, in other public organizations.

On keeping cool and calm The NT exercises a great deal of self-control to keep emotion out of the picture much of the time. It would be a mistake to assume that people of this temperament are less inherently emotional than others. Some may indeed be so, but others may be controlling deep emotions. The major difference is that NTs choose to keep emotions under the control of reason. They don't trust emotion as a way of making decisions.

Special Strengths

These follow directly from their overall characteristics and include independent mindedness, skillful use of both logic and imagination, excellent problem-solving abilities and strong value on honesty and fairness.

Potential Weaknesses

May be bluntly critical of illogical and/or Feeling-based reasoning
It probably can't be stressed too much that the NT has an almost
religious faith in the value of reason. He or she will argue with delight
and enthusiasm with someone who disagrees on logical grounds, but
when it veers off into personal feelings or an argument for upholding
tradition or maintaining the status quo, the NT will feel inwardly
impatient and may convey that feeling outwardly also. He or she is
likely to terminate the discussion early, or to be overly frank in
expressing disagreement

More generally—may seem critical of others. Even when the other
person *is* offering a good logical argument, the NT—who may be
thoroughly enjoying it—will not let the other person off easily. Our
strong NT will not only argue hard, but will press for evidence—
names, dates, examples, and will offer his or her strongest counterarguments. Typically, this is not intended to be a criticism of the other
person, but rather of the idea or proposal in question. However, most
of us have trouble separating one from the other when we are on the
receiving end. NTs tend to be exceptionally verbal and articulate,
adding to the problem.

May be unaware of the feelings of others Many--though not all--NTs,
seem to be genuinely unaware of the emotional feelings and needs of
others. This is particularly true in the world of work, where emotional
restraint is expected of everyone. The NT is unlikely to look below the
surface for unexpressed values and emotions. In the strongest of NT
types, this may constitute a real blind spot that may present problems
in both professional life and personal relationships.

May neglect to show appreciation Related to this, the NT's love of
making things better can cause this individual to pay very little
attention to all the good things that have already been done by others.
It is not that they are not seen, but they are simply absorbed as a
foundation for the next step. Those who contributed to all the positive

results and accomplishments to date may easily feel unappreciated. Many NTs are so busy looking toward the next great project that they simply forget the small acts, kind words, and interpersonal caring that keep the world rolling along. As a result, they may seem cold and unfeeling to others.

Can be a true misfit in certain situations The most obvious, of course, is a position where tact and high level skills in relationship areas are critical. The NT is not likely to seek this, but if promoted to such a position, will be restless, impatient and relatively ineffective. A second job area that would be all wrong would be one that required enormous attention to detail, rather than the natural NT ability to scan the big picture.

The NT Parent

It should not surprise you to know that the strong NT excels in doing demandingness well. This parent brings her fine skills in logical analysis to setting up a very good system of rules and consequences. She is also both willing and able to give good reasons for her rules. When misbehavior occurs this is the least likely parent to shrink from confrontation. As a result of all that, there is usually great consistency in disciplinary actions.

If difficulties occur, they are more likely to be on the responsiveness side. NTs have no problem with the many teaching and learning aspects of responsiveness, often enjoying these very much. They appreciate the unfolding of the child's growth and development, and are certainly cheerleaders for this. However, strong NT parents may be much less talented in understanding the child's emotional ups and downs, and in providing warmth and comfort. Often their first reaction to an upset is to seek a logical solution, where a hug might be the more immediate need. With a strongly Thinking child this may go fairly well, but with a strong Feeling child it may really miss the mark. Little Feelers with two NT parents may feel protected and taken care of, but may not feel warmly loved.

Looking at the four types that share the NT temperament

Here the NT core will be found combined with either the Extraverted or Introverted preference and the Judging or Perceiving preference. You can see the differences that Introversion or Extraversion and Judging or Perceiving make, but the NT core is clear in all cases.

A recap of NT descriptors tells us that NTs have both a passion to understand their world and a passion to use that understanding to change it for the better. In the service of this, they tend to harness creativity and intuition to a firm, demanding respect for logic and factual knowledge. This may take many forms but the underlying drive is always visible.

Below are the differences found in each of the four NT types as a result of the additional preferences in each Type.

ENTJ—Extraverted, Intuitive, Thinking, **Judging--** Of all the NTs this is the most dynamic, action oriented type. The Extraverted and Judging preferences add sociability, gregariousness, and a structured, organized approach to getting things done. Especially likely to be in leadership positions Very decisive and highly assertive Though Extraversion brings delight in others, may still be very blunt.

ENTP—Extraverted, Intuitive, Thinking, **Perceiving--**Combining Intuition with Perceiving makes this person exceptionally aware of new ideas and possibilities. May be the most creative of the four NT types Spontaneous, adaptable up to a point Interesting fallout from this is that they are talented at reading and motivating others, even though, like all NTs they can be argumentative, blunt, and lacking in tact. With Perceiving, better at planning than at follow-through.

INTJ—Introverted, Intuitive, Thinking, **Judging--**Terrific thinkers and visionaries, the INTJ is socially reserved, and likely to exert leadership through ideas rather than through direct management. Often found in science or technology fields. Very tough-minded, with extremely high expectations of self and others May be especially lacking in emotional sensitivity and tact. May seem aloof.

INTP—Introverted, Intuitive, Thinking, **Perceiving--**Quiet and reserved, they are the most likely of all NTs to lead with ideas rather than organizational force, and are best working alone. Great at dissecting illogical arguments Perceiving preference makes them especially dependent on having challenging problems to solve in order to work with vigor and enthusiasm. Poor at routine tasks. Adaptable & flexible until core principles are at issue.

Part V

---

*Polishing the Basic Design—
Integrating Responsiveness, Demandingness and
Temperament*

Overview:

In upcoming chapters we consider how preferences and temperament affect parenting. Here we also think again about why parenting experts disagree and what this means for you.

The parenting expert dilemma In Chapter One we suggested that parenting experts differ in their ideas about best parenting practices because they also differ in their models of human nature. Some see the newborn as the *pretty-nice blank slate*, and others seeing this newbie as *wild, willful,* and in need of taming. We tried to suggest that both views are partly correct. Your child comes into the world both warm and loving and wild and willful, in amounts that may vary a lot from child to child. Now that you have explored the chapters on temperament, you may see that we left out a vital part of *"why experts disagree."* Why would intelligent and well educated people reach different conclusions about human nature? The missing piece is that there are natural differences in temperament between parenting experts, as well as in and between everyday parents.

Imagine a gentle and loving mother who values harmony very strongly, married to a spouse who is very similar. The genetic lottery suggests that they may have pretty gentle, harmony-loving children. If so, the temperament of the parents will lead them to emphasize parenting techniques that stress close bonding above all, and minimize discipline. If this parent-pair *do* have children of a similar temperament, their approach may work reasonably well. In our temperament system we would describe this as a family of Feelers, perhaps NFs. Based on their own temperaments and life experiences, it might be quite reasonable for the parents to assume two things. First, they might assume that children are born naturally wanting to cooperate, and only stray from this if not deeply loved. Second, following logically, would be the conclusion that the right parenting techniques should emphasize very large doses of affection and closeness, and very little that you could call discipline. If they happen to become professional parenting experts, then, their advice would be strongly in the direction that is often described as "attachment parenting." That makes perfect sense.

On the other hand, two very strong minded *doer* parents (let's say strong Thinkers and strong Judgers) might be very conscious of the fact that individuals have to learn to temper their wishes and wills in order to live with others. If the two parents are a great deal alike, the luck of the genetic pool might again give them children much like themselves. They would assume from the beginning that firm discipline is critical, and perhaps that as long as you love your children and look out for their welfare, constant evidence of love is not essential. Their children, again, if very much like them in temperament, might do quite well with this approach. If these two became parenting experts they might be tempted to write a book with a title like "Dare to Discipline". Again, from their viewpoint, and their life experiences, this would make perfect sense.

The real problem This appears when you try to apply either of these extremes to all parents and all children. Several things happen in the real world. First of all, you as parent bring your own temperament to the advice you read about. You may, therefore, reject out of hand anything that just feels wrong to you. That's a fairly reasonable response, but you may miss some important advice along the way. Even worse, you may assume that a particular set of advice is right (after all, this is an expert, yes?) and try desperately to follow it against your natural instincts.

You might find yourself trying to discipline sternly, when nothing in your voice or actions really seems stern. Or, on the contrary, you, as the strong Thinker, might carry your children around constantly for the first six months of life, resenting every moment. (Not good). Later, with your toddler and preschooler, you maintain a sweet gentle tone when things go wrong—but your eyes are blazing. In either case, parent-child communication will be very disjointed.

Another combination Now imagine that the gentle, Feeler parents have strong Thinker-Judger children. They really are likely to discover that love is not enough. Similarly, Feeler children of the Thinker-Judger parents may find their parents fair and reasonable, but hard to snuggle up with on a cold winter's night. Furthermore, clean examples of matching dad-mom temperaments often do not occur in real life. Thinker versus Feeler parents, in particular, will find themselves divided on proper parenting techniques, and find themselves arguing--sometimes bitterly--over who is too soft and too hard. Even more baffling, with several children in the same family, one child may seem to respond very well to the parenting model while another seems designed to frustrate all well-intended efforts. If the two of you, as parents, already differ in your philosophies, the family arguments are going to be world class.

What this means for you

I. The model we have examined at length for Authoritative parenting (responsiveness/demandingness) is an ideal overall approach, but it has to be adapted to your child and to you as parent.

II. Your own temperament may make some parts of the model very easy to carry out and other parts very difficult. You will need to learn to do better in some areas where your child needs your help.

III. You and your partner may seriously disagree on many issues, and need to find common ground for a compromise.

IV. You cannot change your underlying temperament preferences, but armed with insight about possible problems, you can "stretch" to change your behavior to a degree. To see what we mean try the exercise in the box below.

A Quick and Useful Preference Test!

1. Take a pen or pencil in the hand you normally write with (your preferred hand!) and write your full name.

2. Now place the pen in your other hand and again write your full name.

Was that hard, clumsy, frustrating? Of course. you are using your non-preferred hand.

Preferences are naturally-preferred ways of doing things. They are written in our genes.

But—you have had a lifetime of practice with the preferred hand, and much of your skill also comes from that. With enough practice you could begin to use the non-preferred hand if you had to. It would always be harder, and less skillfully done, but you could do it.

What is more, it would become easier and better over time and practice.

Whether you are a Feeler trying to improve in demandingness, or a Perceiver trying to be more organized, a Thinker wishing to be more tenderly nurturant, or a Judger more spontaneously responsive, the idea is not that you should try to change your natural preferences, but that you should, *really should,* try to develop some abilities and skills on your non-preferred side. In this effort, you need to be kind and understanding with yourself, as you try to stretch in new directions. It is baby steps, not one-day miracles. It is being a little more effective, not becoming Superparent.

And one more thought: As you begin these chapters, keep this in mind.

In all these descriptions of preferences, temperament and parenting style, *we are describing parents with at least Clear, and more often, Strong Preferences* (See comment on this at the end of Chapter 8). Also, in the temperament combinations (SP, SF, NF, NT) we are similarly describing parents where both preferences (S and P for example) are Clear to Strong.

So—what does it mean if some of your preferences were rated as Slight—or even tied? This is not a negative thing—it generally means that your behavior is fairly well balanced between the two preference poles. (As an Introvert, for example, you may be talkative and pretty comfortable in social groups, but still want a good deal of down time in between social events.) If this is true throughout the questions for this preference set, you may score as a slight Introvert, but not a strong one. *If so,* the parenting problems described for a parent with a stronger preference in a specific area may not fit you. At least in that area, the responsiveness and demandingness model may be just fine as it is. If the preference or temperament problems don't fit, take a sigh of relief and move on.

What if it does sound like me, even though I rated myself as "slight"? Well, you may have more to learn about yourself in that preference area. If the problems described do sound like you—even though you rated yourself as Slight in that area, you should find the ideas and stretching exercises to be helpful.

The rest of this book is devoted to helping you tweak and stretch, wherever this may be helpful.

195

Parenting by Temperament

Chapter 16

Parent Preferences and Responsiveness

A brief review of Responsiveness

Responsiveness, as you will recall, is the giving side of parenting. It begins with warmth and affection, but continues on to include many varied actions that the parent engages in for the sake of the child. Now we want to look at responsiveness again, in the light of temperament. To be really talented as a responsive parent, you need not only to be loving and caring and willing, but also attentive and smart--aware of what your child is thinking and feeling. That means that you have to be good at understanding your child's unique temperament, your own temperament, and how these forces interact.

In Chapter Three we talked about four different aspects of parent responsiveness. In this Chapter we will look at the different ways in which individual temperament
preferences may affect all of these forms of responsiveness. Since it has been a while since Chapter Three, we repeat the chapter summary here.

Recapping Responsiveness

The gift of warmth and intimacy

- ➤ Providing spontaneous affection to your child
- ➤ Making time for many happy moments

The gift of active parent learning

- ➤ Taking a great interest in your child's development at all stages

> ➢ Spending time just observing and being intimately aware of your child's feelings, interests and joys
> ➢ Learning about yourself and your own strengths and weaknesses as a parent.

The gift of active teaching

> ➢ Speaking and reading to your child early and often
> ➢ Encouraging and actively supporting the child's education and special interests
> ➢ Sharing your own feelings wherever appropriate
> ➢ Offering clear communication on family rules, values, moral issues
> ➢ Listening and responding to your child's ideas, feelings and viewpoints

The gift of structure

> ➢ Providing a comforting and predictable home environment

Warmth, Intimacy and Temperament Preferences

Intimacy comes most easily to Feeling parents and may require the most time and experience to blossom in strongly Thinking parents. Where there is both strong Thinking and strong Judging, the parent's drive to be organized at all times and on top of all tasks may add a level of difficulty. Although these preferences should not affect the inner love that is felt, they may very well affect the way that love is *expressed*, and parent willingness to spend intimate moments in play and other close parent-to-child interactions. Preference differences may also have important effects on even a parent's very best efforts to understand what the child is feeling, thinking, and needing.

Good child/parent relationships These have more in common with adult/adult relationships than we might first think. Both require really understanding the other person, and understanding yourself.

198

Thinking/Feeling preference differences enter in to this. Particularly where parent and child have strong and opposite preferences for Thinking and Feeling, careful attention to your child's signals, and to your own natural preferences, is very important. Feeling children seek and delight in a great deal of interaction—cuddling, hugs, emotionally rich speech. Thinking children may seem much the same in the first few months, but soon turn much more to exploring the world, and developing and testing their own skills. The Feeling parent with a strongly Thinking child may want more constant closeness than the little person is up for, and may feel somewhat rejected at times. Whether your child needs more emotional responsiveness than you would naturally give, or far less, you need to understand what both of you are about, and try to find a healthy middle ground that works for both of you.

Introversion/Extraversion Highly Extraverted children (and parents) share feelings easily, but love to be around a variety of people. The Introverted parent may be at some risk of feeling not all that uniquely important, as his Extraverted child grows older and reaches out to many different people. This may be particularly true in a contrast between an Introverted and Feeling parent and an Extraverted but Thinking child.

The Introverted child, on the other hand, shares his deepest feelings very cautiously, and may be overwhelmed at times by the very Extraverted parent. Family harmony and family happiness across a broad range of differences, requires a great deal of patient understanding.

Active parent learning and preferences

Developing a clear view of who your child is This is a theme throughout this book. Getting to know your child is something that goes on all the time, unless we are too desperately busy and stressed to pay attention. Things that get in the way, though, include being very different in preferences, being biased toward our own preferences and/or trying to "make" a child be the way we want them to be.

Preference bias problems At heart, we all think our preferences are the right preferences. For example, Strong Thinkers see strong Feelers as overly sensitive and often illogical. Strong Feelers see strong Thinkers as rather cold and impersonal. Both think the other has a character flaw. When we hold any of these preferences strongly, the temptation, whether with friend, spouse, or child, is to try to help the other see the light and behave and think more like we do. It is extremely hard work to just look at our children as they are and accept and love them for their differences. And--fair warning--of the various preference combinations, Thinker-Judgers may be the worst sinners in trying to helpfully change another.

Problems with less obvious preferences Intuition and Sensing are harder to see in others because we have less visible behavior to work with. Much of the activity of these preferences goes on inside the Intuitor/Sensor head, and can only be seen if we listen very carefully to what the person likes to talk about, and what sorts of projects they enjoy. To make that work with children we have to be careful not to over-direct their activities and conversations. Nevertheless, the true Sensor has little inner patience with the Intuitive world of theories and ideas, and the strong Intuitive has little interest in the Sensor world of useful, but factual information. In adult groups they are often pushing the agenda in contrary directions.

Showing interest Especially as your child grows and becomes her own unique self, taking pleasure and interest in what interests and excites her may also range from easy to hard. It will depend very much on how your preferences seem to mesh. The dreamy, imaginative parent may find herself struggling to get excited about a Sensing child's most practical interests. That stamp collection may just not resonate with the highly Intuitive parent, but it needs to, as much as possible. Respecting preference differences is an important step in the right direction here. This will be much improved by spending quiet time just listening and observing your child in a truly non-judgmental way. Even with strong and opposite preferences children can open up new worlds to us if we just slow down, take very deep breaths and stop - - - and listen.

Learning more about yourself as person and parent

We hope you have begun this journey by taking the Adult Sorter for yourself and reading about your preferences, temperament, and type. Where you and your child have strongly different preferences, the effort you make to really understand your child will also pay off in seeing the ways in which you are uniquely different from that child. Having your spouse or other co-parent go through this same process will also help, both in understanding one another better, and in seeing the forces behind your disagreements.

Will your own preferences affect your willingness to do this? The honest answer is that in some areas, yes they will. Sensors are more likely than Intuitives to be impatient with the process. Their bias is toward experiencing the present and doing what seems practical. Intuitives, on the other hand may find the process fascinating, but be slow to look for practical ways to apply what they have learned. Judgers may be efficiently willing to go through the process, but then tend to rebel against findings that suggest that strong Judging brings its own problems.

Between Thinkers and Feelers, both will be interested, though they may want to act on the information in different ways. Thinkers may be quicker to want practical applications, Feelers more likely to just enjoy thinking about it all. You can easily imagine what some of these preferences may do in combination. We will look at that in Chapters 20-23. Regardless of your first reactions to your Sorter scores, hold on to your results, try to keep an open mind, and let time and new experiences with child, spouse, friends and self-reflection lead you to fresh insights.

Active Teaching

Reading, speaking and sharing All parents enjoy teaching their childrenthe skills they value most, but these valued skills will differ from preference to preference. Intuitive parents are more likely to adore reading stories, and getting their child's imagination on fire. Sensing parents will take more delight in helping their child advance in practical skills. Thinking parents will especially challenge even the small child's ability to be logical about ideas. Feeling parents early on will on teach lessons about understanding others. This works harmoniously when the child and parent preferences are similar, and is fun for all concerned.

However, a great similarity in parent/child preference may mean that there are important parts of life experience that are being ignored. Sensors do need to have their imaginations stretched; Feelers do need to understand that there is a place in life for self-assertion. Thinkers do need to learn about consideration for the feelings of other.

You should think of parenthood as a wonderful opportunity to add new experiences to your own world. If you have never been big on fairy tales and poetry, perhaps this is the time to try again. If the do-it-yourself world is like a foreign country, perhaps it is time to find out why so many others love it.

When both parents' preferences differ radically from the child's preferences it is particularly important that they try to see not only what they value, but what sorts of learning the child is most engaged and excited about, and then stretch themselves to include that.

Communicating about rules, reasons, and values The specific rules and limits that you decide to have are a part of demandingness. We can't stress too much, however, the importance of reaching a good understanding of why you want these rules and limits. Only then can you communicate them clearly and convincingly to your child. If your child takes something that belongs to someone else, or is store merchandise, the short answer for why she shouldn't is first that it is wrong, and second that it is stealing. That can get pretty circular though. Why shouldn't you steal? Because it is wrong. Why is it wrong? Because it is stealing.

Over lots of discussions like this with five-year-old, would-be family lawyers, I (Nancy) came to the generic explanation that you had to stop and think about what would happen if everyone did it. Not only would individuals be harmed, and individual grocery-stores etc. be harmed, but our whole system would collapse. We arrived at the general rule that you should not do something if it would be a disaster if everyone did it. That's pretty abstract, but I was pleased a few years back to hear it handed down to the next generation. My older daughter was explaining to her daughter why it was wrong to pick oranges from the orchard across the street, and asked her to think about what would happen to the man that owns the oranges if everyone did that!

Will your child find this sort of discussion deeply interesting? Well, yes and no. Your Intuitive Feeler will probably be sympathetic to the plight of the poor orange grower—not the whole point, but important. Your Intuitive Thinker may get the most out of this because it makes systematic, logical sense. But—the eyes of strong Sensors may begin to glaze over if you go on very long. Sensor-Judgers will get the idea that it is socially wrong and respond to that, but not be terrifically impressed by the lengthy logic. Sensor-Perceivers, especially in the early years, will get the idea that you don't like stealing, and probably tune out the rest. That's okay too. They will all get the idea that you have reasons for your rules, and are serious about them.

But how about your preferences and these discussions? The Intuitive parent will probably enjoy such discussions; the Sensing parent will want to say clearly that stealing is wrong, and be done with it. The Thinking parent will enjoy using her own logical powers to make all this make sense, while the Feeling parent will tend to rely more on trying to get the child to put himself in the place of the person who is the victim of theft. And, in turn, the good and bad of these approaches will depend a lot on the child. It is complicated but so important. It is one of many contributions that responsiveness makes to demandingness—easing the way to positive, cooperative family life for all concerned.

The Gift of Structure

Maintaining an orderly household for your child is yet another responsiveness gift that helps children to feel cared for, and makes it easier for them to begin to organize their own lives as they grow older. For the Judger parent, organizing comes easy. If there is a weakness for strong Judgers it would be that it is all too easy and can be overdone. The sort of highly organized household that the Judger loves requires a great deal of cooperation from all family members. For the Perceiver child this may mean pressure beyond what the young Perceiver is ready to face.

For the Perceiver parent, maintaining even a modestly structured household may a very difficult and often neglected area. We offer some helpful (we hope!) hints for Strong Perceivers in Chapter 19 where we discuss the SP temperament effect on parenting. Some advice for strong Judgers is given in Chapter 20 where we discuss the SJ temperament effect on parenting.

The other preference pairs are less involved in this. Extraversion may add to Perceiving to produce a parent who is more attuned to whatever is happening at the moment, and thus still less structured, but the effect is probably not great. Thinkers will be more interested in creating systems for the household than will Feelers, but again the strong differences will come in carrying this out, and these will depend most of all on the Perceiving/Judging preference.

Chapter 17

Parent Preferences and Demandingness

A brief review of Demandingness

Demandingness is the firm, business-like side of parenting, just as responsiveness is the gentle nurturing side. It should be no surprise then that the same parents who are the most naturally talented at responsiveness, may struggle greatly with some aspects of demandingness.

The two broad demandingness areas include the traditional one of setting limits for behavior that is not acceptable and consequences for that behavior, and the less obvious one of setting clear expectations for positive behaviors, and rewards and consequences in that area.

Within this framework the more specific components of demandingness include:

Developing and clearly expressing guidelines:
➢ Setting realistic limits and rules for behavior
➢ Knowing what is reasonable for both age and development
➢ Having well thought out expectations for learning and development

> (We think of calm communication about guidelines and consequences, and the reasons for these, as being part of the work of responsiveness. Here the parent is helping the child to avoid trouble if at all possible. <u>Deciding</u> what the rules, limits and consequences will be, however, is part of demandingness.)

Applying consistent, contingent discipline:

> ➤ Confronting promptly
> ➤ Applying the rules firmly
> ➤ Following through (not going wobbly!)

Consistently monitoring your child:
> ➤ Knowing what she is doing and not doing
> ➤ Knowing where he is and with whom

Effects of Preferences on these demandingness tasks

Developing and clearly expressing guidelines. Intuitives, Thinkers, and Judgers, all for different reasons, are going to do this more deliberately, and often more effectively, than Sensors, Feelers and Perceivers. Intuitives by nature, like to contemplate the future, and should enjoy the planning that goes into rules, limits, and also positive expectations. Whether they will apply them well, will depend on other preferences.

Thinkers also enjoy planning and especially like to apply reason and logic to all problems; child behavior will be no exception. Judgers, finally, want a world that is organized and predictable, so they will be highly motivated to plan for it. The Intuitive, Thinking, Judging parent (**NTJ**) should be awesome here in the right parent/child combination. With a Sensing, Feeling, Perceiving (SFP) *child*, however, this particular parent might overwhelm the child and end up producing a great deal of passive resistance—endless dawdling, forgetting, etc. In that case, the best recipe will be to pull back a bit, reduce the number and complexity of rules and focus on those rules that are most critical.

Applying consistent, contingent discipline The two preferences that will produce the greatest problems here will be strong Feeling and strong Perceiving. For Feelers it is very straightforward. Confrontation is painful. Carrying out a disciplinary measure over a period of time, and with an unhappy child, is even more painful. The ultimate Feeler joy would be to parent in a world in which love and responsiveness really would be enough. They suffer both because the child's anger toward them is hurtful, and because they empathize deeply with the child's own unhappiness. This can be a serious problem, and we will offer suggestions and "stretching exercises" later in the temperament chapter on the Intuitive Feeling (NF) temperament. Feelers in all temperament combinations will find this helpful.

Perceivers (unless they are also Feelers) may not have a special problem in confronting and discussing the problem. However, carrying out a protracted punishment, such as a loss of privileges or grounding, just doesn't fit their moment to moment life style, and is very likely to be discontinued long before the intended date. Obviously, strong versions of both Perceiving and Feeling will make this even harder. The best general advice for that specific situation is to set time limits that you can live with, but carry that through, no matter how you feel about it.

The Thinking parent is less influenced in all discipline issues by the immediate emotional context and more concerned about the lesson that is to be learned and the long-range value of this. If there is a weakness here it would consist of being too comfortable with this, and setting and enforcing stricter limits than may really be needed. Strong **Judger** parents are likely to err in the same direction, simply because they function best in an orderly world themselves, and assume that this is right for everyone. The **Thinker/Judger** combination is going to be particularly strong in confrontation and enforcement. Both preferences contribute to thinking rules through well in the first place, and then having the determination to enforce them. Carried too far, however, this can be harmful to a gentle child's sense of autonomy, and can sometimes backfire with a strong and willful child.

For all parents, but particularly for Judgers, it is so very important to understand the reasons for your rules and to be sure that they are based on what is really needed for your child, and not just on what is comfortable for you. It may be helpful here, also, for these parents to reflect on how much they value their own freedom to design their daily lives in pleasing ways. Children are no different, and do best under the least restriction that is necessary to keep them safe, and keep them developing in positive, cooperative ways.

Between Sensors and Intuitives, the practical Sensor is likely to have fewer rules in the first place, but to be less willing to make changes in rules and consequences. The imaginative Intuitive can more easily be carried away by a persuasive child argument or by what seem to be exceptional circumstances. As we will see in a later chapter, Intuitive-Feelers have a particular weakness in that direction.

Consistently monitoring your child

Pretty much the same array of strengths and weaknesses will turn up here for different preferences. For Feelers who often do really want to keep in close touch with their child, the downside of monitoring is that you may find out something you didn't want to know. If this is the case, you end up needing to confront and perhaps discipline. As we have seen those are not Feeler talents, at least where Feeling is strong. This leads to ambivalent feelings and conflicting actions in this area. In addition, as children grow older, issues of personal privacy come up, and Feeler parents are especially sympathetic to the child's claim that they are not showing trust. Thinkers are much less likely to have problems here.

Perceivers may do only a so-so job here, for different reasons. Monitoring is hard work. It requires a certain amount of future oriented worry, as well as consistent, self-disciplined action on the parent's part. These are not high Perceiver skills. Monitoring is also easiest when household times for homework, play, chores, meals and bedtime are themselves consistent and well organized. Structuring is a responsiveness skill but it is much more likely to be lacking in Perceivers, adding to problems in monitoring. Finally, as you might imagine, the strong Perceiver, strong Feeler combination suggests lots of problems here.

Introversion/Extraversion as a special case.

There is little reason to expect these preferences to have a major effect on demandingness, by themselves. This is especially true for setting limits, though Extraverts might be more generous in specific rules about parties and social events. It is likely that Extraverts would have a somewhat easier time with confronting and monitoring, just as they have a somewhat easier time with social interactions in general, but this would likely be overshadowed by the other preferences. We can imagine, however, that Introversion and Feeling in combination would increase the problem that Feelers have with enforcement and monitoring.

Coming up

In the coming chapters we will look, in turn, at the most typical parenting style for each of the four temperament combinations, (SP, SJ, NF and NT) and the strengths and weaknesses of each style. We will also offer some "stretching" advice where it may be needed, and some consideration of how parent temperament and child temperament may interact

Chapter 18

The SP (Sensing and Perceiving) Parent in Action Strengths, Weaknesses, Problems and Stretches

Recapping the SP:

Sensing and Perceiving together in the SP temperament family greatly enhance both living in the present moment and giving minimal thought to future plans and possibilities. The SP places a high premium on feeling free and unconfined. It is not hard to imagine the effect of these priorities on some areas of responsiveness and many areas of demandingness.

What might the SP parent be most concerned about in their child's development?

Our guess is that the typical SP would most of all look to see that their child was enjoying life while growing up. Signs of boredom, lack of hobbies, interests, or compatible friends might send up red flags for this parent.

Where might they be less concerned? Routine misbehavior, common to children everywhere, would not be of intense concern unless it continued well beyond the average age. SPs tend to be philosophical about this, assuming most problems will simply be outgrown in time, and remembering their own escapades with an occasional smile.

How would this affect responsiveness?

Warmth, intimacy and daily interactions Being focused on the here and now, highly spontaneous and flexible, SP parents are ready for all sorts of interactions with their children. With their focus on the present moment, they spend less time dreaming about the person their child might grow up to be and more time enjoying the small person the child is right now. These parents may excel in responding to the child's moment to moment interests, questions and needs. SPs are probably the most spontaneously playful parents of all the temperament groups.

Active parent learning SPs will learn a great deal about their children simply by having a lot of cheerful interaction with them. They are less likely than other temperaments, however, to spend a great deal of time in analyzing and interpreting behavior. Similarly, they are the least likely to wish to dwell on their own strengths and weaknesses through lengthy self-observation. In many parent/child combinations this works well. Most small children would rather have a parent who plays joyously with them than one who takes the parent role with great seriousness.

Where there are real parent/child conflicts, or more serious behavioral or emotional problems, however, the SP style can present problems. SPs are less likely to recognize serious problems early, and less likely to be clear about their own role in conflicts. Because long periods of reflective thought are not their favorite occupation, they may also be baffled by a child whose temperament is very different from their own.

Active parent teaching

Reading, learning, understanding emotions SPs typically would not be likely to see parent teaching as something to plan for in advance. On the other hand they are probably *more* willing than most parents to interrupt whatever they are doing to answer a question, play a game, or show a child how to do something.

Sensor/Perceiver parents will enjoy reading to their children, but will be far more energized when they can teach them to ride the first tricycle, color a picture, or catch a ball, and later to use tools skillfully and build, design or otherwise create real-world objects. Depending on their own attitude toward school as they grew up, they may be very good at helping with school work, or may tend to do this minimally. In either case, they will stress the basics—reading, writing, arithmetic and later math--more than theoretical topics such as social studies. Depending a lot on whether they also have the Feeling preference, they may discuss emotional issues in some depth, or may just look for practical ways to help a distressed child cheer up.

Communicating about rules and limits It is not likely that the typical SP parent will want to spend a great deal of time discussing reasons for rules and expectations. Having explained a rule a few times, a practical SP parent would see little point in repeating it or elaborating on it. Lengthy discussions regarding morals, limits, and appropriateness of behavior (especially after the fact) have no great fascination. In addition, SPs may tend towards much more lenient and tolerant definitions of acceptable and unacceptable behavior, again because they tend to feel that things generally work out here, as in all things.

Providing structure

This area is the part of responsiveness that will give SPs the most trouble. Maintaining a highly organized environment for the child is an unlikely SP strength. It isn't appealing and the necessity may not seem at all obvious. The strong SP, by definition, has avoided strict orderliness for a lifetime.

However, the first child brings orders of magnitude more mess and disorder for all parents. Additional children pile it on wider and deeper. If nothing is done to counteract this, we can imagine one of two possible outcomes. ***If everyone in the family is a determined SP***, things can progress to total and glorious disarray, at least until dad's mother, or mom's mother or the neighborhood social worker gets on the case. This happy chaos might feel good, but a lot of negative things are happening just the same. First of all, the SP parent is probably more stressed than he or she begins to realize. Babies do have to be fed, diapers do have to be washed, and it *is* wonderful to have every child in the house asleep once in a while. These things simply do go better with some system, and household chores go much better when older children have learned to help out.

Now, consider the alternative outcome where one parent is a Judger, and one or more children are Judgers, and as a group, they are not happy with the antics of the SP parent. The SP longs to spend the morning (if at home) with coffee and a newspaper, or the internet, or a pet project she/he is longing to do. But—the baby needs to be fed and the preschooler can't find her socks. Soon the school calls about the fact that the eight-year-old forgot her lunch. The walls are still reverberating from last night's quarrel about undone tasks and whose fault that was. In short, the SP in this situation has both high job load and very high stress—an SP's nightmare.

Wisdom says that some changes really are needed for any SP parent who has let everything get out of hand. It is not a question of making this parent into a Judger, or getting the SP to say "Ah, I feel so much better now that I have my to-do list right in my breast-pocket." The Sensor-Perceiver will always have the heart of an SP. At this point in life he or she simply has to realize that some changes have to be made and some compromises accepted—at least for the duration. We call those compromises "stretches" and make suggestions below.

Overall--SPs are likely to:

- Be playful with their children and have frequent and positive interactions
- Be less devoted to consciously observing and analyzing a child's behavior, but still absorb much about their children.
- Be excellent on-the-spot teachers, but not structure this in advance
- Be disinterested in long discussions on rules and limits
- Be relatively weak at organizing and structuring the child's environment

Good areas for SP stretches toward the responsiveness model

Thinking about rules: In general, most SP parents would benefit from taking some time to really think about what their expectations are for good behavior, and why they have the rules they have. This is particularly true for the positive behaviors related to school work, chores, and the development of more mature behavior.

Targeting the most important rules, and giving clear reasons, will likely result in increased respect and cooperation from children of all temperaments. SPs might find it surprisingly useful to have some parent-to-parent sessions to discuss their ideas together. This is particularly true if one parent is a Perceiver and the other a Judger. Here the goal must be a realistic compromise, since their ideal situations will be very different. The Perceiver must try to do more, and the Judger must try to expect less. Two SPs, however, would be wise, also, to deliberately reflect on how they are doing, and what might be done better.

Becoming a part-time Judger. For the SP, the wise approach to acquiring a few organizational habits, is clearly through small changes—baby steps. Once we humans admit to any shortcoming, we all tend to try for dramatic and immediate reform—lose 70 pounds before June (and it is May), spend an hour a day on the treadmill and lift weights before bedtime—etc. etc. This is never a sane course. For our SP, for whom the spontaneous life is a built-in preference, radical change is a self-defeating idea. Life in the moment is energizing; life on a scheduled routine is depressing. Like all other preference problems, what is needed here is a reasonable compromise.

Perhaps start by picking two events—for example, dinner time and bedtime--to be put on a timetable. Keep it simple and minimal but then try to really stick to your plan. With this, add one time for toy pick-up every day, and involve everyone that toddles or walks. You and your toddler would need to do it together, but that is good practice for both of you. ***In our house*** we had what was called the "fink" basket. The origin of the name is lost in history, but the idea was that anything not picked up before bedtime, was confiscated in this basket. Depending on age and responsibility level, participants had to pay a fine to get the item, or lose its use for some period of time.

Household neatness at bedtime was really remarkable! The SP parent who feels overwhelmed with home, work, and child rearing, would be amazed to see the amount of help that a good SJ or NT parent can summon from a well-organized family!

 If this becomes a reasonably comfortable routine, Monday through Friday, try adding a Saturday chore time for everyone in the family, and try to make it as much fun as possible. Add music if that is a family joy, and maybe celebratory treats after. Then let the weekend be structure-free for the rest of the time.

The point is--make some changes that will help, but leave yourself plenty of stretches of unstructured time. If finances are comfortable, all Perceivers, and especially SPs, should happily hire cleaning service, yard service etc. and save the organized moments for more personal tasks.

In Summary: SPs should try to stretch a bit toward the responsiveness model by:

> Taking time to really think about their demandingness rules, limits, and expectations, and give the child clear reasons for these.
> Focusing particularly on explaining the value of long-range behaviors—getting things done, keeping up in school
> Beginning some small steps toward routines, schedules, and household organization. The big focus should not be on any elaborate plans (they will not last) but on doing a few simple but important things very consistently.

The SP temperament and demandingness

216

In General SP parents typically have a relaxed view of parenting. They could be considered permissive to some degree, in the sense that they don't set down large numbers of rules or expectations. and focus more on real and immediate behavior. It is not that they are opposed to discipline, in principle; rather they are simply more laid-back in the worry department. SP parents tend to be optimistic (maybe even overly optimistic) about outcomes. This is a natural SP bias. Just as they feel they can always meet a deadline by working madly at the last moment, and solve most any crisis by their resourcefulness, they also expect that their children will find their way eventually.

Setting rules, limits and expectations.

SPs love freedom. As adults they often question rules and limits themselves, and will not only struggle with enforcing consistent limits, but also with defining sufficient limits. They may tend towards much more lenient and tolerant definitions of acceptable and unacceptable behavior. This affects the time they are willing to spend discussing limits, as we saw earlier, but it also affects the rules and limits themselves. When a situation erupts that can't be ignored, SP parents may tend towards the "because I said so" strategy, not because they are authoritarian or strongly controlling, but because they are interested more in stopping bad behavior quickly and moving on to something more interesting.

Consistent contingent discipline SP parents are likely to be quite comfortable with disciplining their children when there is obvious misbehavior. Their sense that most problems will be outgrown means that misbehaviors that are *not* disruptive at the present moment may not receive the attention they should. Noise, destructiveness, and fighting are immediate problems that will get swift SP attention. Undone homework or neglected chores may not receive similarly firm treatment.

Following up on a lengthy punishment with older children, such as a grounding, is another area that tends to be weak. It is not so much that the SP is undone by the child's continued unhappiness, in the way that a strong Feeler parent might be; more simply the episode soon becomes yesterday's problem. Keeping Tuesday's punishment going on Friday seems a bit silly and unnecessarily burdensome. If the SP is also a strong Feeler, of course, this problem will be multiplied by the emotions involved.

Monitoring To the extent that successful monitoring requires maintaining an reasonably organized household, having consistent and clear expectations (from cooperative behavior to homework), and then keeping close tabs on all children in the family, the strong SP parent can be expected to struggle here, for all the reasons we have discussed before.

Overall--SPs are likely to:

➢ Define fewer and less clearly defined limits
➢ Be comfortable with confrontations but not go looking for them
➢ Focus on immediate and disruptive behavior and take swift action
➢ Neglect enforcing certain behaviors that do not have an immediate impact
➢ Be less careful in seeing that extended punishments are enforced
➢ Be less careful about monitoring behavior of all kinds

What is needed The SP parent may never want to have a chalkboard full of rules, limits, and orderly schedules, but should try to take time out to develop a simple system of rules and limits that matter. This may seem entirely out of character, but in many families run by an SP, it very much needs doing. This is particularly true for rules related to positive behaviors (getting chores done, completing homework and other projects). The trick is to find the rules that seem to matter most and apply monitoring and consistent contingent discipline to these. A two day grounding that is enforced thoroughly may be more useful than a two week grounding that is disintegrating by the third day. Whatever the rules are, the child needs to know that the SP parent really means it. If this parent has had problems in his or her own life due to unfinished tasks, neglected education, etc., a little thought might indicate that all children need a lot of help to come through in these areas. It just isn't good enough to assume they will outgrow their problems.

In summary--SPs should try to stretch a bit toward the demandingness model by:

> ➢ Taking time to establish a limited set of rules, limits, and expectations that they believe in and are willing to enforce.
> ➢ Focusing particularly on long-range behaviors—getting things done, keeping up in school
> ➢ Making a plan to enforce these more consistently
> ➢ Being careful *not* to select a longer period of punishment than they have the will power to enforce
> ➢ Fully carrying out any punishments given.
> ➢ With small steps again, trying for more consistent monitoring

Interaction of your child's temperament with the overall SP parent responsiveness/demandingness style.

NF child:

The Intuitive-Feeling child is likely to receive the needed warmth, positive feedback, and personal interactions that motivate good behavior from the SP parent—especially with the SFP parent. However, NF children--needing to understand the reasons behind expectations and actions--will be frustrated with the lack of explanations from SP parents. In addition, when the NF child does wander into behavior that the SP parent will not tolerate, this child may find the swift disciplinary actions of the SP parent somewhat disturbing. It is such a contrast to the otherwise fun and free spirited nature of this parent.

Strongly Sensing parents (both Perceivers and Judgers) will always struggle in trying to understand the more dreamy NF child, and may feel impatient with what seems like impracticality. A good understanding of the Intuitive preference can be very helpful here.

NT child:

We would expect the older Intuitive-Thinking NT child to be critical of the SP parent's lack of explanation for rules and limits, and lack of thoroughness in discipline. We might imagine all sorts of challenges between NT children and SP parents. Issues around authority and respect, lack of organization, and even lack of sufficient parent control (all from the NT child's view) may create problems between the NT child and SP parent.

This will be even more true with an NT child who also shares the Judging preference. NT children, seeing weakness in consistency and logic, may disrespect the parent's authority and misbehave more often because of this. With this child, SP parents particularly need to try to stretch toward more systematic rules, better explanation for these rules, and more consistent enforcement. It bears repeating that fewer rules and more moderate consequences, combined with strong consistency for these rules, may be the best compromise for the SP parent.

SJ child:

The strong SJ child looks for order and routines and is most cooperative (and comfortable) when expectations are clear and predictable. Lots of discussion regarding your reasons for expectations and action are not needed frequently; consistency and predictability are. Hence, SJ children may not have a problem with the lack of reasons for rules and expectations from the SP parent, but they are likely to be frustrated by the lack of consistency, organization, and routines. The absence of a clear and predictable environment may result in less cooperative and more pushy or controlling behavior on the part of the SJ child. Again, there is a need for the SP parent to try to stretch toward greater orderliness and consistency.

SP child:

The SP child will appreciate the more permissive style of the SP parent (lots more freedom to enjoy the here and now), and the warmth and spontaneous interactions typically provided. Neither SP parent nor SP child will wish for lengthy discussions and explanations either before or after a disciplinary episode. What's done is done, and both are quickly ready to move on to happier activities.

At the same time, it is likely that the SP parent does not provide sufficient limits and expectations to help to contain and direct this uninhibited, live-for-the-moment personality. The best advice is to establish at least the most important rules and expectations, to know what your own reasons are but not be too repetitive about them, be good about warmth and interactive fun, but very firm on contingent, consistent (and quick) discipline measures. Simple rules, clear consequences, and swift and consistent action are the keys.

All children will benefit from a more orderly household, but SP children with a strongly SP parent, need this in a special sense. No matter what our preferences, we all have to learn to get things done when required by the outside world. School demands this of the child, and work demands it of the adult. It is possible, as adults, to find careers that fit our needs for change and excitement to a degree, but there is always a bottom line—some minimum that must happen on time and on schedule. The SP parent, who sets no model for this, makes it much more difficult for the child to learn a few Judger skills. Any parent with a Perceiver child would be wise to make a few organizational behaviors absolutely routine for both child and parent.

SP parent—you are joyful and great fun for yourself and your child. Your good qualities as a parent are many. But, here and there, a stretch toward more organization and a little more self-discipline is called for! Hard to believe as it might be, your child will be better for it, your entire family will be better for it, and your own life will be better for it.

Chapter 19

The SJ (Sensing and Judging) Parent in Action
Strengths, Weaknesses, Problems and Stretches

Recapping the SJ:

The classic SJ, who greatly values well-learned and proven ways of doing things, strongly prefers order and predictability. With this, the SJ feels responsible for keeping home, work, and community running well, Sensing adds a strong preference for the here-and-now world of doing, rather than any world of the imagination, and a greater reliance on accepted and traditional ideas, including those about child behavior.

What might SJ parents be most concerned about in their child's development?

In the early years they will look especially to indications for good physical development and health, and with that, the establishment of good habits of grooming, orderliness and cooperative behavior. As the child grows they will pay especial attention to the development of good manners, respect for others, and conscientiousness regarding school work, chores and helpfulness at home.

What might they be less concerned about? While SJ parents will certainly be concerned about good grades and hard work in homework and projects, and about a successful future for their child, they are less likely to have a deep interest in the unusual or imaginative aspects of their child's thoughts and projects. SJ's are highly grounded, and approach most ideas with the (perhaps unspoken) question "what is it good for?"

How would this affect responsiveness?

Warmth, intimacy and daily interactions There is nothing in the SJ temperament that would result in any less warmth and caring for children than is true for other temperaments. However, the strong SJ parent is likely to take less time for spur of the moment interactions. In this, SJs are perhaps the least playful of the four temperaments. Although all Sensors focus their attention on the present moment, when strong Judging is added, the focus is on getting the things done that were *planned* for this present moment. Parenthood is full of unavoidable distractions and unexpected mini-crises, but the SJ is wired to cope with these promptly and get back to the planned program.

The strong drive to get things done may also work against the development of easy parent/child signals and rhythms. The SJ parent certainly wishes to understand the needs the child is trying to communicate, but haste really can get in the way here. Especially, if the need being communicated is simply "Hold me, mom", and that is not on the schedule for 2 PM, it sometimes won't get the attention it should.

This will vary though with the SJ's Feeling or Thinking preference, with Feeling pulling the SJ much more toward emotional synchrony with the child's needs, and Thinking pushing in the other direction. SJs need to look at themselves carefully here, and see if they can manage more time just "hanging out" with both baby and older child.

Active parent learning

About the child The SJ, being a strong traditionalist, is more likely than other temperaments to see the child as she ought to be, or will eventually be, rather than as the complex person who is actually there. Fairly commonly, the underlying Judger belief goes in the direction of seeing the child as starting out with a slightly wicked blank slate, to be guided and improved upon. With this belief the parent tends to focus on the goals—behaviors to be developed through discipline and maturity—rather than the child's inner essence.

Neither SPs nor SJs are given to lengthy analysis in this area, but the laid-back, "no worries" SP is more likely to see the child as he is through many playful interactions, than is the dutiful, concerned SJ, who is sometimes overly worried.

About the self For both SPs and SJs the very practical Sensing preference often reduces the person's interest in self-study, and this would be equally true of examining strengths and weaknesses in parenting. However, the SJ differs from the SP cousin, in being much more concerned about doing the right thing. If the SJ parent comes to feel that self-study is important to good parenting it will get on the to-do list, and become a useful tool.

Active parent teaching

Reading, learning, understanding emotions The SJ can be expected to be very good at reading to and with their child, and later, at helping with problems in school work. It will probably be done at scheduled times rather than on the spur of the moment, but there is no harm in that, other than occasionally missing what educators call a "teachable moment" (These are the instants when some event or object has vividly caught the child's attention, making him or her especially open to a new concept). SPs would be good at catching these, but the SJ dedication to making organized time for learning certainly balances it out. Emphasis on discussing feelings and emotions would vary greatly with the Thinker or Feeler preference.

Clear and detailed communication about rules, and limits This is less likely to be part of the SJ repertoire. SJs often assume that it is not necessary to explain the obvious. Even praise and rewards for good behavior may be somewhat reduced in the SJ family, since there is a strong sense that it is the child's responsibility to behave well, rather than the parent's responsibility to nurture this with frequent rewards. This will vary though, depending on Thinking and Feeling.

The Feeling parent is more likely to use praise, in particular, simply out of a desire to be close to the child—a sort of verbal hug. The strong Thinking parent combines Thinking with Sensing and Judging to become a pretty stern and formidable guardian. At the same time, Thinking will tend to increase the willingness to communicate the reasons for rules, limits and discipline in the SJ, where Feeling will tend to soften it, especially where consequences are involved.

The Structural Side Here the strong SJ absolutely shines. An orderly home, on-time meals, children's checkups scheduled well in advance and never missed, homework time kept sacred, pens, pencils, paper, glue, project materials always at the ready—all are likely to be shipshape in the SJ home. This is often underrated as an important part of parenting, and the typical SJ parent does a beautiful job here.

Overall—SJs:

> Find that the need to get things done may push them to be less spontaneous, and less sensitive to the child's early signals and later unique needs, than is true for other temperaments.
> May praise less often
> May be somewhat more likely to think of the child in terms of their preformed ideas about children, and less likely to just observe the actual child.
> May or may not spend time in self-study, depending on how it is viewed
> Have lots of rules and expectations, but may be relatively brief or even impatient in providing lengthy reasons for these
> Provide outstanding structure and organizational support in the household

Good areas for SJ stretching toward the responsiveness model.

Strong SJs would be well served by rethinking their daily, weekly and monthly/annual to-do lists to see if they can whittle down the number of tasks they set themselves, and leave spaces in every day for just letting things happen. SJs generally feel that the more they get

226

accomplished in a given stretch of time, the better people they are, and the better that time has been spent. For parents, that is not true if it means that productive down-time with children is squeezed thinly between a mountain of work chores, home chores, community obligations, etc. Taking a long look at what is really essential is a good first step.

Although SJ parents highly value respect for authority, their lack of emphasis on communicating expectations and reasons may serve to *undermine* their authority, especially with older children and with certain child temperaments. Children need to understand parental expectations, the reasoning behind them, and the idea that there is a direct relationship between punishment and seriousness of infraction (as well as rewards and good behavior). SJ parents would benefit from trying hard to balance their need to maintain authority with a willingness to provide the child with greater opportunity to express his or her viewpoints. In addition, SJ parents will need to learn to verbalize the good reasons behind traditional standards for behavior. There is nothing wrong with the SJ faith that maintaining order in society is critically important. The parent just needs to think this through and be able to talk about it. Sometimes, in this process, the SJ parent may find that the rule has more to do with parent comfort than any real problem. If this is so, this may be a rule that can be discarded.

In Summary: SJs should try to stretch toward the responsiveness model by:

Finding a way to pause in the rush through the day's to-do list to:

- ➤ Watch and listen to the child
- ➤ Observe what the child is thinking, feeling and spontaneously doing
- ➤ Find time for parent-child play, and enjoy "teachable moments"
- ➤ Think through rules and limits carefully to avoid overdoing it

> ➢ Communicate reasons for actions
> ➢ Be open to listening to the child's viewpoints
> ➢ Be open to rethinking a rule if it really can't be justified
> ➢ Provide more positive feedback for good behavior

The SJ Temperament and Demandingness

Setting rules, limits and expectations. SJs are more likely than other temperaments to assume that children are not naturally motivated towards acceptable behavior. The strong SJ has an inner feeling that the world is unruly, and needs constant work at keeping it in order. This feeling certainly carries over to the unruly behavior of children. Especially where Judging is very strong, there will be rules aplenty, and they are likely to be fairly uncompromising. Because SJs tend to respect authority and organization themselves, they are likely to expect children to respect their authority, often with little questioning.

Consistent, contingent discipline The typical SJ parent is likely to confront unacceptable behavior promptly, and take swift action whenever misbehaviors occur, using consistent discipline that is directly linked to behavior. The one exception to this might be the SJ who is also a strong Feeler. There is going to be some ambivalence in that case, with a real drive toward enforcement, but emotional hesitation in carrying this out. One quite reasonable solution, if the other parent is a Thinker, is to shift some of the enforcement duties in that direction. As long as both parents are supportive of the discipline strategy, there is nothing wrong with letting the more talented parent handle more of the job.

Monitoring This is likely to be a strong area. Because SJ parents tend to provide an organized household with clear expectations and responsibilities, they are able to monitor behavior in the home readily. They also can be expected to monitor behavior away from home efficiently as a part of their overall organizational talent.

In sum: We would characterize the strong SJ style as high in demandingness and generally effective. An exception to this effectiveness might occur if the demandingness level is extreme, and provokes rebellion in some child temperaments. Feeling will soften the demandingness somewhat, while Thinking is likely to enhance the trend toward strong rules and limits.

Overall--SJs are likely to:

> ➤ Have lots of rules and expectations
> ➤ Assume that children are somewhat "unruly" and need lots of oversight
> ➤ Be relatively impatient with providing reasons for actions
> ➤ Be willing to confront misbehavior
> ➤ Be good at monitoring and provide lots of household structure

What needs to be done To the extent that SJs need to make some changes in demandingness, or stretch toward the model, it would be in such areas as examining their rules and expectations to be sure that they are not *over*-doing it. It might be helpful, also to examine their assumptions about just how unruly their children are. (An SP child is probably pretty unruly, but an SJ?)

SJs should try to stretch a bit toward the ideal demandingness model by:

> ➤ Thinking through rules and limits carefully to avoid overdoing it
> ➤ Being particularly careful not to impose rules purely for parent comfort
> ➤ Observing and reflecting on the child's actual behaviors to see if:
>   o Specific actions are being effective
>   o Specific actions are truly needed

Interaction of your child's temperament with the SJ parenting style

NF child:

The Feeling child really needs warmth, positive feedback, and happy interactions to feel secure and to be motivated for good behavior. NF children also strongly need to understand the reasons behind expectations and actions. For this child there is a real need to balance the SJ demandingness strengths with greater responsiveness, and especially greater willingness to listen and communicate. In the worst of cases, the NF child with a very strong SJ parent may feel unloved. This is especially true where the parent combination includes the Thinking preference. SJ parents would benefit by really spending some time understanding the NF temperament.

NT child:

The Thinking child also has a great need for clear and thorough explanations for rules and limits. The older Intuitive and Thinking child is the one most likely to become rebellious and disrespectful if there is not a serious effort to explain rules, and to make those rules make sense. Though this is a responsiveness task, it will have a strong effect on this child's willingness to accept SJ discipline. Frequent praise is not greatly sought, but NTs do long for signs that you take a real interest in their ideas and reasoning about things.

The role of Intuition for both NT and NF An additional roadblock to responsiveness here may be the Sensor-Judger parent's lack of sensitivity to Intuitive thoughts and Interests. It is hard to show responsiveness to a child's interests in areas that seem foreign to the parent. It is particularly useful here for the SJ parent to read about and try to understand the Intuitive preference, and come to recognize the kinds of things that delight the Intuitive child.

SJ child:

In many, many areas, SJ parent and SJ child will be a very good pair. They will easily understand what the other values, and the SJ child will be easy to parent in areas related to being on time, getting things done, and keeping things tidy. The strong SJ child, whether Thinking or Feeling, will not need constant repetition on the value of orderliness and doing things in accepted ways. Nevertheless, the SJ parent will do well to try harder at good responsive communication, so that this SJ child will grow up with an understanding of why rules and customs exist.

One thing to keep in mind, however, is that all Judgers want a good deal of control over how things are done. Two strong Judgers can clash, not because either is poorly organized, but because each wants to do it "her" way. When that happens it is time for both to acknowledge that temperament is driving this, and stop, and smile.

SP child:

The SP child will be your greatest challenge—things won't be quite so bad if the Thinking Preference is there, but the S*P* Feeler just wants to enjoy life here and now. This child will not be wild about tradition and order as reasons for rules, will not be wild about rules, no matter what. SJ parents will have strong expectations for tidy and orderly behavior, even from fairly young children, and will be increasingly frustrated and perhaps, angry, when there is constant resistance. The best advice here is, of course, first of all, know your child. If and when it becomes clear that this is a strong SP, "don't fence me in" child, the parent should settle on a few things that are critical, enforce those firmly, and learn to be more tolerant about how this child prefers to spend time

As SP children move on into the school-age life, Judging parents (who have a great tendency to over-schedule themselves), are also likely to try to over-schedule their Perceiver's outside life. At most they should suggest just one or two extracurricular activities in sports, art, music or other projects and let the child be the best guide as to whether anything more is desirable.

Little SPs do best when there are not too many rules and not too much structuring of his or her life, coupled with *extreme firmness* about those rules and structures that the SJ parent sees as critical. Discipline has to be clear, predictable, highly consistent, and prompt (an hour later is another world for a young SP). The SJ parent needs some real soul searching to arrive at a set of rules that are truly needed, but are as minimal as possible. A heavy SJ hand here will just be smothering for the SP nature, and most likely will lead to endless evasion and procrastination

SJ parent—you are a model parent in many ways, excellent in discipline, in monitoring your child's activities, and in providing a home structure that works wonderfully. You just need practice in slowing down, letting yourself be fully in the moment from time to time, and (at least occasionally) letting events and people evolve as they will.

Chapter 20

The NF (Intuitive and Feeling) Parent in Action Strengths, Weaknesses, Problems and Stretches

Recapping the NF:

Both Intuitive and Feeling, the NF is well described as Humanity's Champion. As Intuitives they are in love with the possible, fascinated by the future, and always looking for the hidden meanings behind surface events. As Feelers, they are deeply motivated to maintain harmony in their interpersonal relationships, and a peaceful environment in their larger world.

What might NF parents be most concerned about in their child's development?

NFs will be especially concerned that their children feel loved, have high self-esteem, and are kind and considerate of others. In the child's behavior it is the wish to be cooperative that matters, more than whether or not they literally say "please" and "thank you" at an early age.

What might they be less concerned about? Where the SJ parent worries that the undisciplined child will naturally misbehave, the typical NF parent often has remarkable confidence that the child is naturally good, needing only warm, affirming responsiveness from the parent in order to grow and develop well. Firm disciplinary strategies are a much lesser concern. If anything, there might be worry for this parent that firm discipline could disrupt the parent-child bond.

How would this affect responsiveness?

Warmth, intimacy and daily interactions It should come as no surprise that Feeling parents are usually very responsive to their children's emotions, and highly supportive of their emotional needs. Intuition adds a further plus in being skillful at understanding the young child's signals. All of the responsiveness components, from lots of warmth and affection, to getting in synchrony with your child's signals, come very easily to the NF parent. The only likely exception would occur if the parent were also a very strong Judger. In that case, this parent might be torn between being willing to drop everything and respond to the child's interests, and getting things done efficiently.

Active parent learning

Observing and learning about the child. The NF is intensely motivated to do this. The fascination with theories and patterns means that there will be a natural tendency to apply these to the child. NFs tend to read widely on parenting issues, and to devote a great deal of thought and parent discussion to understanding the child they have been given. Like parents of all temperaments, however, they will be somewhat baffled by a child of very different preferences. This will be mildly true of a Sensing child, resulting in a parent who is forever trying to interest the child who loves doing and making, with thinking and imagining instead. However, the larger problem is likely to be with the strongly Thinking child. The NF takes the desire for close (and pretty constant) emotional ties as fundamental to all human nature, and is likely to interpret the cooler Thinking preference as a problem in need of fixing, rather than a human difference.

Because of their own relatively gentle natures, NFs are likely to be more than a little mystified by assertion and strong shows of willfulness or aggression. If they make a mistake here, it will be in seeing all self-assertion as a problem to be overcome rather than channeled in healthy ways. The Thinking child who adds Judging and perhaps Extraversion to the mix, may seem very strong-willed and uncompromising. This child will need plenty of advice in finding practical compromises in the world between what she wants at any given moment and what is possible in the real world. In order to be of help here, though, it is very important that the parent not assume that a reasonable amount of assertion (like a cooler emotional disposition) is a basic character flaw--or the result of insufficient parent love, or some other parent imperfection.

Parent learning—self understanding This, again, comes absolutely naturally to the NF, who has probably done a great deal of self-searching long before parenthood. If there is a flaw here, it is that this tendency is so strong that it may go on endlessly, sometimes to the detriment of reaching some conclusions and acting on them. If the NF is also a Perceiver, the Perceiver love of keeping all options open will probably increase the tendency to keep searching.

Active parent teaching

Spending time on reading, learning, emotional understanding This should be another strong plus for the NF parent. This parent should be especially skillful in helping the child understand turbulent emotions in himself, and deciphering the emotional reactions of others. This may be more difficult, though, with a strongly Thinking child.

The NF will enjoy teaching and mentoring in many different areas, and will delight in reading to, and reading with the child. The only caution in this area might be that with a Sensing child, there is a need for the Intuitive parent to take time to understand what delights a Sensing child and how that might differ from what delights an Intuitive parent.

Communicating about rules and limits Highly Intuitive parents often talk to their children more frequently and in somewhat different ways than do Sensor parents. Their general fascination with understanding and explaining why things happen may also carry over to a greater interest in talking about the whys and wherefores of rules and limits.

Thus, they are often highly motivated to discuss these issues in advance as a way of preventing later problems, and are willing to spend a great deal of time communicating, about this, as long as it can be done pleasantly. They take great care to respect their children's feelings, wants, and ideas, and are typically open to discussion and negotiations.

However, time spent communicating about good behavior, and even about bad behavior and its consequences, is based on the belief that the child who understands the rules and the reasons for the rules, will naturally want to behave well. The one area they would tend to minimize would be discussion of consequences if all does not go well. This comes from the Feeler passion for peace and harmony. They hate to spoil a good moment with painful discussion, and even in a bad moment, want to pass over it as quickly as possible. Carrying out consequences, and even having a painful discussion about them after a crisis, is a whole other matter, as we shall see in the demandingness section.

What this parent will very positively communicate, however, is pleasure in the good things the child does. Positive feedback is a very strong part of the NF parenting style, and does provide a lot of information about the parent expectations on the positive side.

The Structural Side

Here we are talking about keeping an orderly environment, having family meals and other events occur at a predictable time, etc. Except for the fact that those with the Intuitive preference tend to be more caught up in ideas or long-range plans than Sensors are, there is not much in the NF temperament that would determine the outcome here. Instead, it is pretty much up to the Perceiving or Judging preference that the NF has. Perceiving NFs (NF*P*s) will likely be quite weak in this area, with Intuition adding a little to the Perceiver effect, while Judging NFs will not have this problem.

Overall-- NFs are likely to:

> Be very strong and talented in emotional and interactive aspects of responsiveness
> Have a clear view of the positive aspects of the child, but have problems with understanding the Thinking child, and in understanding highly assertive behavior.
> Be somewhat conflicted about communication about rules and limits, doing it well as calm discussion, but avoiding it if this is likely to lead to conflict.
> Be good at appreciating the child's accomplishment, and praising good behavior
> Be good at the structural side if Judgers, but poor if Perceivers.

Good areas for NF stretches toward the responsiveness model.

Most of the stretches that the NF will really need, come in the area of demandingness, rather than responsiveness, as we discuss in the next section. If there is a weak area in responsiveness, it might be communicating about consequences. NFs will be very clear about rules, and reasons for rules, but may avoid the painful work of laying out specific consequences for those times when things go wrong.

One piece of advice for NFs, though, would be to work really hard on understanding preferences that are not like their own. Precisely because the NF is idealistic, he or she may be slow to accept the idea that not everyone fits (nor wishes to fit) the somewhat dreamy idealist model. As we have noted, with the Sensing child it is mainly a matter of using imagination to see the things that excite and energize that child differently from the Intuitive. With a Thinking child it goes further. Here the NF really needs to struggle with the Thinker's cooler emotional style and greater mental assertiveness, to see that this is a different but equally valid way of experiencing the world, and to keep from being (however gently) critical of the Thinker qualities.

Finally, if the NF is also a Perceiver, there is likely to be work to be done on organizational (structural) skills. Here we include some advice on this from the SP chapter:

> ***"Becoming a part-time Judger.*** For the SP, *[and NFP]* the wise approach to acquiring a few organizational habits, is clearly through small changes—baby steps. Once we humans admit to any shortcoming, we all tend to try for dramatic and immediate reform—lose 70 pounds before June (and it is May), spend an hour a day on the treadmill and lift weights before bedtime—etc. etc. This is never a sane course. For the Perceiver, for whom the spontaneous life is a built in preference, radical change is a self-defeating idea. Life in the moment is energizing; life on a scheduled routine is depressing. Like all other preference problems, what is needed here is a reasonable compromise.
>
> Perhaps start by picking two events—for example, dinner time and bedtime--to be put on a timetable, and try to really stick to this. With this, add one time for toy pick-up every day, and involve everyone that toddles or walks. You and your toddler would need to do it together, but that is good practice for both of you. In our house we had what was called the "fink" basket. The origin of the name is lost in history, but the idea was that anything not picked up before bed was confiscated in this basket.
>
> Depending on age and responsibility level, participants had to pay a fine to get the item, or lose its use for some period of time. Household neatness at bedtime was really remarkable! The SP parent who feels overwhelmed with home, work, and child rearing, would be amazed to see the amount of help that a good SJ or NT parent can summon from a well-organized family!
>
> If this becomes a reasonably comfortable routine, Monday through Friday, try adding a Saturday morning chore time for

everyone in the family, and try to make it as much fun as possible. Add music if that is a family joy, and maybe celebratory treats after. Then let the weekend be structure free for the rest of the time. The point is—make some changes that will help, but leave yourself plenty of hours of unstructured time. If finances are comfortable Perceivers should happily hire cleaning service, yard service etc. and save the organized moments for more personal tasks."

In Summary: NFs should try to stretch toward the responsiveness model by:

➢ Making a special effort to gain insight into Thinking children, and any child with substantial assertiveness.
➢ Becoming more aware of what interests and delights a Sensing child.
➢ Being careful about "paralysis by analysis"—thinking endlessly about the child's nature and their own, and failing to reach useful conclusions to act on.
➢ Disciplining themselves to explain consequences to the child in advance of problems
➢ If strong Perceivers, also, working on building in some household structure, small step by small step.

The NF Temperament and Demandingness

The main effect of the preference for Intuition on demandingness is not huge in itself, but **Intuitive** parents will tend to be somewhat more flexible in rethinking a rule and hearing the child's arguments out. Carried far enough, this undermines efforts at consistency. The **Feeling** Preference usually has a much larger impact on demandingness style. The strong Feeling parent can be expected to struggle with demandingness, so the NF combination has its problems here.

Setting rules, limits and expectations. NF parents don't mind setting
rational rules and limits, but confrontation is likely to be painful, and
disciplining a misbehaving child is even more so. The NF parent may
do a perfectly adequate job here, but also may know that in his or her
heart the rules are just guidelines, to be used with discretion in
differing circumstances. With the possible exception of strongly NF
children, this is going to lead to any number of problems.

Consistent, contingent discipline The willingness to confront
unacceptable behavior firmly is a key element of demandingness. In
general, NF parents are likely to be distinctly uncomfortable with
confrontation and enforcement when children behave in unacceptable
ways. Loving harmony, they find nothing harmonious about the
disciplinary encounter, and are likely to waver on their stated or
implied consequences in the face of an emotional disruption.
One outcome of this is falling into what we have called the "Feeler
Trap" during discipline sessions. As a parent who is open and willing
to discuss issues, it may be easy for the NF to feel as if the discussion
itself was sufficient to solve the problem. Thus, a heart-to-heart talk
on why a behavior was wrong, misguided, or otherwise in error, may
evolve into a substitute for disciplinary action. This is especially true
when the child seems to show impressive understanding and regret.

For some children, this may be effective in itself, but for many it may
become part of an endless cycle of misbehavior, discussion, regret,
parent/child making up, followed by more misbehavior—truly a
Feeler trap for the overly-gentle parent. Other negative outcomes may
range from passively to actively defiant behavior in the child, and to
disrespect and even contempt on the part of children of some
temperaments.

Monitoring behavior Monitoring behavior has the same inherent
problem—if you find misbehavior it logically leads to unpleasant
confrontation and discipline. In addition, the idealistic NF may feel
that monitoring implies a lack of trust in the child, and consider this
the more important issue. NFs who are also strong Judgers are more

likely to do a fair amount of monitoring, just as an organizational issue, while NF Perceivers are most likely to be avoiders in this area.

Overall: In all probability the NF probably comes closest of all temperament groups to preferring the permissive parenting style by nature. If convinced that this is not working in the family, the NF has some real stretching to do here.

In summary: NFs are likely to:

> Be good at thinking about rules and talking about them, but hate to set them in stone (or even firm clay!).
> Be relatively uncomfortable with confrontations
> Be relatively poor and/or overly flexible in enforcement—therefore inconsistent.
> Be especially ineffective in administering swift contingent punishment
> Be very susceptible to falling into the "Feeler trap"

Good areas for NF stretches toward the demandingness model. NFs may need to work to develop some clear outcomes and enforcements for their
expectations on rules and limits. This requires careful (but not endless) thought. As in all temperament-related problems, honest compromise is a key point, but the compromise should come in the planning, not the actual enforcement.

Recognizing their aversion to this whole area, NFs should aim to develop rules that they truly believe to be necessary, and enforcements that they truly believe are reasonable. They will never have the long and serious list that an SJ parent might, and that is quite okay. But—and it is a large "but"—once the list is developed, there should be no compromise on consistent enforcement. What any child needs most, in order to cooperate, is clarity and predictability in the rules and consequences.

Though it may not feel right to the Intuitive Feeler, balancing a nurturing responsiveness style with clear limits and some consistent enforcement is a positive thing. It is far more likely to result in the cooperation and harmony the NF parent seeks. Having clear and articulated reasons for actions gives credibility to parent intentions. Providing consistent enforcement and consequences gives credibility to parent authority. Both are necessary. Does this imply that rules, once set, cannot be changed? No. What it does mean is that they should not be changed in the heat of battle.

After both confrontation and consequences are completely out of the way, a parent can always be open to rethinking a given rule or consequence, based on both its fairness and its usefulness. And, there is no harm in letting the child be in on the discussion, as long as the decision belongs to the parent.

NF parents may need to examine how much their relatively permissive approach is really a very personal desire to keep harmony and peace, at the cost of an appropriate amount of demandingness for the child.

Consistency itself is a quality that NF parents should give particular attention to, as their desire to be flexible and understanding tends to clash with this. As is true with all temperaments, NFs need to find some middle ground that they can both live with and use in successful parenting.

NFs should try to stretch a bit toward the model by:

> - Targeting the most important types of misbehavior and establishing clear consequences that fit personal values.
> - Confronting firmly in those areas
> - Using contingent punishment immediately and consistently
> - Keeping discussions minimal prior to enforcement (avoiding the Feeler Trap)
> - Being willing to reconsider rules and consequences only when there is no on-going disciplinary event.

> ➢ Becoming more self-aware about the temperament-based reasons for their problems with demandingness.

Interaction of your child's temperament with the NF style

NF child:

The Feeling child really needs a lot of warmth, positive feedback, and affection as motivation for good behavior, and with an NF parent, there is likely to be lots of it. NF children also strongly need to understand the reasons behind expectations and actions in order to have some idea that there is more than parent cruelty at work here. Again, this is a mostly good fit with the NF parent. Because the NF child also hates emotional conflict, there are two very important things to do here. First, the rules and consequences should be absolutely clear, in advance of any problem. Unpredictability is likely to cause far more emotional trauma in the long run than any punishment, so avoid surprises. Secondly, the parent should make every effort not to add anger or loud reprimands to the situation. Just evoke the rule, and the consequences, and let that speak for itself.

In addition to this, avoid the "Feeler trap" action of allowing prolonged discussion to occur between confrontation and enforcement. This brings unpredictability back into the mix, as the little NF senses some opportunity to manipulate the situation. However dear that little NF is, she can learn to do this, if you give her good reason. In the long run this will just increase the emotional conflict.

NT child:

A strong NT child will never completely understand the way the mind of the NF parent works. The little NT will appreciate parental interest in her life up to a point, and certainly see the kindness behind this, but may never seek as much parent/child closeness as would be ideal for the NF parent.

In this, it is the parent's role to be observant and sensitive.
Similarly, while the NT child will appreciate the NF parent's
willingness to provide reasons and justification for expectations, this
child may be critical of the NF parent's occasional lack of cool logic.

Demandingness problems may be more serious. Weak and
inconsistent discipline will convince the NT over time that the NF
parent lacks the intention, and probably the strength, to take action. At
the least, it will diminish the child's respect for parent authority. A
willful older child may perceive this parent as easy to control or
manipulate. Either of these outcomes may lead to more serious
problems in the adolescent years.

SJ child:

This child will greatly appreciate your warm responsiveness, and
especially so if he has the Feeler preference also. However, the strong
SJ child looks for order and routines and is most cooperative (and
comfortable) when expectations are clear and predictable. Often-
repeated discussion regarding your reasons for expectations and action
are not needed, while consistency and predictability are, so this will
not be a natural temperament fit. Problems are maximally likely here
if what the parent communicates about rules and limits is not borne
out in demandingness consequences. Things will go better though if
the NF parent is also a Judger.

SP child:

The SP child will be your strongest challenge. Although the SP child
will
relish the more permissive style of the NF parent (lots more freedom
to enjoy the here and now), and the warmth and frequent interaction
provided, there is very little in the NF parent style that will help to
contain and direct this free spirit. In fact, those long heart-to-hearts
about expectations and reasons may be more frustrating to the SP
child than informative.

The best advice for NF parents and for all parents of SP children is to know what your own reasons are, but try not to be too repetitive about them, and be good about warmth and overall responsiveness, but very firm on contingent, consistent, and prompt discipline. Nowhere is consistency more critical than with the SP child.

NF parent—you are the epitome of warmth and caring, and your children are fortunate to have you for that. You just need to strengthen the demandingness side to help your children reach their full potential, and to maximize genuine harmony in your home.

Chapter 21

The NT (Intuitive and Thinking) Parent in Action Strengths, Weaknesses, Problems and Stretches

Recapping the NT:

Strong Intuition leads the NT to be a creative and imaginative person, but this is anchored to earth by strong Thinking. The NT who comes upon an interesting idea or theory will then turn it around and ask—but is it logical, is it realistic—is it true? The end product is a person who is very much interested in new ideas, but then wants to use them to make things happen in the real world. The passion for logic is accompanied by a desire to keep emotion restrained and under control.

What might NT parents be most concerned about in their child's development?

Because skill in logical thinking and analysis are very important to the NT, they will certainly wish to see this developing well in their children. The same is true for high standards of fairness and honesty. Beyond this, NT parents are likely to approach parenting as they might any major undertaking, wanting the whole system to work extremely well. Quite likely they will have a broad idea of this that includes competence in school and in sports, music or other interests, and the ability to make satisfying friends.

What might they be less concerned about? High levels of popularity would not be a particular concern nor would the NT parent especially stress empathy and compassion, beyond their own standards of fairness. The great need for interpersonal closeness and harmony that is so important to the NF, would also be of lesser concern to the NT.

How would this affect responsiveness?

Warmth, intimacy and daily interactions Showing intimacy outwardly is not likely to be the NT's greatest strength. It is not that they are less loving, or less interested in the child; attachment may, in fact, be very deep. However, the NT typically neither displays as much emotion as other temperaments, nor is as good at sensing subtle emotion and mood shifts in others. Love will be shown in their deep interest in the child's well being, and their very considerable devotion to helping the child to grow and develop. NT parents will, typically, take great pleasure in the child's activities and accomplishments, and be quick to say so, since this is such a basic NT value.

NT parents may be somewhat less concerned with their children's immediate emotions or feelings. As a result, less attention may be paid to this area. This parent may struggle here, and especially so with a strongly Feeling child who is unusually sensitive and emotional. NTs by nature tend to believe that the answer to emotional distress is to solve the problem, buck up and get on with things.

The ability to read communication signals from the young infant may also not be an area of special Thinker expertise. Again, that has to do with picking up social and emotional cues--an area where the Thinker is pretty ordinary. Intuition does help here, however, and so does just taking time to observe and learn. All of this gets much easier for strong NTs as the child begins to use words.

Active Parent Learning

Observing and learning about the child. Like the NF, NT parents are likely to read widely about child development and give considerable thought to good parenting and creating a positive environment. However, both Sensing and Feeling will be somewhat foreign to NT nature, and easy to misunderstand as faults to be remedied. An understanding of temperament differences will be very important for good parent/child rapport, as is calm, non-judgmental observation. Understanding what the child is thinking will come easily; understanding what the child is feeling will require more work. *Parent learning—self understanding* This is not the life-long passion for the NT that it is for the NF, but NTs generally do have respect for it. Being creatures of logic, they are most likely to spend time on this when they begin an entirely new role or have a new problem with something they have been doing. Thus, the NT as a new parent or the NT with a baffling problem in child behavior is likely to do a fair amount of reading and thinking in this area, but then move quickly to make any desired changes.

Active parent teaching

Spending time on reading, learning, emotional understanding NT parents are generally fascinated with their child's thoughts and ideas and tend to spend considerable time in the whole area of reading, skill building and discussion. However, they are sometimes better talkers than listeners. The typical strong NT is always up, always involved in a variety of compelling ideas and interests. This may make it harder to slow down and really listen, especially if this is not an equally strong NT child who insists on being heard. It is also true that the strong NT parent has lots of definite ideas on nearly everything. While an NT child may learn to delight in this, other temperaments may find it overwhelming.

In the area of sharing emotional wisdom, the NT may not do a great job. Children need to understand their own feelings and reactions to others, and they need to gain insight into what is going on with friends and family. This is a natural area for parent teaching, just in the course of every day happenings. Strong NTs, however, do their best to keep emotion under wraps. As a result, they are not the most talented mentors in this area. Often times they miss subtle emotional cues from others, including family, and thus don't see some of the teachable moments that occur every day.

Communicating rules and limits As strong Thinkers, NT parents typically have clear and logical ideas about right and wrong, and as strong Intuitives, will wish to communicate their reasoning and expectations in depth. Because of their reliance on logic, NT parents will generally be willing to engage in discussion and debate, and allow for the possibility of changing an opinion or rule, based upon reasonable arguments or requests. (Such arguments have to meet high NT standards for "reasonableness", however.) Being highly Intuitive, NT parents will work hard to explain why rules, limits, and expectations are important, using rational arguments and lots of discussion.

The Structural Side

Preferences for either Judging or Perceiving will affect how well the NT parent maintains an organized and structured home. In general, NTs tend to think ahead and organize, but those who also prefer Judging will find this easier and more natural to do, while those with very strong Perceiving may struggle. (See the SP chapter for stretching suggestions here.)

Overall--NTs are likely to:

➢ Be highly responsive in many areas, but struggle somewhat with expressing emotions and interpreting the emotions of others.
➢ Be very good at sharing their reasons for rules and limits
➢ Be willing to consider the child's viewpoint
➢ Spend lots of time mentoring, teaching, discussing, but not do as well in emotion areas.
➢ Be better talkers than listeners, and stand to benefit from reflecting on this
➢ Overlook the real interests of Sensors, and be inwardly impatient with highly sensitive Feelers.

Good areas for NT stretches toward the responsiveness model

Most NTs would be well-served by spending some time monitoring their own responsiveness style, and trying to gain real insight into their children's preferences and temperaments. They should look carefully at how much they tend to direct conversation with a child, compared to how much they relax and let it flow. Similarly, they should try to see whether they tend to ignore or shift away from emotional areas when the child is expressing feelings.

The NT parent also should realize that parents are the most central role models for empathy and compassion toward others. NTs are notoriously just and fair toward others, but may easily fail to teach children to reach beyond that when it is needed.
With children of very different preferences, they need to take time to really understand how the child sees and experiences the world. This includes knowing what is important to the child that may not seem important at all to the NT parent. With this should come new respect for differences and a willingness to alter some aspects of responsiveness to fit the child's needs. The NT really should increase awareness in this area, and be sure that there is lots of active listening going on.

Especially with a Sensing child the parent needs to be very aware of the child's natural interests and not bombard him or her with theories and abstractions. Similarly the parent needs to pay attention in reading, and later in buying books, to the things that are exciting to the child, not simply the stories that excited the NT as a child.

It is even more important that NTs really work at understanding the very different values and experiences of the Feeling child, as this is often the source of the greatest misunderstanding in their parent/child relationship.

If the NT parent has a strong Perceiving preference, they need to look at the same advice given for other Perceiving parents—target a few organizational areas and time management areas in the child's world, and try to make improvements one small step at a time. For NT Judgers, this will not be a problem.

NTs should try to stretch a bit toward the responsiveness model by:

> Examining strengths and weaknesses of their own responsiveness style
> Working on any tendency to ignore or downplay emotional issues
> Trying to be a good model for kindness and empathy
> Learning to listen in a more relaxed, non-pressured way
> Working hard at understanding and respecting the ways in which the child's preferences, needs, and view of the world are very different from their own
> (If Perceivers,) working toward a more organized and scheduled household (See specific stretching suggestions in the SP chapter or in the NF chapter).

The NT Temperament and Demandingness

Setting rules, limits and expectations. As we noted in the section on responsiveness "NT parents typically have clear and logical ideas about right and wrong, and as strong Intuitives, will wish to communicate their reasoning and expectations clearly." As a group, they may come the closest to the Authoritative style of parenting in this area. Problems that they do have appear more frequently on the responsiveness side, rather than in demandingness.

However, in establishing standards, the one area that the NT parent may treat too lightly is that of expecting the child to be tactful and considerate of the feelings of others, since this is not usually a high NT priority. If asked, the NT parent would certainly agree that tact and consideration matter, but it might not occur to them even to mention it, unless a problem came up.

Consistent, contingent discipline Typically, the NT parent is comfortable and confident about taking a stand when necessary. NTs are not likely to shy away from confrontation. Having clear standards about expectations and acceptable behavior, and being less influenced by the emotions of the moment, NT parents are not likely to waver without compelling reasons. As individuals who are future-oriented, NT parents want both to correct the immediate problem and to ensure the right behavior for the future.

NTs place a heavy emphasis on logic and reason, and as a result, tend to establish consistency between rewards/punishment and positive or negative behavior. In general this is entirely a good thing, but problems can arise with children of a very different temperament. Feeler children, in particular, may find the very calm, very firm NT discipline style to be impersonal, and see the parent as uncaring. The most helpful change for this might be in greater efforts at responsiveness, rather than a change in demandingness.

Monitoring Preferences for either Judging or Perceiving will have the greatest effect how well the NT parent maintains an organized and structured home. This, in turn, affects monitoring, since consistent routines and clearly assigned responsibilities make it much easier to keep track of what is and is not getting done, as well as where children are at a given moment. In general, NTs do this well, as they are not bothered by the fact that it may lead to confrontations, but those who also prefer Judging will find this easier and more natural to do, while NT parents who prefer Perceiving will likely find it to be more of a struggle.

Overall--NTs are likely to:

> Have clear and consistent rules and consequences
> Be comfortable with confrontations
> Enforce the rules promptly and decisively
> Be good at monitoring, generally

But also

> In some cases, fail to be clear about expectations in areas of tact and empathy

> In some cases (especially combined with Judging) tend to overwhelm their more gentle Feeler children.

Good areas for NT stretches toward the model

As we have seen, NT parents can be expected to do a very good job in most areas of demandingness. If they have a strong Perceiving preference, and are neglectful about household management, they also need to look at the same advice given for other Perceiving parents in the SP chapter. They should try to target a few organizational areas and time management areas in the child's world, and try to make improvements one small step at a time.

It is also the case that extremely firm and impersonal discipline may be seen by the child as a lack of understanding and respect. This is particularly true for Feeling children, but carried to the extreme this may be true for any child, and may backfire by reducing the child's inner desire to please. This is especially likely if the NT parent has problems in conveying a deep sense of warmth in responsiveness, and is very firm and impersonal in demandingness areas.

For some children the result may be both a drop in the child's sense of being loved, and reduced compliance with demandingness requirements. In this situation, the NT parent would do well to work harder in responsiveness areas, be more quiet and thoughtful in disciplining, and to take time out after a discipline encounter is over, to give reassurance to a disheartened child.

NTs should try to stretch a bit toward the model by:

> Working hard at understanding and respecting the ways in which the child's preferences, needs, and view of the world are very different from their own
> Taking care to include kindness and empathetic behaviors among the qualities they are asking of the child.

➤ (If Perceivers,) working toward a more organized and scheduled household
➤ Looking at their responsiveness skills to see if a problem *there* is producing a problem in the child's willingness to follow the rules.
➤ Being more thoughtful during and after discipline encounters.

Interaction of your child's temperament with the NT parenting style

Feeling children in general With a naturally cuddly baby and toddler, the NT parent of a young child often needs to slow down and make more lap-time. A smart Thinking parent may make this more mutually enjoyable by introducing songs, poems, or picture books into this time and having such tools always ready. With an older Feeling child this parent needs to remember to be generous with touches and supportive and loving comments.

NF child:

NF children will appreciate the NT parent's efforts to explain the reasons for rules and limits, and the parent's willingness to consider the viewpoint and arguments of the child. However, these children may be frustrated by their own lack of influence in arguing their case, as a result of the NT's relative disregard for arguments based upon feelings and values.

The NF child will appreciate praise and attention from the NT parent regarding good behavior and achievements, but the Thinker's approach of the NT parent may make the NF child feel less valued. Without being able to articulate it, the child may perceive his or her emotional side to be disrespected, or at least seen as less important. Similarly, while NT parents are usually very open in being willing to discuss their reasons for rules, their disregard for arguments based upon feelings and personal values may frustrate NF children. The best advice here is to be sure that the NF's responsiveness needs are being met, and to be sure that all discipline is done quietly and calmly.

NT child:

___

In day to day interactions, the NT parent and NT child should be very compatible, wanting similar things from one another. However, though they may have great respect for one another, this will not necessarily mean fewer arguments. In fact, we might expect that spirited debate would be occasionally elevated to an art form between the parent and the older child. At the same time, if NT parents have proven their competence and authority, cooperation will follow.

If some areas are neglected in the child's development, it will likely be those of ensuring polite and gracious behavior and understanding and valuing the feelings of others.

SJ child:

___

The strong SJ child looks for order and routines and is most cooperative and comfortable when expectations are clear and predictable. This child does not, however, care much for lots of discussion regarding reasons for expectations and action. The emphasis here should be on consistency and predictability, as the SJ child will just be frustrated by too much talk about reasons and rules. If the SJ child has a strong Feeling preference, some of the difficulties noted for the NF child may also occur here in emotion areas.

SP child:

___

The SP child will continue to be the strongest challenge for parents of every temperament, so advice is pretty similar for all parents. It helps if the little SP has the Thinker preference, but the SP Feeler just wants to enjoy life here and now, will not be wild about lots of discussions regarding reasons for rules, and generally will not be wild about rules no matter what. The best advice is to know what your own reasons are but don't be too repetitive about them, be good about warmth and reciprocity, but very firm on contingent, consistent (and quick) discipline.

In responsiveness areas, it is vital for the NT parent to gain insight into the things that get the SP juices running, and work with these in appreciating the SPs interests and helping in the development of SP skills.

NT parent—you are a tower of reason, logic and systematic planning. Your commitment to your children is not to be questioned. In many different areas you are a fine teacher and a fine disciplinarian. You do, however, need to give thought and reflection to the emotional side of life, on understanding and responding to feelings, and on helping your children to take care with the feelings of others.

Chapter 22

What about Introversion/Extraversion Effects on Parenting Style?

This preference pair does not alter parenting style nearly as much as the four temperaments do, as we have noted in other places. Below are a few differences that are common, however.

I. Introversion, Extraversion, and Responsiveness.

Warmth, intimacy and interactions

Highly Extraverted children (and parents) share feelings easily but just naturally love to be around a variety of people. The Introverted parent may be at some risk of feeling not all that uniquely important, as his Extraverted child grows older and reaches out to many different people. This may be particularly true in a contrast between an Introverted Feeling parent and an Extraverted but Thinking child. The Introverted child, on the other hand, shares his deepest feelings very cautiously, and may be overwhelmed at times by a very talkative, Extraverted parent. Family harmony, and family happiness, across a broad range of Preferences and temperaments, requires a great deal of patient understanding.

The Strongly introverted parent will be more quiet in parent-child interactions, but not less engaged, especially with a young infant. One need of every Introvert, however, is some space and peace in each day. The very fussy infant or very active toddler may pose greater problems in summoning up the needed patience and strength for Introverted than Extraverted parents. The Introverted but strongly Feeling parent may be more compelled to go the last mile here than the Thinking parent, because he or she shares the child's great need for closeness, while strong Introversion combined with Strong

Thinking, may result in a parent whose resources may be more readily depleted.

There can also be a mismatch in the direction of the highly Extraverted and Feeling *parent* and the strongly Introverted and Thinking *child.* Here the problem may be that the parent's constant desire for close interaction is greater than the child's needs, especially by toddlerhood and on. If this difference is large the toddler and preschooler may quickly wiggle down from a lap and resist being picked up when happily occupied. For the child, this is a good thing, and the parent needs to learn to be sensitive to it.

The strongly Extraverted and Feeling parent needs to notice and respond if her child often pulls away when picked up, and spend a little more time peacefully watching, and a little less time being actively involved in the middle of the child's activities. This parent is sometimes likely to intrude on a perfectly contented child when it would be wiser not to do so.

Children generally love it when you notice and comment on what they are doing (not as a good/bad judgment—just as an observation that shows you took an interest). The Extraverted-Feeling parent can substitute some of this for the extra hugs that are stored up. This is particularly sound advice with the Introverted Thinking child, who really wants to develop her own agenda a good part of the time.

It is also the case that Extraverts may spend less time interacting with their children one-on-one as they grow older, and more time on the interaction of the family as a whole. This will be fine for the Extraverted child, but the strongly Introverted child may fail to get some of the close individual socializing that this child thrives on.

Active parent learning

Learning about the child In being observant about the child, the Introverted parent is likely to be the better of the two. Extraverts tend to be busier just being themselves, and interacting with others, and therefore are often less observant of small happenings and small differences in others. These are not large differences, however, and minor compared to effects of other preferences.

Learning about the self All else being equal, Introverts would probably have a small edge in being willing to examine their own preferences and their strengths and weaknesses as parents, simply because they tend to be somewhat more observant and reflective in general.

Communicating about rules and limits In terms of the responsiveness task of discussing reasons for rules and limits, **Extraverts** might talk more freely, but this is not a big difference within the closeness of the family.

The Structural Side

Differences in tidiness, meal schedules etc. depend most of all on Judging/Perceiving. Extraversion may combine with the Perceiving preference to slightly increase the tendency to live in cheerful chaos, but Extraverted Judgers usually will show pretty typical Judging organization and orderliness. However, Extraverts of both types may create lively and noisy environments for their children to enjoy. This is fine for the Extraverted child, but the strongly Introverted child may long for (and need) some area of peace and quiet.

In Summary –The most meaningful differences may be found in the area of Warmth, Intimacy and Personal Interactions.

➢ In terms of parent/child interactions, the Introverted child with an Extraverted parent may feel less deeply connected than he or she might wish. The Extraverted child might feel right at home with the same parent.

➢ Introverted parents with the highly Extraverted child may weary of the endless cheerful chatter and tend to withdraw at some moments. Similarly they may not provide the amount of outside social action that the young Extravert longs for.

➤ Introverted parents may be better listeners and observers and for that reason, may know their children somewhat better than Extraverts, and may also be somewhat more reflective about themselves.

➤ Extraverted parents will just naturally create a more busy, noisy and socially interactive household than Introverted parents will. This may be great for the Extraverted child but stressful for the Introvert if the parent does not provide a good amount of quiet time. And while the Extravert may talk more easily and often to the child, he or she may not listen as carefully and attentively as the Introverted parent.

Introversion, Extraversion and Demandingness

Setting rules and limits The most that can be said about Introversion and Extraversion in demandingness, is that these preferences may add a little something or subtract a little something from the influence of other preferences. In setting rules and limits, it seems unlikely that these preferences would affect the clearness or firmness of these. It is possible, though, that types of rules in specific areas might be affected.

All else being equal, Extraverts are generally more bold and fearless than Introverts, and that suggests several things. In the area of limits related to both physical and emotional safety, it is likely that Introverts might restrict dare-devil behavior more, and in older children, Extraverted parents might give more freedom in the parties and social events in which their children are allowed to participate. In combination, Extravert-Sensing-Perceivers are the most likely to permit more adventurous behavior, and Introvert-Judgers less likely.

Consistent, contingent discipline and Monitoring Fearlessness also suggests that Extraverts might be more comfortable with confrontation and with monitoring, but that will depend a lot on the strength of the Feeling preference. You can expect Extraverted Thinkers to confront very readily, Extraverted Feelers, much less so, and Introverted Feelers to have a very difficult time in this area.

Much the same would be true for monitoring. And, just as Extraverted children are more physically active, the Extraverted parent may be more ready to go into action than the Introverted parent, in carrying out disciplinary measures. In combination, the Extraverted and Judging parent may be very active and effective in many demandingness areas, and this might be almost over the top with a strong Extraverted, Thinking and Judging parent.

Just a little stretching for Extraversion/Introversion

➤ Mainly here, the advice is to get to know your own and your child's Introversion/Extraversion comfort level well, and try to work with that. For each parent/child pair, be sure that there is a good balance of talking and listening, and that this balance works well for the particular child.

➤ For the Extraverted parent and Introverted child, be very aware of your child's need for quiet time and time alone with you.

➤ For the Introverted parent, be aware that parenting young children is physically and emotionally strenuous—try to protect your own needs for some quiet time and some time to recharge your energy level.

➤ It is important for this parent to get a handle on bedtime, so that there is quiet time to look forward to. If there is a young child and older preschoolers, it is wisdom to have a quiet time for all concerned during the baby's major nap time.

➤ Grocery shopping and other errands should ideally be done when one parent can baby-sit, to reduce the chaos. If feasible, using a baby sitter to make room for a once-a-week outing is wise, even if that outing is a simply trip to the park or a quiet library room. This is good advice for all parents, but especially for the Strong Introvert.

➤ Extraverts should be wary of a tendency to allow too much risky behavior, whether physical or social, and Introverts should be sure that they are not restricting activities unnecessarily as a result of their own anxieties.

➤ Introverts, and especially Introverted Feelers, should also be wary of failing to discipline or monitor simply because confrontation is unpleasant.

Chapter 23

Two Parents, Two Temperaments--
When Moms and Dads Disagree

The Scene

It's nearly 9 p.m. and Joe is getting the last child settled in for the night, having taken the task over from his wife who was clearly getting nowhere. He is once again feeling both angry and guilty. It has taken most of the evening to calm down the excitable five year old, and a similar amount of time to shepherd the eight year old through his homework.

Joe's patience reached the breaking point when his wife, Sandy, was still sweetly coaxing the 5 year old to bed after an hour. At that point he yelled, lost his temper and took over. Soon that five year old was wailing and his older brother was calling dad a mean- tempered monster. As he escorted the eldest through the living room, to finally put him to bed, Joe caught his wife, Sandy, giving him an icy stare. Obviously, his troubles weren't over.

He is absolutely certain it is his wife's fault. She will not take a firm hand with the problem and the boys have learned to play endlessly on her patient nature. At the same time, she is furious when Joe steps in to take charge. She criticizes his "loud" voice, and constantly accuses him of being utterly indifferent to the children's needs and feelings. And now, there they are again, ready for another bout of recriminations.

Does this sound familiar?

Of all the preference differences, the Thinking/Feeling pair has the greatest influence on your demandingness and responsiveness balance. Obviously here, Joe is inclined to lean heavily on demandingness, while Sandy emphasizes responsiveness. And, although it sounds like a tired stereotype, chances are that in any parent pair, the mother will be more skilled and more naturally inclined toward responsiveness, and the father toward demandingness. This is certainly not always true; some couples may both be high in responsiveness, some both high in demandingness, and some may show greater male responsiveness and female demandingness. The odds, however, are tilted in this male-demandingness and female responsiveness direction.

No doubt this stereotypical male/female pattern is partly the result of social learning during development. However, there is good evidence, accumulated over many years of research, that inborn temperament also plays an important part. In particular, data collected with the Myers-Briggs Type Indicator[22] shows that there are common male/female differences in preference for Thinking versus Feeling. The Myers-Briggs findings, gathered over many years, indicate that about 56% of all men, versus 25% of all women, fall in the Thinker category. Thus, by the law of averages, dad is more likely to be the Thinker, and mom the Feeler.

Let's look at a simple example, with dad as the Thinker and mom as the Feeler. In deciding whether a bed time rule could be stretched for a child who wanted to watch a particular TV program, our Thinker dad would be concerned about the precedent it would set, and the problems that this might produce on other nights. Feeler mom might have greater concern for how important this particular program was to the child, and be more willing to make an exception. His concern

---

[22] Myers, I. B., McCaulley, M. H., Quenk, N.L. & Hammer, A. L. (1998). *MBTI Manual, 3rd Ed.* Palo Alto: Consulting Psychologists Press.

would probably be that she would be willing to do this over and over again—making not one, but an endless series of exceptions. Her concern would be that he thinks abstract rules are more important than the happiness of his children.

If you, as the reader, already are certain that one or the other is right, you are at the heart of the problem. As we have noted before, we see the world so clearly and strongly from our own perspective—a perspective given by both experience and temperament—that it seems unimaginable that someone we care about sees it differently. The repetitive fights over the same issue start from the assumption that the other person is just misguided. If you can just find the right, really convincing words, or just say it more strongly, or, or, or, then the beloved other will surely see the light.

Not going to happen! The first hard step in reaching a better understanding is the acceptance that this can never be true. If you are really a very different Thinking/Feeling pair, this difference is not going to go away. More generally it is useful information to recognize this. When you are having the same fight over and over again, temperament differences are nearly always somewhere at the bottom of it.

Well, so then what?

Each of you might start out thinking that the other person should just let you handle it all, you with your superior wisdom! Even if you could pull off that trick, it would be the wrong answer, because children do need both responsiveness and demandingness—and they need you to uphold a common standard together, as far as you possibly can. So, as you look at your spouse across a Thinking/Feeling divide, the first thing you need to acknowledge is that the difference is not going to go away. The second thing you must take to heart is that you each have something vital to contribute.

The very things that our fictional couple has been fighting over do matter. The dad needs to recognize that firm discipline that ends only in a state of rage is not working well. We hope that our children will end their days ready for a peaceful night's sleep, and we hope that for ourselves as well. On the other hand, everything we know about demandingness tells us that inconsistency, vacillation, and lack of rules that children will respect, is a recipe for family chaos.

Once both parties admit that they bring their share of problems to this, they will have to hammer out serious compromises to make sure the children get what they need. This will take lots of respect and lots of thought. What sorts of rules and consequences can the Feeler accept and live with? Where can the Thinker compromise those unbending standards? Which parent may be better at handling certain situations?

Advice for this pair

With this couple, several possibilities come to mind. Let's look at the simple issue of having or not having exceptions to rules. If rules need exceptions, from mom's point of view, and rules need to seem firm, from dad's point of view, perhaps this couple could agree on having bedtime exceptions on a pre-planned basis. One night per week? Only on weekend nights? That may still seem too rigid to mom and too loose to dad, but that is what compromises are all about.

More broadly, within this framework, they might both realize that firmness is dad's natural strength. If they can agree on the rules and the exceptions, perhaps the dad really could take over the bedtime discipline. He would be far less likely to do this in anger if it were his task from the start. Quite possibly another compromise might be that mom agrees to this, *contingent* on his bringing it off without losing his temper. As long as it is clear that the partners are in agreement in principle, there is nothing wrong with letting the better disciplinarian handle certain situations—provided he/she really *is* the better disciplinarian.

***Preferences and temperaments are real. They cannot be argued
away.*** The better arguer in any pair may succeed in making the
partner feel in the wrong, or guilty or some messy combination of
both, but like murder, temperament will out. The behavior will return,
the issue will return, the fight will return until you find some
acceptable compromise. If you both open your hearts to the reality of
your differences, there will always be creative ways to compromise
that will benefit your partnership, your children, and your joy in
family.

Other preference problems?

Thinking and feeling, of course, are not the only preferences where
there may be serious parent disagreement. With respect to
demandingness, Perceiving and Judging would run a close second. A
houseful of scattered toys may reflect happy play to one parent and
nerve-wracking chaos to another. Certainly, if our Thinker dad were
also a strong Judger, and our Feeler mom a strong Perceiver, their
road to compromise would be even harder and more painful. We have
emphasized Thinking/Feeling here simply because this difference
seems to stir up the most deep seated anger among parents who differ
radically on this. In truth, compromise is critical wherever there are
strong preference differences.

Part VI

Adding Grace to Your Parenting Design—Working With Your Child's Preferences

---

Overview: *Things to Work on.*

I. Accepting and Honoring Preferences.

Parent Expectations If you were the perfect parent you would wish for your child only that she or he might be the very best possible and most successful model of her natural preferences. In the real world, what you naturally tend to do is wish and expect that your child will have all of the qualities that you like in yourself. These may or may not have a great deal to do with who this child is. One of the things that is hardest to wrap our minds around is the fact that we basically like and approve of the behaviors in ourselves that come from our deepest preferences, and usually like and approve of the same behaviors in others. We have commented on this before, but let's think about it in more detail.

Imagine that you are a strong Perceiver. You hate being prescheduled, would never willingly make a to-do list, and want to cope with each day and each hour as they come. A strong Judger would look at you and wonder how on earth you could stand to be like that. You might look at the strong Judger, moving dutifully from task to task, checking off the old to-do list, and hurrying to bed to be fresh for the morning's work, and wonder how *he* could stand to live like that.

The Perceiver might sigh in a harried moment and wish he were more organized, and the Judger might admit from time to time that she doesn't take enough time for play or recreation, but the fact is, they wouldn't trade. Miss Perceiver relishes the openness of her unscheduled life, and Mr. Judger finds deep satisfaction in daily tasks he has accomplished. Neither can really experience what the other feels, and neither really wishes to.

This makes life pretty complicated when it comes to parenting children with preferences that are strong and different from our own. Good parenting cannot be aimed at changing the child's basic preferences or temperament. That will not happen, no matter what you do. The most you can achieve if you try to do this is to create a child who remains the person he is but feels guilty or ashamed (or worse from your point of view) angry and rejecting toward you.

Moving toward acceptance In the best of worlds you can do two things when your child's temperament differs from your ideal model. First you can support and appreciate the positive contributions (from your point of view) of your child's natural preferences. That is generally the easy part. Second, you can go to war with yourself, if need be, to be sure that you accept the qualities that your child has, and relishes, which do *not* please you. It doesn't mean that you have to love those qualities. It does mean that you understand and accept that they are natural and important to your child. That is *not* easy, but ever so important. David Keirsey has sold over 10 million books on temperament with the title *Please Understand Me*. The books speak for themselves, but so does the title; we all long to have others see us and accept us as we are. Nowhere is this more critical than between child and parent.

But—having said that, as you can see from the descriptions of each preference, every preference has its advantages and its potential problems, and every child can use some help in getting comfortable with needed behaviors that would not be his or her first preference.

II. Helping *your child to build skills on the non-preferred side.*

This is tricky, because it requires you to hold, and act on, two rather different ideas. The first is that this is who my child is, and her temperament is not going to change in terms of how she is most comfortable in the world and how she prefers to do things and react to things. If I respect her, I should not be trying to change her fundamental nature. The second is that, preferred or not, she needs to become reasonably good at some non-preferred behaviors. Each of us live in a social world in which many things determine what we do at a given moment besides our personal wishes. Parents have their own needs for calmness, control over situations, time to themselves, etc. Siblings have their own needs. Schools, teachers, community organizations and eventual employers have their own needs and make demands on us to find ways to fit into this. This means that both adults and children with strong preferences will benefit from learning enough of what we call "skills on the non preferred side" to function in everyone else's world.

Coming up

In the next chapters we invite you to look at three things for each set of preferences—the qualities that should be easy to appreciate for a parent of any preference, the qualities that will be harder to appreciate, mostly for parents of opposite preferences, and some possible problems that may be present with strong one-sided preferences. We then suggest some tips to help your child develop skills on the non-preferred side in problem areas.

Chapter 24

Working With Your Introverted or Extraverted Child

The Extraverted Child's Special Characteristics

Qualities that are easy to appreciate
Makes friends easily
Likes others—friendly
Likes to communicate
Shares feelings readily
Enthusiastic, usually good humored

Qualities that may be harder to appreciate
May talk constantly
May seem too noisy, too active
May be easily bored when alone

Possible problems
May lack close and lasting friendships
Impulsive, can be too bold—do risky things
May lack ability to work and play independently

The Extraverted child: Being an Appreciative Parent

The Extraverted Parent will likely delight in the Extraverted child. Both are likely to thoroughly enjoy a busy people-filled household. Parents will delight in their child's willingness to share thoughts and feelings, and relish the generally upbeat nature of this child. Chances are, unless overactive classroom behavior results in teacher concerns;

the Extraverted parent will see no potential problems and no need for "skills development."

The Introverted Parent This parent will also relish this child's positive, friendly and talkative nature—up to a point. Endless chatter and near-constant activity, however, will be wearing on the quiet, Introverted parent. In addition, with a rather different set of friendship values, this parent is much more likely to have concerns about frequently- changing friendships that are perceived as lacking depth and closeness. Similarly, the strongly Extraverted child may be seen as a risk-taker by the Introverted parent, in need of close monitoring. In some cases this may be a legitimate concern, but in other cases it may simply reflect the parent's own more cautious nature.

The Extraverted child: Developing skills on the non-preferred side

Our American love of the outgoing, extraverted personality makes it hard to see why the person with this preference needs skills development at all. Certainly, the more gregarious and upbeat Extravert generally has an easier time in the world. The Extraverted parent may see little need for developing the non-preferred, Introvert skills, while the Introverted parent may see it as essential. However, the ability for depth and intimacy is certainly very important in the formation of major adult relationships, and the practice ground for that lies both in the family and in the formation of close friendships in childhood. Your strongly Extraverted child can be something of a social butterfly.

Being comfortable working and playing alone from time to time is another area worth thinking about. Fulfilling the Extraverted child's desire for playmates 24/7 may not be doing them a favor in the long run. A side benefit of becoming more skillful at spending some time alone is that this ability makes it possible to be a more independent person. If the light goes out your day when you have to spend an hour or two by yourself, it is very hard to hold an opinion or take a position that differs from your friends. This is doubly true for a strong Extravert who is also a strong Feeler.

Finally, another problem with the very Extraverted child's love of talking, moving and doing, is that listening skills tend to be neglected. Most obviously, this includes listening to others, and paying attention to that, but it also, in a sense, includes listening to oneself. As we have noted, the little Extravert in class is the first to raise a hand to answer a question, but generally does this before thinking about her answer. That answer gets worked out as she goes along. This is charming at age seven, but less delightful in a work-group discussion at age thirty. Below are a few suggestions for the strong Extravert that you might want to try wherever they seem appropriate.

Encouraging the development of close relationships

This is really in your child's hands, but you can try to maximize possibilities by setting the scene here.

- Encourage occasional sleepovers with just one friend
- Encourage just one additional friend on some family trips or outings.
- Protect family time together and do parent/child one-on-one special events periodically

With respect to time spent alone.

- Encourage some playtime or quiet time alone—you might want to set aside some small segment of time each day for this—no TV, no video games, no playmates. This needs to feel like a normal part of life, not a mini-crisis.
- Regularly encourage quiet reading time. A half-hour of reading time just before going to sleep could be offered as a staying-up privilege.

General noise and exuberance:

This will bother the Introverted parent considerably, and will bother the Extraverted parent very little if at all. In either case, however, if your child is strongly Extraverted, you will want to make clear that there are limits in any situation, and times and places where everyone has to learn to be calm.

It is most likely to be the Extravert in the classroom who will bring teacher reports home that stress this need. Strong Extraverts tend to be noisy and sometimes disruptive in class, talking out of turn and moving around even during quiet times. Every child needs to learn to exert some control over this.

- Try having moments of family silence. Religious families often say grace at meals. Others might simply have a moment—or two, or three—of silent reflection before meals. It is good practice in being quiet and your Extravert could benefit from practicing this regularly.
- Stress indoor and outdoor differences in voice, and in activities like running, jumping etc. Try to make it clear that noise and activity are wonderful in some settings, hurtful in others.
- If it is an appropriate style for your family, yoga, and brief meditation exercises might even be good for your exuberant little Extravert!
- With all of this, be sure you are respecting and providing plenty of outlets for your child's need to talk and shout and run out all her energy.
- Remember that you are trying to establish a bright line between places for joyous chaos, and places for calm control.

With respect to listening

- In order to listen you have to quiet yourself, so quietness practice is actually the first step.

- Find ways to make listening practice a family game. Tell stories and see who can tell them back the best. Discuss something that happened during the day and see who can repeat that.
- You might try adding self-listening (listening to your own thoughts) to moments of family silence before meals. This means asking each person to think of something during the silence that they would like to talk about during the meal. Then praise clear ideas, but don't praise unorganized rambles.
- Talk to your Extraverted child about the usefulness of good listening skills in school and in life. Make the point that listening to others is basic courtesy and not listening is (at least subtly) disrespectful.

With respect to risk taking

The Extraverted parent may not see danger signals that are there with that Extraverted child. It is wise here to listen to comments by your child's school and other organizations and/or other parents. If others are consistently flagging bold, impulsive behaviors in your child, action may be needed.

- In young children this simply means that there is a need to be especially aware of behaviors that could be dangerous in home or neighborhood and careful in monitoring them.
- In the older child it means paying special attention to what they are asking permission to do, and being sure that you have the whole story.
- When problems arise from impulsive behavior, try to help your child find a strategy for better self-regulation, even if it is just a slogan like "look before you leap".
- For yourself—It may mean some self-analysis is needed. Did you have a history of derring-do? If so, do you still feel some pride in this? Is it possible you take secret delight in your child's antics when you shouldn't?

Especially for the Introverted parent and Extraverted child

- ***Handling general Commotion*** Recognize that your child's love of noise, activity, motion is not your thing. Your aim should not be to suppress this passion in your child, but to find ways to channel it that will work for both of you.
- The well-known requirement that children use "indoor voices" when inside, and confine all running to outdoors, are reasonable requirements. Coupled with that though, is the need to provide enough rough and tumble outdoor time, both in the neighborhood and in parks and other outdoor areas for your younger child, and plenty of extracurricular activities for your school-age child.
- ***Carving out time for yourself.*** Your little Extravert will chatter whenever she is with you. You will love her much more for this if you can create islands of quiet time for yourself. For the parent at home, even 15 minute segments in your day where no one is to interrupt could be godsends—and good for all concerned. For any parent, a quiet period before dinner, or planned early bedtimes with books allowed, will smooth things out a little. You don't want to remake your child—just find some compromises that will work for both of you.

- **Handling impulsiveness/Riskiness** If this is genuinely your child's nature, it will be something you need to be sensitive to, just as we suggested for the Extraverted parent. At the same time, you need to realize that you, as a strong Introvert, may be overly sensitive to reasonable risk. It is good to talk your doubts over with others and pay careful attention their reports and comments

The Introverted Child's Special Characteristics

Qualities that are easy to appreciate
Quiet and calm
Often enjoys playing alone
Excellent listening skills
Makes close friends and is loyal
Not easily distracted

Qualities that may be harder to appreciate
Shy—reluctant to join in groups
Slow to make friends
May get tired and cranky with too much socializing
Hesitant about new experiences
May seem overly cautious

Possible problems
Too shy—unwilling to enter groups, make new friends
Too fearful—unwilling to try new experiences

The Introverted child—being an appreciative parent

Extraverted parents often feel considerable concern when they find that their child is quiet and perhaps shy. This parent may fail to notice the strengths and be overly concerned about the seeming lack of perky sociability, and about possible over-
cautiousness. It is vital to realize that this child is just as happy in his or her own way as a more exuberant-seeming child. In this situation it is extremely important that you recognize and accept the child's natural temperament.

This young person will not be a big group joiner, nor a bold adventurer. He will very likely, however, make lasting friends, enjoy interests in depth, and cope quietly but happily with life.

Nevertheless, if shy and cautious behaviors are more extreme, then gentle skills-building is definitely called for.

Introverted Parents will find their Introverted child very comfortable to be around, generally. They enjoy the relative quiet, and are usually understanding about letting the child talk when ready. The one exception here might be the Introverted but Feeling parent who may look for more communication about inner emotions than an Introverted and Thinking child is willing to give.

If the parent is strongly Introverted, the main problem that may arise here is in over-indulging the child's social wariness (see below).

Some do-nots for the Extraverted Parent:

- Do not try to turn your quiet introvert into a glad-hander, cheerleader.
- Do not run roughshod over her when she is not ready to try something new.
- Especially do not allow yourself to be critical of her quiet ways.

Some Dos for the Extraverted Parent

- Do provide quiet social experiences from infancy onward
- Do plan for a gentle introduction to play groups, preschool, etc. Watch for readiness for each adventure
- Be understanding when your child clearly has had enough in any social situation. Find a calm quiet area for her to restore energy and good nature.
- *Do* read the more detailed suggestions below for the Introverted parent. As an Extraverted parent you will probably do these things without any prompting, but the list may be helpful *provided* you don't get carried away with it.

Dos and Do-nots for the Introverted parent

When Introversion is strong in a young child, there is a natural tendency for the Introverted parent to sympathize and sometimes go too far in helping the child avoid stressful situations. As the Introverted child reaches preschool age there may be tears or tantrums when being left with the group, that don't seem to go away over time.

The concerned parent may feel that this child is simply not ready, and therefore keep him or her at home for awhile longer. This relieves everyone's stress and anxiety, but also removes the child from social experiences that are very necessary for the development of social skills.

Preschoolers learn these skills fundamentally from one another. They involve how to get another child's attention, how to say something that that child will be interested in, how to share toys and play together, how to resolve simple conflicts, and so forth. If a child is, by temperament, not motivated to socialize in this way, and is then not given this experience early on, the task simply becomes harder as other children become more proficient. A brief postponement for preschool may be helpful, but if you find yourself extending this you may want to get professional advice.

The Introverted Child: Building skills on the non-preferred side

As you look at some possible ways to do this, remember that you want to stretch your child's social interaction skills a little, but you are not trying to turn him or her inside out, nor make daily life miserable. *So consider these suggestions here carefully and thoughtfully*, and with a good ear for how your child is taking it.

Tips for your Toddler

- Here, lots of early experience with other children is a very positive thing to provide—but in careful doses. The trick is to make the presence of other children and adults a normal part of your child's life, at the same time that you keep the total amount of time spent this way modest and tolerable for your child. You need to plan for this, but also allow plenty of time with just family, or even alone play.

- If you are, yourself, a strongly Introverted parent, the obvious opportunities may not be your natural thing, but you need to stretch yourself here, especially if there are no other young children in your household.
- Getting together with friends who also have young children is one good way to do this. If that is impractical, there are organized playgroups for parent and child. In reality these are mostly "Mommy and Child," activities, but are worth looking into even for dads.
- Public parks are a third opportunity. What is important is that your young child is well accustomed to other children before that first, traumatic preschool day. You need to do this without, at any time, turning that into an unhappy experience.

Tips for the Preschooler

- It may be even more important for the child with the Introversion preference to have a good and lengthy preschool experience than for the Extravert. If your little Introvert is highly resistant, you need to get the best advice you can on how to handle this. A good preschool teacher will usually be able to help here.
- If the child is under three, you may want to wait a few months and then try again, but continuing to delay this experience indefinitely is not likely to be in your child's best interest.
- Take the trouble to get to know some of the other parents and their children, and encourage play dates for your child with others.

- Even though there may be one special friend that your child always asks for, encourage more than one friend to come over from time to time.
- Similarly, arrange enjoyable outings with several small friends from time to time.
- Again, the trick is to make this a normal, low key part of life.

Tips for the early grades

- Continue to encourage play dates and social get-togethers that include several children. Interesting outings—movies, zoo, pool, beach, theme park—can be used as natural motivators.
- Encourage your child to play at friends' houses from time to time rather than focusing everything around home. Explain that this is only fair.
- Talk about friendships, and help your child with good reasons for trying to have several friends. (For example, the different things you might like to do with each one, the different ideas and interests that they might bring to you, the fact that friends do quarrel sometimes, do move away sometimes, etc.)
- Make some types of birthday invitations a requirement. When your child has been invited but is reluctant, and it is for a *good* friend, the lesson needs to be learned that there are some things we just do for others.
- Strongly encourage at least one extracurricular activity that involves others, whether music, sports, or a school activity.
- If you child tends to sit in the very back of the classroom, challenge him or her to sit in the front in classroom circle-times, once in a while, as a deliberate act of bravery.

Tips for little Introverts of all ages

- Be sure that you have a reasonable number of social events in your home that include family members and friends.

- Give your child social responsibilities early on—opening the door for guests, greeting them and bringing them to you, and so forth.
- Similarly, at an appropriate age, it is good to have your child learn to answer the telephone well, and to take messages. Learning some basic phone etiquette is simply useful.

The Temptation of the Extraverted Parent

The tendency here is to look at the list and launch a full-scale program immediately using every item. In her heart of hearts a highly Extraverted mom, for example, will believe that, with the right effort, she can liberate the little Extravert inside. Not so. It isn't in there! Your child needs to have most of his or her free time to spend as preferred—playing alone, being with family, being with one friend. The list is intended to help this child develop social skills that might otherwise be avoided, but it is not intended to change preferences. Items should be tried slowly and judiciously.

And the Introverted Parent This parent will not be tempted to overdo it. If anything, Mom or Dad (and especially if it is Mom *and* Dad) may be largely unaware of the contribution they are making to preference strength here by sheltering a very strong Introvert too much. If somewhat aware, they still may feel too protective of the child to demand any significant effort in this direction. We believe that this may be a mistake. Helping your highly Introverted child to become more comfortable in the social world may be one of the best gifts you can give as a parent.

Chapter 25

Working with your Sensing or Intuitive Child

The Sensing Child's Special Characteristics

Qualities that are easy to appreciate
Very aware of the here and now
Good memory for facts and detail
Conscientious about facts and details—rarely makes careless mistakes
Likes to get good at things—polish skills

Qualities that may be harder to appreciate
May be disinterested in past/future
May have little interest in abstract ideas
May respond poorly to vague instructions
May resist change in well-learned ways of doing things

Possible problems
May under-perform in school in some subject areas due to lack of interest
May have little interest in anticipating and planning for the future

The Sensing Child: Being an Appreciative Parent

Sensing parents will find that appreciation comes very easy. The child is practical, present-focused, and good at the things that Sensors enjoy being good at. If there is any problem for the Sensing parent it would be in being sufficiently alert and concerned if some aspects of academic learning do not go well, or if and when the adolescent does not begin to plan for the future.

Intuitive parents may miss the spark of imagination that they had been hoping for. If so, they need to deal with this feeling ruthlessly, accepting and enjoying all the good qualities that the Sensor brings, and realizing that their child's developing mind is the child's own gift, not a fulfillment of parental wishes. "You may give them your love, but not your thoughts, for they have their own thoughts."[23]

The Sensing Child: Developing skills on the non-preferred side

The downside of the Sensing preference is that a fascination for factual details tends to obscure larger patterns. You become very good at knowing what is so without worrying about why it is so. As a result the Sensor is often not very skillful or interested in understanding causes or in predicting future changes. Skills development on the non-preferred side, here, is hard to influence, because it is a way of thinking, more than a way of behaving. This is somewhat true for both poles of this preference pair.

The Extravert and Introvert, as they get older, can see that they behave differently from some of their friends. Particularly for *young* Sensors, the behavior is a much less visible fact, and the suggestion that they somehow should think in new ways is likely to merely feel like criticism. If you can do so without seeming critical or without offering it as "schoolwork", family discussions that revolve around the simple whys of things could be helpful. (Just be careful not to end the discussion with your own "right" answer).Why do ants follow each other around?" or, "Why does Mom always go to bed early when Dad always stays up?" may be the right idea for the five-year-old—so long as you don't finish this by smartly giving a definitive answer of your own.

When your Sensor reaches the upper elementary grades, telling mystery stories around the dinner table and trying to guess "who did

---

[23] Kibran, Kahlil, (1923). *The Prophet. New York: Knopf.*

it" and "why" might be a way of encouraging mind-stretching. Our family has an old tradition of starting an adventure story at the table and then having each person keep adding to it, going around in order. Basically, anything that makes imagination and speculation fun will be good; anything that makes it punitive or humiliating will be just the opposite—and will drive your young Sensor back to "Just the facts, Ma'am." So, this one takes a lot of care and thought.

In the list below we suggest some possible ways to encourage playing with ideas. The Intutivie parent should not, however, be too surprised or disappointed if the young Sensor finds a lot of this a waste of time. If so, take that as a wise guide and don't push.

Always stress that there are no wrong answers, and do not give in to the temptation to hog the limelight with your own brilliant, Intuitive ideas. Finally, these are intended as stretching exercises to try once in a while—definitely not as something to do on a daily basis. All that you should be trying to do is to help your Sensor be more comfortable with situations that are uncertain and require exploring unknown possibilities.

So (carefully) try:

- Asking lots of "why" questions with no definitive answers
- Playing the adventure story game with family and friends, where someone begins it and each person adds something
- Looking for games that encourage associations, (Apples to Apples, Jr., is great for the grade school years)!
- Brainstorming wild and ridiculous ideas for writing projects
- Brainstorming inventions—a car that also flies and sails?
- Encouraging them to dream about what might happen in the future (what will they do, where might they live, and what the world will be like).
- It might even be fun to have them speculate on the future life of friends and family members.

- Using *Aesop's Fables* to practice finding the meaning of stories. These are very short stories, each with an intentional moral, so it is easy to read the story and then speculate on the moral. Although they are easily found in book form, there is also a very nice Web site with more than 600 of the fables at: **http://www.aesopfables.com**

For the Sensing Parent:

You may see little reason for all this effort to help your Sensor reason more intuitively—and you may be right! There are certain kinds of jobs that do require the abilities of the Intuitive, but there is also a world of jobs that do not, and do require the skills that the Sensor has in abundance. Don't push it if these stretching exercises are not fun for your child or for you and the rest of the family.

For both Intuitive and Sensing Parents:

You do need to recognize that your Sensor child, while very good at observations and facts, may show a slump in school in later grades. Spelling, arithmetic and related skills should go well, but in later years school work becomes less practical, less related to everyday life, and your strong Sensor is likely to show less interest. This may be especially true in such areas as history, or social studies. Here you may need to acknowledge the truth of this child's feelings, but go on to insist on adequate work regardless of interest level. At the same time, you should begin to think of the fields where his/her special talents may be very helpful—where natural interests will win the day. Such varied careers as accounting, statistics, sports, construction fields, technical writing, graphic art or computer technology would probably be a better fit (depending on other talents and preferences) than scientific research or the literary arts.

Because Sensors tend to spend little time dreaming about the future, it would be wise to contribute some ideas early on about the many

careers that are possible, and the varied pathways to these. Of the various imagination stretching ideas we have
listed, those that ask your Sensor to imagine his own future, and the future of others he knows, may have the most lasting value.

The Intuitive Child's Special Characteristics

Qualities that are easy to appreciate
Vivid imagination
Generates interesting ideas
Good at thinking about why things happen
Loves to learn new ideas, new ways of doing things

Qualities that may be harder to appreciate
May have little interest in details and dull facts
Can easily be bored by routine and by routine memorization
More interested in trying something new than in perfecting old skills
May be poor at following detailed instructions
Possible problems
May be a poor learner in areas that require mastery of fact and detail
May under-perform on tests by not reading instructions or by making careless errors

The Intuitive Child: Being an Appreciative Parent

Intuitive parents usually delight in their Intuitive child, even to the point of ignoring the Intuitive's (sometimes) unwillingness to tackle facts, details and instructions. However wonderful their creative imaginations may be, though, these children will benefit from parental emphasis on the less interesting factual matters, as we detail below.

Sensing parents, particularly if sensing is very strong may not see much to delight in at all. The child may seem too fanciful, head in the clouds, not suited for the real world, and the parent may secretly long for a more practical child.

It is easy to become rejecting of your child's greatest strengths in this situation. As with all preferences, the parent who feels this way needs to step back and really work to accept that the child brought these talents and not other talents into the world. It is well and good to teach your own down-to-earth life skills to this child.

Your Intuitive child: Developing skills on the non-preferred side

The most important skill-building for your Intuitive child would involve reminding her in many different ways that she needs to acquire facts to support her interesting ideas. It is very useful for young Intuitives to see a clear distinction between what they can imagine and what they factually know, and to practice making this distinction in varied settings.

Your child's other preferences will considerably affect the relationship to facts and details. The Intuitive child with Thinking/Judging preferences will show this problem least because their Thinking preference gives them a strong desire to be accurate and competent in their ideas, and their Judging preference influences them to be organized and systematic in all that they do. At the other extreme, the Intuitive, Feeling and Perceiving child is likely to the most carried away by imaginative ideas, because the Thinking and Judging constraints are not there.

Some possible ways to encourage skill development include a few ideas in the categories below. You will find that most of them focus on the school-age child.

Taking Care with Instructions

- Practice reading instructions slowly and carefully—and then doing it again.
- You could make a game of this by challenging your child to read them very fast and then tell you exactly what they are, and then try it again, slowly.
- When there are errors in test papers and homework, these should be gone over carefully by child and parent to see if instructions were poorly followed.
- Practice reading test questions twice, circling key words the second time.

Gaining respect for the power of facts and details

Here, as in ideas for the strong Sensor, the focus is on finding fun ways to exercise the non-preferred side. You want to strengthen both the ability to look for facts and recognize them, and respect for the power of accurate and detailed information.

Some possible suggestions:

- Playing memory-based games: The visual memory game "Memory" is one example. "Trivial Pursuit" is another. A third might be the whodunit game "Clue," where the murderer, location of murder and weapon must be identified. (Although this sounds like a task for Intuition, it actually relies on the ability to remember all the wrong guesses that have already been made.)
- In dinner-table discussions, have fun with a "Three facts or you're out," rule when discussing ideas and beliefs on just about any topic. If your child can't come up with three verifiable facts to support a belief—he's outa there!
- With older grade schoolers try analyzing stories, crime dramas, etc. to separate the factual content from ideas and theories. .

Keeping Imagination Under Control!

- With a great creative imagination sometimes comes a great ability to dream up things to be afraid of. It is sometimes useful to help your child analyze imaginary fears by asking for the factual evidence. (Do you know anyone who ever saw a monster under the bed? Where would bed monsters come from? Where do they disappear to when parents look for them? Where do they go during the day?)

This does not mean, of course, that all fearfulness is due simply to hyper-imagination. If your child's fears are severe and are disturbing his daily life, that is very different. It may be time to seek counseling help in that case

Chapter 26

Working with Your Thinking or Feeling Child

The Thinking Child's Special Characteristics

Qualities that are easy to appreciate
Good at logical thinking/good problem solver
Makes reasoned decisions
Has a talent for fairness
Values honesty
Loves accomplishment

Qualities that may be harder to appreciate
Can be too blunt and outspoken
Can be insensitive to the feelings of others
May come across as critical
Decisions may ignore needs of others

Possible Problems
May be actually inconsiderate of others
Bluntness, competitiveness may lead to friendship problems

The Thinking Child: Being an Appreciative Parent

The Thinking parent will readily see the many good qualities of the Thinking child. This parent will treasure the child's ability to reason clearly, and find good solutions to everyday problems. This is a very comfortable pairing, as both child and parent place high values on fairness and honesty and on speaking your mind rather than saying one thing and thinking another. In this context insensitivity may seem to be a trivial problem, and the parent may easily dismiss bluntness or insensitivity as just part of truthfulness. However, where Thinking is very strong, this area may need some serious skills development.

Most of the time Thinking child and Thinking parent should be very comfortable together. Conflict may occur when the Thinking child bluntly and fiercely disagrees with the Thinking parent's views but if overall responsiveness and demandingness are going well, they both have the skills to sort these issues out.

The Feeling parent will struggle much more with this child's seeming lack of sensitivity. As a good Feeler, the parent may work very hard at accepting and appreciating this child's strengths, but it will be a struggle. Honesty and fairness will be admired readily, as will the child's good logical mind, but outspoken frankness will not be seen as a virtue. A critical-seeming remark made to a friend will cause this parent to say (or think) "Why on earth did you say that?" and the child's answer "Because it is true" will not clarify things at all for the Feeling parent. This is going to be a life-long struggle for understanding, for this pair.

Because Thinking and Feeling impact decision making and our core values more than any other preference, you can see the process at work throughout society. Political parties split on this, as do educational philosophies, and our most profound ideas of fairness and social justice. It is also the one preference set with strong male-female differences. As we noted in an earlier chapter, about 56% of adult males are Thinkers, while nearly 75% of adult females are Feelers. Thus, in a mom/child Feeler/Thinker pair, the mother with a young male Thinker, who blames it all on maleness, may have a point. That doesn't make it any less innate, however.

The Thinking child: Developing skills on the non-preferred side

The potential weaknesses of very strong Thinking often do not become conspicuous until adolescence and adulthood, although they may have caused considerable annoyance within the family before that. In some cases, the Thinker may be a person who is exceptionally unflappable by nature. In other cases, the individual simply prefers the calm state as the best way to cope with the world, and manages to keep emotion strongly under control.

Either way, he or she may be remarkably insensitive to the importance of emotion and personal feeling in others. It really can constitute a "blind spot" in the perceptual world of otherwise very savvy individuals. Just as the very strong Sensor does not experience what a world of imagination and Intuition might be like, the strong Thinker cannot imagine the world of a strong Feeler, nor see any sense in making decisions that are not based on logic and rationality.

For adults, this creates a number of problems in the workplace, especially when Thinkers are in supervisory or other leadership positions. They want to get right down to business, whatever that business might be, and tend to zip past the social amenities. They disagree forcefully when the occasion arises, and may not soften their words when they need to evaluate or reprimand others. In making decisions they may fail to consider the Feeling needs of others and, therefore, make leadership mistakes. Similar problems may occur in intimate relationships, if the Thinker has not learned a fair amount about the feelings of others.

Helpful approaches

So, your budding, strong Thinker needs to be guided to realize that there is a world of feeling that is somewhat foreign to him or her, but very real all the same. In helping in this skills development, it is sensible to use the good, logical processes of the Thinker to explore Feeling. Many natural opportunities should occur when there are conflicts with family or friends. Here the young Thinker may genuinely not understand why others are so upset. Exploring this (logically) may be helpful. If friend Joe got mad and stormed out of the house, then why did he do that? What set him off? Might your

297

child have handled things differently? If so, how? It is important to try to bring home the fact that people really are different and have different needs. If your child felt that a friend was wrong, was it really important to say so? What would happen had he or she said nothing? If something did need to be said, how might it have been done less hurtfully?

It may help, with this logical and reasonable person, to make it clear that there are costs involved for each of us when we make others angry. Sometimes these may be costs that need to be paid, but sometimes they are not, and the smart Thinker should begin to distinguish between them. At best this sensitivity and tact will be a hard-earned skill, rather than a natural behavior, but that doesn't diminish its usefulness.

Much of what we suggest as skills development for the Thinker involves engaging their good abilities to reason, and using this, to look at themselves.

- Using their own personal conflicts with others is very helpful once the moment has passed. They should consider what their own feelings were when the friend seemed unfair or hurtful, what they thought the other child was feeling, and how they might feel if the situation were reversed and they were in the other child's place.
- Also use stories, movies, and current events to talk about why people do the things they do, and why they get upset and angry with each other. The logical Thinker should respond to the idea that you are more likely to reach an agreement with others if you understand and take their feelings into account.
- Talk about individual differences and the fact that we each experience the world in our own way. With the older Thinking child it may be useful to talk directly about inborn preferences and temperament differences, especially in Thinking and Feeling. Encourage respect for people who are different.

- Talk about the practical usefulness of compassion and
  empathy. Help them to see the vital role that strongly Feeling
  people play in keeping the whole nurturing side of life
  together, from health care, to teaching, to conflict resolution.
  Help them deeply respect their own clear and honest Thinking,
  while also understanding the words of a famous 17th-century
  philosopher-mathematician, "The heart hath its reasons, which
  reason knows not of."[24]

The Feeling Child's Special Characteristics

Qualities that are easy to appreciate
Warm and considerate toward others
Empathetic—able to understand emotional distress in others
Often an active peacemaker
Agreeable by nature and willing to compromise

Qualities that may be harder to appreciate
Very strong need to be well-liked
May have difficulty asserting personal needs, feelings, opinions
May be unduly influenced by others
Decisions may be too much influenced by emotion

Possible problems
Strong feeler may have harmful self-assertion problems
If lacking in direct self-assertion, may be manipulativ

The Feeling child: Being appreciative

The Thinking Parent, almost as much as the Feeling parent, will find
this child to be very dear. Kindness and agreeableness do shine here
and would be hard not to appreciate. This child is a natural friend-
maker and peacemaker. He is usually able to read emotion in others
and sense what they are feeling. This talent for empathy often is

---

[24] Pascal, Blaise (1670). *Pensees.*

visible very early in life. Conflict may come, however, if the little Feeler tends to keep the peace by manipulating the truth in difficult situations. Similarly it may seem hard to a Thinker to accept this child's seeming lack of a central core. "But what is it that you think?" may find this child casting about for the most acceptable answer rather than her deepest truth. The parent must understand that gentleness and kindness are a package that goes with the less admirable desire (from a Thinker perspective) to please at all costs. On the bright side, this parent should be good at helping the Feeler child work on skills for the non-preferred side.

The Feeling parent will also delight in this child, and do so even more completely than the Thinking parent. What the Thinking parent sees as problems, however, the Feeling parent is likely to see as all part of the child's inherent sweetness. The parent/child combo will find much joy in one another, but in the process, some opportunities for growth on the non-preferred side may be missed.

The Feeling child: Developing skills on the non-preferred side

Very strong Feelers will have problems that are diametrically opposed to those of Thinkers. The approval of others, the sense of peace and harmony in relationships at all levels, is so vital that many other needs that the person has may be ignored in order to avoid conflict. Others may exert too much influence over them in many different ways, and they may refuse to face hard realities at times, especially if that means more interpersonal conflict. Reasoned analysis may be ignored if the consequences are painful.

At the extreme, this strong preference may be a serious source of stress when conflicts arise. Your child needs to know that you perfectly understand his or her wish to be well liked and at peace with everyone. However, she also needs to know and understand that this is not always possible. Help your child to discover that the world will not end if he or she quietly, but firmly, disagrees with a friend or a group of friends from time to time. A friend may get angry, but a good friend will get over it. Sometimes two friends will try to pull your little Feeler in opposing directions. This is a good time to suggest that many decisions need to be made on the grounds of fairness and logic (Thinker skills), since it is impossible to please everyone.

You can also point out that the Feeler will be tempted to tell each person what they want to hear, because it seems less painful—even kinder—in the short run, but this may only lead to more trouble in the long run. If the problem arises you should also make it clear that there will always be people who will not respect others' wishes and will not take your child's gentle "no" for an answer. Wise Feelers need to learn that such people should not be allowed to play a large role in their lives. Much of this will seem scary, and feel as unnatural just as tact and diplomacy does to the strong Thinker. Be assured, though, that over all the growing-up years, such discussions will surely help your Feeler child to develop a more independent self.

Summarizing ways to encourage skills development here:

Harmony problems

- The simplest point is that different people will want you to do conflicting things. Helping one may hurt or anger the other. Trying to please both may just alienate both. This needs to be emphasized.
- A related point is that people may do things, or want you to do things, that are not kind, just, or fair. When this happens you need to be able to say no, no matter how precious the friendship.
- A third point is that some friends will prove to be consistently disrespectful of the views and values of others. Such a friend may not be one the child should stay close to.

Reasoning about fairness

- As we have suggested for reasoning about other things, you might take fairness as a sort of theme in stories, movies, current events and the events of your child's own life, and discuss this often, letting your child try to reason out what is most fair in a given situation.
- Help them to see that feelings are sometimes a very good guide to what is fair, and sometimes a wickedly bad guide. They need to see that their own discomfort may tempt them to make decisions based only on what will please others or get them out of an unpleasant situation.

Developing gentle self-Assertion

- We stress the word "gentle" here. It would never be productive to try to teach your Feeler child the ways of corporate bosses. Self-assertion may be very difficult, painful and aversive, especially at first. But if this child can learn to disagree calmly and quietly, but firmly, time and experience will help to show that the world will not come to an end.
- Encourage resilience, remind them that they are strong and can survive friendship disappointments.

Chapter 27

Working with your Judging or Perceiving Child

The Judging Child's Special Characteristics

Qualities that are easy to appreciate
Organized, neat, prompt
Good follow-through
Dependable
Decisive

Qualities that may be harder to appreciate
Resistance to change
Fussy over neatness
Hasty Decisions
Pressured style

Possible problems
Can be excessively rigid about change
Can be excessively rigid about neatness
Can become bossy toward others in these areas

The Judging Child—Being an Appreciative Parent

The Judging parent may feel that they won the lottery with this child. Not only does this serious, hard-working child share this parent's values, he also eliminates half of the things that parents and children stress over, together. Do your chores? Done! Homework? Done. Brush your teeth; make your bed? Done. Don't forget your lunch? Be home on time? Done, done. Well, no child is that perfect, but the strong Judger comes close in these areas, to the delight of the Judger parent. For young children the more problematic and harder-to-appreciate behavior may be a surprising resistance or emotional upset when plans are changed. This goes hand in hand with wanting to keep life well-planned and orderly. In the school years a very strong Judger may also show bossiness with friends and siblings which may be hard to accept even for the Judging parent. The parent, whether Judger or Perceiver, needs to be understanding about the Judger child's earnest desire to promote good order in the world, while also recognizing that this is an area for skills development.

The Perceiving parent will also marvel at the many tasks that need little or no reminder, and at the efficiency this child brings to the world. However, this parent is also likely to feel that something is wrong in an area that would not bother the Judger parent—that a person so earnest cannot really be enjoying life. This is another one of those preference bridges that is very hard—perhaps impossible to see across.

The Perceiver parent's desire to enjoy the day as it unfolds, see the flowers while they are blooming, enjoy a laugh and a smile when it happens, is a way of seeking momentary joy that is hopelessly opposed to finishing up the to-do list in record time. That this accomplishment gives the Judger an equal amount of pleasure, is unfathomable.

As a result, the Perceiver parent may be forever trying to lure Judger child into a slower, more spontaneous pace. Judger child may humor this parent from time to time, but soon go back to whatever she was doing. Respect is again the keyword.

The Judger child: Developing skills on the non-preferred side

This is not a child whose organizational skills are likely to need your attention. On the downside, there is a sense that very strong Judgers keep themselves so continuously booked that they don't develop the playful side of life. By adulthood very strong Judgers may be fiercely serious people. This is one preference where developing some skills for letting the clock roll on without watching it, getting good at a few games that have no long-term objective, and just learning to stop and see the sunset—are skills worth developing.

It is also true that when the Judging function is very strong, there is often a tendency both to literally judge others on their performance (including that Perceiver parent) and to be somewhat controlling of others. It is not that the Judger specifically wants to control others for the joy of it; instead this issue simply crops up when the wishes of others threaten to interfere with the plans the Judger has made, or the orderly environment the Judger has created. A strong Judger would not be greatly bothered by the messy house next door (although she might be secretly a little critical), but could be seriously annoyed by sharing a room with a hopelessly untidy Perceiver. This is seldom a great problem in childhood, but by adolescence, and in adult work and marriage it can be quite another matter. In close relationships, Judgers have a great tendency to do the planning for both members of the partnership, feeling maximally comfortable that way.

What may help

Getting back to practical strategies, we can't, in good conscience, recommend practicing sloppiness, lateness and disorganization as skills development here. However, a large dose of self-understanding, and a budding understanding of temperament differences, is a very good idea as this child grows older.

Natural occasions will occur when your child is critical of another, has a quarrel with another over plans, and so forth. This Judger needs to understand that human beings really do come with a wide variety of differences, and not everyone finds the structured life to be pleasing. This is going to sound pretty improbable. At best your Judger may be willing to accept that this is so, but never understand what it would feel like to live in glorious disarray. You are making real progress, though, if the little Judger does take your word for this.

Building on this base, the next step is to stress that we must each respect these differences in others. We have the right to organize our own lives in the ways that are most pleasing, but not to impose this on others. In the short run, this means accepting others for what they are willing to give and do, and biting the tongue from time to time when critical thoughts arise. In the longer run, it means using our understanding of self and others to select work situations, personal friends, and marriage partners that are compatible with our own temperaments.

Another possible area of concern arises from the fact that children with a strong preference for Judging are more likely to be stressed when things do not work out as they had planned. Whether this involves expecting an *A* on a history test, having the bedroom in order, or having family plans suddenly change, Judgers do experience more stress when their expectations are not met than do others. Helping a very strong judger weather disappointment, change and unpredictability without breaking out in a stress rash will be a challenge for both of you!

Finally, Judgers feel so much more comfortable when life is certain, that they sometimes tend to make quick decisions, just to get something settled. When this happens they are likely to end up frustrated and regretful. And yet, temperament being what it is, in a similar circumstance they may do it again. Help in making more careful and systematic decisions may be a good thing.

The below are some possible ways to encourage some skills development on the non-preferred side:

Living with the Judger Self

- Because good organization and effort can carry the Judger a long way, Judgers sometimes tend to believe that there is not anything they cannot accomplish, if they try hard enough. This may or may not be realistic, and can produce a person who is chronically hurried and chronically stressed. So—

- When hard work does not produce some desired outcome, discuss the fact that expectations have to be realistic. Where the Perceiver needs to be convinced that hard work will produce results, the Judger sometimes has to come to terms with the fact that we all have to accept limits in our abilities.
- Knowing your capabilities and setting realistic goals is important here. Some Judgers also need to see that the drive toward accomplishment, when it spreads out in all directions, can become a mindless frenzy. They need to think through their goals and work hard at those that are truly close to the heart, while just letting go of things that are not really that important.
- We suggested for hyper-active Extraverts that using Yoga and meditation (by school age) might be another way of practicing quietness. For slightly different reasons, this might be useful for Judgers too. And if this is a strongly Extraverted Judger— well there you go!

Encouraging some spontaneity/flexibility (*Most of this is intended for grade school and older children*)

- Schedule time for fun. This sounds pretty structured and Judger-like, but you want to start by being sure your little Judger does not totally fill the day with work and obligations. Be sure they take some time each day to just hang with friends, go on an unplanned bike ride, or play a video game.
- Introduce deliberate last-minute re-planning from time to time. You might have a weekend day (unpredictably) in which whatever the family had planned is now totally changed. It offers a chance for the young Judger to experience how displeasing this feels initially, and to discover (usually) that it is quite okay once it is underway. If this change of plans is a delight to other family members, there is another lesson for the Judger to learn there.

- If your Judger is making unreasonable demands of others, have him practice identifying his real needs as opposed to his temperament-based *wants*. When the difference becomes clearer, have him practice using negotiation and compromise in place of demands.

Practicing Delayed Decision-Making

- Turn failed expectations into learning experiences. When a decision has not worked out well (for example, precious savings were used to buy something that was not all that great), talk about the decision process, ask why the decision was made, what would have been good to know first.
- In upcoming decisions, get your Judger child to take time to list possible pros and cons before coming to a conclusion. It might be useful, also, to have her look back at these after the decision has been made and carried out

The Perceiving Child's Special Characteristics

Qualities that are easy to appreciate
Easy going—enjoys the moment
Flexible, welcomes change
Responsive to new events
Can work heroically at the last minute
Not critical of others

Qualities that may be harder to appreciate
Easily bored by routine
May hate to make firm decisions
Procrastinates on chores, homework, etc.
Likes to start new things—hates to finish

Possible problems
May go beyond procrastination to failure to finish
May seriously neglect school work if bored

The Perceiving child: Being an Appreciative Parent

The Perceiving parent will generally find this child to be a pleasure, as the parent/ child pair will share a great desire to enjoy the moment, and an easy ability to change plans as needed. If the Perceiving preference has gotten mom or dad into serious hot water in the school years or in the later work life, however, the parent may be more critical of these Perceiving traits in the child. On the other hand, if the parent has always been able to pull things together just enough to satisfy the world, possible Perceiver problems may be dismissed as something the child will grow out of. Experience says that this may be true for some but not for all. This depends on the strength of the preference, the child's other preferences, and overall abilities.

The Judging parent will also enjoy the child's many good Perceiver qualities, appreciating especially the adaptability and relaxed, easy-going nature of this child. Obviously, however, the Judger desire to maintain good order, keep things running on schedule, and see that tasks are done well and on time, is going to clash with any strong Perceiver style. As a parent, it is the Judger who is going to have to do the greater amount of attitude adapting.

This is an area where understanding and accepting differences in temperament are critically important. Since we know that Judgers have a natural tendency to control the events and circumstances of their own lives, and therefore to control others to some degree, and we know that they tend to be somewhat critical of disorganization in others, this is not going to be easy for the Judger parent. There is certainly an important role for this parent in helping the Perceiver child acquire some of the skills on the Judger side, but----no amount of effort will turn this child into a true Judger. The first, and most important thing, is to take a deep breath, and all the way to the bone, acknowledge the truth of this, and accept it.

The Perceiving child: Developing skills on the non-preferred side

As long as the outside world does not interfere, the strong Perceiver can be quite happy and content, moving from interest to interest at will, letting the day/week/year flow by peacefully. The problem, of course, comes from the fact that the outside world does—and sometimes must—intrude on this Perceiver's Garden of Eden. The child has schoolwork, homework and chores. The adult has a living to make and employers have certain expectations. Families have timetables for meals, bedtimes, and even family outings. Family members complain if your organized chaos slops into their areas of the house. Moms do far more than just complain about clean rooms, clean clothes, combed hair, etc.; they demand you do something about it. Even friends want you to commit to what you will do next Saturday.

To one degree or another, the Perceiver lifestyle will clash with others' expectations. And so, to survive in one piece, the Perceiver must acquire some Judger skills. It is wisdom to recognize that the going-with-the-flow style will be a life long preference, and as this young person grows older it will be important to guide the Perceiver toward a lifetime career that will be the best possible fit for this style. On the other hand, adult life in our society absolutely demands a certain amount of organization, and our Perceiver clearly needs some skills development here.

Suggestions

The general approach that we would suggest is to first, take temperament into account and keep your demands very simple at every age and stage, but second, expect those limited demands to be met completely and promptly. For the young child, you might allow toys to remain out all day, at least in certain parts of the house, but when it is time to pick them up (dinnertime, bedtime, or company-time), insist that it be done at that time.

As we noted in an earlier chapter, our family enforced this by collecting any possession left around after the clean-up deadline, in a holding basket. The owner could redeem leftover treasures immediately by deductions from the weekly allowance. Alternatively they were simply confiscated for a specified period of time. (This will sound fiercely Judging to Perceiver parents, but believe it—it worked like a charm.)

Similarly, if an older Perceiver child is expected to tidy the bed each day, you might try to have relaxed standards about the quality of the work (no hospital corners), but insist that it be done immediately on getting up. The idea is to take just a few organizational tasks and try to make those into prompt habits. Perceivers don't need to learn to love organization and getting things done—but they do need to practice both as useful life-skills. As you can tell by the long list of suggestions below, the very strong version of this preference is likely to cause the greatest frustration in parents, teachers, and later on employers and marriage partners. Some possible ways to encourage skills development include:

In General

- Keep your demands at the minimal level that is acceptable to you at each age and stage of your child's development.
- Expect these limited demands to be met completely and promptly (this requires your diligence and consistency).
- Be sure that you structure reasonable order into household routines—meals, bedtime, homework, chores, etc. (This has already been discussed in several places, but be aware that it is very hard to stay on top of your Perceiver's tasks and

deadlines if there is not a fair amount of predictability at home.)

Home Chores

- Have consistent routines for household chores, and complete chores as a family (for example—Saturday morning before everyone is free to have fun).
- Make all tasks, chores, etc., as much fun as possible. If your family is working together and likes to sing, keep a song going. Offer riddles to solve, play a great CD, or some other family entertainment.
- Rotate chores for your Perceiver (remember, change is Perceiver fun).
- Try the "Fink basket," technique—at the end of day clean-up time, all possessions that have not been put away are placed in a basket and can only be redeemed by allowance deductions.
- Use the "scrape your plate and something extra" technique for cleaning up after meals where everyone takes a plate and something else to the sink to rinse or to put away. (This is not too bad as a philosophy of life, either!)

Schoolwork and Homework

- Stock up on school supplies (include lots of poster boards, paints, glue sticks, and markers). You want to be sure that being out of something critical is not a valid excuse.
- Keep your grade-school Perceiver nearby while doing homework and take an active interest in his/her accomplishments.
- Break up homework assignments into small bites and provide breaks.
- With young children, actively help them plan and decide how to complete chores and homework, and, as they mature, review their plans and ensure they stay on track. Although the

frequency and time involvement should gradually decrease, you should expect to participate to some degree and to cheerlead all the way through high school.

- Reward homework with favorite activities, only after it is successfully completed.
- Try not to criticize last-minute hero efforts; they often produce good results for Perceivers. At the same time, by staying on top of what this child needs to get done, try to make these heroics unnecessary.

Does the sink or swim technique work for young Perceivers?

It is obvious that helping Perceiving children develop organizational skills, and complete chores and homework, will require a great deal of effort on your part—effort that doesn't end until they are off at college. By the beginning of 3rd grade it is popular for teachers (and parents alike), to try the "sink or swim" approach. The theory here is that if the child experiences enough negative consequences (no allowance, bad grades, etc.), they will see the light and be motivated to complete chores and assignments.

No doubt motivation is a major issue here, and the "sink or swim" approach may work, at least temporarily. However, this approach assumes that once-burned, the Perceiving child will continue to be motivated to complete future chores, assignments, etc. In truth, Perceivers are not good at worrying about consequences or about the future in general. They may be devastated when they find that their own failings have lost them a major reward or privilege, and this will be motivating in the short run, but probably not for long.

Thus, we suggest that you approach the "sink or swim" philosophy very slowly, just gradually reducing your involvement over the years as you see your Perceiving child taking greater responsibility. Our suggestions for limited requirements, set times, expectations of promptness for these limited requirements, and a great deal of

313

participation on your part—all are intended to build a set of habits that should be useful as your child matures. If you are a Perceiver parent, it will be doubly hard. We can only suggest that you look carefully at the chapters and sections on doing demandingness that apply to you.

Some final thoughts about preference combinations

In these chapters we have often discussed parent/child similarities and differences by thinking about just one preference pair at a time in an effort to keep things clear, and fairly simple. At the most we have considered pairs of two preferences in the temperaments. But, of course, we are all Introverted or Extraverted, Sensing or Intuitive, Feeling or Thinking and Perceiving or Judging at the same time. If we share two or three preferences with a child, these similarities bond us in understanding, in spite of the remaining differences. If, on the other hand, we differ on most or all preferences, the job of understanding will be harder, and require more effort by all parties.

To give just one extreme example, imagine that the genetic lottery handed out two absolutely opposite types. The parent is Extraverted, Sensing, Thinking and Judging (ESTJ) while the child is Introverted, Intuitive, Feeling and Perceiving (INFP where N stands for Intuitive). The ESTJ parent is outgoing, energetic, down to earth and practical, cool and logical, and well organized. The INFP child is inward and quiet, imaginative and dreamy, guided strongly by emotion and given to letting life happen rather than taking strong actions. The parent will seem like a rather overwhelming force to the child, and perhaps somewhat blunt and unfeeling (something that simply would not be true for an ESTJ child with this parent). The child may seem passive, impractical, emotional and unfocused to the parent. This child will need help and guidance in finding a good place in the world, compatible friends, and creative things to do. It will take love, deep understanding and long sustained effort for *this* parent to be a strong supportive friend to *this* child.

This example is exceptional, but makes the point that the greater the number of differences between parent and child, the more work there may be in bonding together, and understanding and appreciating one another in all the different glory we bring to the world.

Conclusion: The Happy Family

Leo Tolstoi, the great Russian novelist, once said, "Happy families are all alike, every unhappy family is unhappy in its own way."[25] In a certain sense, we believe that this is true. Some of the underlying values that we think you would find in most happy families (and would truly not find in unhappy families) include:

> *Respect for one another*
> *Acceptance of differences*
> *A good grasp of the art of compromise*
> *Mutual affection*

It all begins with mutual affection—nature's gift to families. However, we suggest that *affection cannot continue to thrive without the other three values—respect, acceptance and compromise*. Our feelings of love and caring are the reasons that we try very hard to make relationships work, but loving kindness will wither in an atmosphere of disrespect and endless criticism. As we have said many times in this book, our own natures speak to us so strongly that it is often impossible to believe that our way is not the only right way. Equally, it is very difficult to imagine that others have the same feelings about their "way." Instead, we assume that they simply need to gain a better understanding of our true view of the world—and we tell them that over and over and over. It doesn't take, so we try harder. Then we begin to categorize them as lazy/compulsive, too plodding/too dreamy, too cool/too emotional, etc. Strangely enough, this doesn't make things better.

As the best overall design for parenting we have strongly emphasized the authoritative approach—a rich blend of responsiveness and demandingness. We feel that it is the very best foundation for highly effective parenting. In the end, however, a system, however wise, is a road map that only comes alive in the actions of the travelers. No

---

[25] Tolstoi, L. N. (1875). *Anna Karenina*, pt. I, ch. 1.

system can be greater than the character and commitment of those who use it. No parenting system can be better than the willingness of parents and families to truly understand one another, accept one another and work together.

What truly defines a happy family then? We believe that most happy families share a respect for differences that allows each person to feel valued and accepted. With that, they have worked out ways to solve difference-based conflicts. They have learned to compromise.

We hope the view of temperament that we have explored throughout this book will help you to better see the world through one another's eyes. Happy families surely love one another, but the simple truth is—most of all—happy families *like* one another.

Your authors,

Nancy Harkey and Teri Jourgensen

About the Book, Authors, Websites

The Book

<u>Parenting by Temperament: Full Revised Edition,</u> is a revision and extension of two earlier books by these authors—<u>Raising Cuddlebugs and BraveHearts, Volumes I and II</u>. In this revision, readers of the earlier works will find both familiar material and newer ideas. We have expanded our description of basic parenting strategies for "responsive" love and "demanding" discipline, and have streamlined our description of some aspects of temperament, in order to give the reader a single volume that covers these topics effectively.

The Authors

<u>Nancy Harkey</u> lives in Claremont, California, and is retired from California State University, Pomona, where she was a professor of psychology for many years. She received her Ph.D. from Claremont Graduate University, where she studied both developmental and physiological psychology. She later taught a variety of courses in child development, biological psychology and experimental methods.

<u>Teri Jourgensen</u> lives in Oakland, California. She has a Master's Degree in public administration, is a certified Myers-Briggs Type Indicator Trainer, and is employed by the City of San Francisco as an Organizational Development Trainer and fFacilitator.

We (Nancy and Teri) are mother and daughter. Teri has two brothers and one sister. Teri and her siblings, together, have given Nancy eight grandchildren, currently ranging in age from 13 to thirty-two and providing lots of vivid temperament examples and personal experiences for both authors.

Our Websites

The major website that accompanies this book is at http://www.parentingbytemperament.com Here you can explore pictures of temperament types, take our adult and child sorters, and buy both print and Kindle versions of our books. It is also possible to ask questions of the authors through our forum at http://forum.parentingbytemperament.com

Finally, there is also a broad, general blog on temperament at http://www.temperamentMatters.com This is not specific to parenting, but covers all sorts of issues centered around temperament and personality.

INDEX

AUTHORITATIVE PARENTING
....*18*
Demandingness *18*
Responsiveness..............................*18*
BAUMRIND STYLES
Outcomes...*24*
BAUMRIND, DIANA..............*13*
BAUMRIND'S FOUR PARENTING
STYLES
Authoritarian...................................*20*
BEGINNING OF ATTACHMENT
....*11*
CHANGING RHYTHM OF
DEMANDINGNESS *95*
CHANGING RHYTHM OF
RESPONSIVENESS *37*
DEMANDINGNESS AND
PREFERENCE EFFECTS
consistent monitoring *208*
consistent, contingent discipline....*206*
developing guidelines *206*
Introversion/Extraversion *209*
DEMANDINGNESS/DISCIPLINE
TOPICS
discussions during discipline.........*84*
doing grounding well.....................*83*
good tactics at all ages *86*
misbehavior in public *82*
other things that help....................*91*
simple habits of obedience.............*73*
HAPPY FAMILIES.................*318*
HUMAN NATURE — VIEWS
behaviorist view...............................*4*
blank slate *3*
Freud...*4*
native depravity................................*3*
pretty nice blank slate.....................*5*

INBORN MOTIVATIONAL
TOOLS *9*
MARSHMALLOW STORY *62*
PARENTING
conflict will occur.........................*15*
PASCAL, BLAISE *299*
PREFERENCE BIAS PROBLEMS
we prefer our own preferences....*200,
267, 271, 317*
PREFERENCES
Extraversion/Introversion
adult...*122*
child...*118*
parenting interactions.............*123*
Judging/Perceiving
child...*148*
parent interactions *153*
Sensing/Intuition
adult...*131*
child...*128*
parenting interactions..............*133*
Thinking/Feeling
adult...*141*
child...*137*
parent interactions *143*
when they are slight *195*
RESPONSIVENESS GIFTS
active parent learning
about your child..........................*28*
about yourself...........................*30*
preference effects *199*
active teaching
clear communication *33*
preference effects *202*
sharing thoughts......................*31*
providing structure
preference effects *204*
providing structure.........................*37*
warmth and intimacy.....................*27*
preference effects *198*
SELF-CONTROL AND SELF-
REGULATION

how children come to accept our rules................ *46*

steps in learning emotional control *50*

steps in learning social control *53*

SORTERS

children above age 12................... *114*

STRETCHING

the concept *194*

TALES FROM THE RAT LAB ... *62*

TANTRUM SPIRALS *77*

TEMPERAMENT AND

PARENTING

Introversion/Extraversion effects

demandingness.........................*262*

responsiveness *259*

some stretches.........................*263*

the NF parent

demandingness.........................*239*

demandingness stretches.........*241*

parent/child interactions *243*

parenting concerns...................*233*

responsiveness *234*

responsiveness stretches.........*237*

the NT parent

demandingness.........................*252*

demandingness stretches.........*254*

parent/child interactions *255*

responsiveness *248*

responsiveness stretches.........*250*

the SJ parent

demandingness.........................*228*

demandingness stretches..........*229*

parent/child interactions *230*

parenting concerns...................*223*

responsiveness *223*

responsiveness stretches.........*226*

the SP parent

demandingness.........................*216*

demandingness stretches..........*219*

parent/child interactions *219*

responsiveness..........................*211*

responsiveness stretches.........*215*

when parent temperaments clash

gender differences...................*266*

step 1--acceptance...................*267*

step 2--compromise.................*268*

TEMPERAMENT AND

TODDLERS

big smilers and old souls.............. *106*

cuddlers and non-cuddlers........... *106*

daydreamers and down-to-earthers
.... *108*

interesting combinations.............. *112*

structure-lovers and freedom lovers
.... *110*

TEMPERAMENT GOLDEN-
MEAN IS RARE.................**102**

TEMPERAMENTS—THE BIG
FOUR

NFs Humanity's Champions

NF adult................................... *177*

NF child *175*

NF parent................................. *180*

NTs Passionate Achievers

NT adult *185*

NT child *183*

NT parent................................. *188*

SJs Keepers of the Flame

SJ adult *169*

SJ child.................................... *167*

SJ parent.................................. *172*

SPs Masters of the Moment

SP adult *161*

SP parent.................................. *163*

TOLSTOI **317**

WATSON, JOHN B. **5**

WHY PARENTING EXPERTS
DISAGREE................... **6, 191**

WORKING WITH YOUR
CHILD'S TEMPERAMENT

your Extraverted child

building skills on the non-preferred
side *276*

your Feeling child

*accepting and honoring
preferences* *299*

*building skills on the non-
preferred side* *300*

your Introverted child

accepting and honoring
    preferences 281
your Intuitive child
    building skills on the non-preferred
    side.....................................292
your Judging child
    building skills on the non-
        preferred side......................304
your Perceiving child

building skills on the non-
    preferred side 310
your Sensing child
    accepting and honoring
    preferences 287
    building skills on the non-
        preferred side 288
your Thinking child
    building skills on the non-preferred
    side 296

CPSIA information can be obtained
at www.ICGtesting.com
Printed in the USA
FSOW04n2045190916
25192FS